Diversity in Human Interactions

Diversity in Human Interactions
The Tapestry of America

EDITED BY
JOHN D. ROBINSON
LARRY C. JAMES

OXFORD
UNIVERSITY PRESS

2003

OXFORD
UNIVERSITY PRESS

Oxford   New York
Auckland   Bangkok   Buenos Aires   Cape Town   Chennai
Dar es Salaam   Delhi   Hong Kong   Istanbul   Karachi   Kolkata
Kuala Lumpur   Madrid   Melbourne   Mexico City   Mumbai   Nairobi
São Paulo   Shanghai   Taipei   Tokyo   Toronto

Copyright © 2003 by Oxford University Press, Inc.

Published by Oxford University Press, Inc.
198 Madison Avenue, New York, New York 10016

www.oup.com

Oxford is a registered trademark of Oxford University Press

Library of Congress Cataloging-in-Publication Data
Diversity in human interactions : the tapestry of America / edited by
John D. Robinson and Larry C. James.
   p. cm.
Includes bibliographical references and index.
ISBN 0-19-514390-6
1. Social interaction—United States.   2. Pluralism (Social
sciences)—United States.   3. Minorities—United States.   4. United
States—Race relations.   5. United States—Ethnic relations.   I.
Robinson, John D.   II. James, Larry C.
HN59.2 .D59 2003
302'.0973—dc21   2002152362

9 8 7 6 5 4 3 2 1

Printed in the United States of America
on acid-free paper

There is very little difference between one person and another, but what little difference there is, is very important.

—William James

Contents

Contributors   ix

Introduction: Weaving the Tapestry   xv
John D. Robinson and Larry C. James

1. What Difference Does a Difference Make? Societal Privilege,
   Disadvantage, and Discord in Human Relationships   3
   Beverly Greene

2. Becoming Americano: Has the Sleeping Giant Awakened?   21
   Miguel A. Ybarra

3. The African Diaspora   33
   A. Toy Caldwell-Colbert, Jessica Henderson-Daniel,
   and G. Rita Dudley-Grant

4. People of Asian Descent: Beyond Myths and Stereotypes   63
   Asuncion Miteria Austria

5. On Native Soil: The Forgotten Race: American Indians   77
   Diane J. Willis and Dolores Subia BigFoot

6. *Na Kānaka Maoli*: The Indigenous People of Hawai'i   93
   Cynthia Kanoelani Kenui

7. A Place for God's Children: On Becoming Biracial in America   111
   Dawn L. Cannon

8. The Wisdom of Years: Understanding the Journey of Life   123
   William E. Haley, Claire Robb, Yuri Jang, and Beth Han

9. Under a Rainbow Flag: The Diversity of Sexual Orientation   145
   Douglas C. Haldeman and Robin A. Buhrke

10. One God, One Faith, One Humanity   157
   Steven M. Tovian, Bowyer G. Freeman, and Abdul R. Muhammad

11. The Visible and the Invisible   175
   Irene W. Leigh and Patrick J. Brice

12. The Enriching Experience   195
   Samuel M. Turner and Deborah C. Beidel

Index   207

Contributors

Asuncion Miteria Austria, Ph.D., is Professor, Chair, and Director of Clinical Training in the Department of Psychology at Cardinal Stritch University in Milwaukee, Wisconsin. She is a graduate of the University of the Philippines, Columbia University, and Northwestern University. Her postdoctoral training was done at the Neuropsychiatric Institute at the University of Illinois Medical Center.

Deborah C. Beidel, Ph.D., ABPP, is Professor of Psychology, Associate Director of the program in clinical psychology, and Co-director of the Maryland Center for Anxiety Disorders, Department of Psychology, University of Maryland, College Park.

Dolores Subia BigFoot, Ph.D., is Director of the Native American Programs at the Center on Child Abuse and Neglect in Oklahoma City. This center provides training for mental health professionals serving Native children who are victims of physical and sexual abuse. Dr. BigFoot has a long history of promoting Native cultural practices in the delivery of clinical services to Native communities.

Patrick J. Brice, Ph.D., is currently Professor of Psychology and Director of the clinical psychology doctoral program at Gallaudet University in Washington, D.C. He received his doctorate in clinical and developmental psychology from the University of Illinois in Chicago.

Robin A. Buhrke, Ph.D., is a Staff Psychologist at Counseling and Psychological Services and Assistant Clinical Professor in Psychiatry and Behavioral Sciences at Duke University. Her special interests include the psychology of lesbian, gay, and bisexual college-age students.

A. Toy Caldwell-Colbert, Ph.D., ABPP, served as Associate Vice President for Academic Affairs at the University of Illinois. She is currently Provost and Chief Academic Officer at Howard University in Washington, D.C. She also holds an appointment to the faculty at Howard University as Professor of Psychiatry and Psychology. Her area of interest is in multicultural issues and the training and preparation of psychologists to work with diverse populations.

Dawn L. Cannon, M.D., is a pathologist and Assistant Dean for Student Affairs at the Howard University College of Medicine. She is a graduate of the University of Pennsylvania and the Howard University College of Medicine. Dr. Cannon is board certified in Anatomic and Clinical Pathology and in Blood Banking and Transfusion Medicine.

G. Rita Dudley-Grant, Ph.D., ABPP, is a graduate of Adelphi University and has served as Commissioner of Mental Health for the U.S. Virgin Islands. She is currently in private practice in St. Croix.

Bowyer G. Freeman has served as Director of Pastoral Care Services for Howard University Hospital (Washington, D.C.) since 1996. He is presently completing the requirements for his doctorate in Pastoral Theology at the Howard University School of Divinity. His ministry within the health care setting asserts that health is the state of physical, mental, social, and spiritual well-being and not just the absence of disease or infirmity. Reverend Freeman facilitates multireligious awareness in all settings.

Beverly Greene, Ph.D., ABPP, is Professor of Psychology at St. John's University in Jamaica, New York. She is a nationally known expert in the area of discordance in human interactions. Dr. Greene is a graduate of Adelphi University.

Douglas C. Haldeman, Ph.D., is a Counseling Psychologist in Seattle and serves on the clinical faculty of the University of Washington at Seattle. His primary publication interests have involved the competent and ethical treatment of lesbian, gay, and bisexual clients in psychotherapy, with a particular focus on sexual orientation conversion therapies.

William E. Haley, Ph.D., is Professor and Chair in the Department of Gerontology at the University of South Florida. He serves on the editorial boards of a number of prominent journals in gerontology and is former president of the Section of Clinical Geropsychology of the Society of Clinical Psychologists.

Beth Han, Ph.D., MPH, completed her doctorate in Aging Studies in the Department of Gerontology, University of South Florida, as well as an MPH in Epidemiology and Biostatistics. Her special interests include statistics, secondary data analysis, and the relationship between disease, depression, and self-rated health.

Jessica Henderson-Daniel, Ph.D., ABPP, is Assistant Professor of Psychology in the Department of Psychiatry at Harvard Medical School and Co-Director of Training in Psychology at Children's Hospital, Boston. Dr. Henderson-Daniel is an expert in the area of multicultural competency training.

Larry C. James, Ph.D., ABPP, is Chief of the Department of Psychology at the Walter Reed Army Medical Center in Washington, D.C. As a senior officer in the U.S. Army, Dr. James is well known for his work with military personnel concerning issues of psychological care and disease prevention. He focuses on positive health behaviors and maintenance of a healthy lifestyle. He is recognized nationally for his work in telehealth and telemedicine. As a graduate of the University of Iowa, he completed a postdoctoral fellowship in health psychology at Tripler Army Medical Center in Hawaii. He holds board certification in both clinical psychology and in clinical health psychology.

Yuri Jang, Ph.D., completed her doctorate in Aging Studies in the Department of Gerontology, University of South Florida. She is currently a postdoctoral Fellow at the Institute on Aging, University of South Florida, whose research interests include cross-cultural gerontology, and the relationship between aging, disability, and depression.

Cynthia Kanoelani Kenui, M.A., a Native Hawaiian scholar, is a doctoral candidate in clinical psychology in Honolulu, Hawaii. Her research concerns and areas of interest include cross-cultural psychology, health psychology, ecological and systemic psychology, and complementary and alternative medicine in indigenous people. She serves as a consultant to various organizations interested in the history and culture of Native Hawaiians.

Irene W. Leigh, Ph.D., is a professor in the clinical psychology doctoral program at Gallaudet University in Washington, D.C. Her research and writing has focused on deaf people and issues related to identity, multiculturalism, parenting, attachment, depression, and cochlear implants.

Abdul R. Muhammad was affirmed into the U.S. Army as the first Islamic Chaplain in December 1993. Imam Muhammad has served in San Diego, Buffalo, Ft. Lee, the New York State Department of Corrections, and numerous other locations. He is a graduate of the State University College of New York at Brockport, San Diego State University, and the University of Michigan in Ann Arbor. Having served as a religious leader and human service professional throughout the United States for the past 25 years, he was formerly assigned as Imam and hospital chaplain at the Walter Reed Army Medical Center in Washington, D.C.

Claire Robb is a doctoral student in the Aging Studies Program, Department of Gerontology, University of South Florida, and is pursuing an MPH in Epidemiology and Biostatistics. Her research interests include mental health and aging, gerontology and economic issues, and well-being in older couples.

John D. Robinson, Ed.D., MPH, ABPP, is a graduate of the University of Texas at Austin, the University of Massachusetts at Amherst, and Harvard University School of Public Health. Currently, he is Chief Transplant Psychologist and Professor and Chief, Interdepartmental Treatment Programs, Departments of Psychiatry and Surgery, Howard University College of Medicine, and Clinical Professor of Psychiatry, Georgetown University School of Medicine. His major areas of interest are in the psychological aspects of medical illnesses, the training of health care professionals, and interdisciplinary training. Dr. Robinson has received numerous national awards for his work in the psychological aspects of ethnic, racial, and cultural diversity and has served as President of the American Board of Clinical Psychology of the American Board of Professional Psychology (ABPP). He completed his residency training at the University of Texas Health Sciences Center at San Antonio. He holds the honorary degree of Doctor of Humane Letters from the Massachusetts School of Professional Psychology in Boston. He holds board certification in both clinical psychology and clinical health psychology.

Steven M. Tovian, Ph.D., ABPP, is Director of Health Psychology and Chief Psychologist in the Department of Psychiatry and Behavioral Sciences at Evanston Northwestern Healthcare in Evanston, Illinois. He is also Associate Professor of Psychiatry and Behavioral Sciences at Northwestern University Medical School and is board certified in clinical and in health psychology.

Samuel M. Turner, Ph.D., ABPP, is an internationally known researcher and clinician in the area of anxiety disorders. He is Professor of Psychology, Director of the program in clinical psychology, and Co-director of the Maryland

Center for Anxiety Disorders, Department of Psychology, University of Maryland, College Park.

Diane J. Willis, Ph.D., a Kiowa Indian, is Professor Emeritus, Department of Pediatrics, University of Oklahoma Health Sciences Center in Oklahoma City. She serves as a consultant to the Indian Health Service, the American Indian Head Start Quality Improvement Center, and Chi Hulli Li, a substance abuse center for American Indian women and their children.

Miguel A. Ybarra, Ph.D., currently is a staff psychologist in the Counseling and Psychological Services Center at the University of Houston. He is a graduate of the University of Wisconsin at Madison.

JOHN D. ROBINSON
LARRY C. JAMES

Introduction

Weaving the Tapestry

Genetically, we are more similar than we are different. However, no two people—not even identical twins—are exactly alike, so there are necessarily differences between people. We all perceive these differences and make judgments about others based on them, whether they are in race, age, disability status, ethnicity, religion, socioeconomic status, or sexual orientation. Some differences are more visible than others. Particularly, if we meet those of a different ethnicity or race, we initially notice what can be called visible factors, that is, physical differences that are easy to pick out visually. Differences that escape immediate visual notice, what can be called invisible factors, also have an impact on our interactions with others. Some of these invisible factors are religion, sexual orientation, and, occasionally, disability status. Age also plays a role in our relationships, as does socioeconomic status. Although most of us are aware of only some of these differences, the quality and effectiveness of our interactions with others can be affected by all of them.

America is made up of people from many different cultures, races, ethnicities, religions, sexual orientations, levels of ability, and ages, which is why it is so often described by melting-pot metaphors. For example, it has been described as completely different entrees that happen to be served on the same table (Bugg, 2001), and as "the American salad," with many distinct ingredients making up the whole, while maintaining individual tastes. We had better learn to accept and deal with our diversity, because it is increasing with each passing year. Our nation has not only become much more diverse in 2000 than it was in 1990, but this diversity has also become more difficult to measure. Minorities now make up roughly one-third of the nation's population and are growing significantly faster than the white, majority population.

Through contact and discussion, individuals do develop more positive feelings about and become more accepting of others. Conversely, without contact and discussion, individuals tend to develop misconceptions and harbor resentment about those who differ from them. For example, people with majority status may feel that those with minority status—whether by race, sexual orientation, disability, or other differentiating factors—have too much attention paid to their status and its concomitant problems. For example, an 11 July 2001 *Washington Post* survey reported that 52% of whites, but only 17% of blacks, believed that there is too much attention paid to racial issues. The report went on to say that whites believe blacks have more or about the same opportunities in life as whites, that there is less discrimination against minorities in society today, and that minorities are not worse off in society than is generally reported in terms of health care, employment, education, and income. On the other side, minorities who are not visually white may feel that it is unfair for those who are visually white to consider themselves to be members of a minority to reap advantages through the enforcement of anti-discrimination laws, referring to them as "minority by convenience."

Although America is very diverse, we have more in common across lines of race, ethnicity, age, religion, and sexual orientation than we generally like to admit. Our goal should be to celebrate our similarities and our differences in equal measure. The chapters in this volume address how interactions among people are affected by differences in their race, ethnicity, sexual orientation, religion, disability status, and age. Although gender is a very important factor in our interactions, and thus cannot be ignored, we do not discuss it in this book because it is a very extensive topic that has been addressed in several other books.

Several chapters in this book address issues of race and ethnicity and are written by authors who identify with that group. For example, Native Americans write the Native American chapter, while the chapter on the African Diaspora is written by Americans of African descent. Race has been defined as being related to natural skin color, while ethnicity refers more to cultural heritage. We frequently have difficulty deciding what to call people when referring to race and/or ethnicity. Political correctness has played a major part in defining terms. The authors of these chapters address these issues as well as current issues within these groups. Skin color among blacks has always been, and continues to be, an issue. Some of the history of this is discussed.

In the first chapter, Beverly Greene discusses general problems brought about by the discordant structure of interactions. When two people meet, a discordant structure is immediately apparent: each person jockeys for the upper hand through dominance in factors such as power, position, and privilege. It is natural for humans to act in this way. If we are in the majority, after establishing the power basis in a relationship, we tend to homogenize the differences pointed out to us by the minority. In doing so, those in the majority may say, "that's not true" or "that never happens" when those in the minority comment on an incident of discrimination or difference. The majority tends to be uncomfortable with differences and experiences of discrimination noticed by the minority, thus tending to try to minimize them by seeing them as simply false or inaccurately conceived because of an incorrect appraisal of a situation. The minority may see this reaction as an attempt to downplay their perceptions, make their concerns unimportant and exaggerated, and diminish their problems to a level where they are either irrational or nonexistent. For example, when those in the minority mention their experience of being stopped by the police and assert that it happens because of their race, those in the majority may claim that as they have also been stopped by police, it cannot be a racial issue, as the minority contends. However, research and media data on those stopped by police clearly show that more of those in the minority are stopped for nonviolations than those in the majority. So why is there a disagreement? It could be because it is too painful for the majority to acknowledge that minorities are really treated differently, that the majority feels that minorities are too sensitive to the problems of daily life, or that these experiences are not part of the majority's reality, or perhaps even that they feel they are being accused, feel the need to defend the status quo, so they have extreme difficulty acknowledging them and tend to minimize them.

Chapters 2 through 7 focus on issues of race and ethnicity. "Race" generally refers to natural skin color, while ethnicity generally refers to cultural heritage. An author who identifies with the group described writes each chapter. These chapters address both issues involving external relations, that is, how particular ethnic and racial groups relate to those outside their group, as well as relations that are internal to particular ethnic and racial groups. When referring to a person's ethnicity or race, individuals often have problems deciding which term to use. These problems are mirrored on a national level, which is clearly demonstrated by the Census Bureau's difficulties with defining race. Our definitions of particular races tend to be vague, making it hard to decide which category people fall into. Hispanics, for example, can be of any race, but are generally considered to be people whose ancestry is from countries where Spanish is spoken and Roman Catholicism is the dominant religion. A black Cuban is visually a black person but may identify as Hispanic, as would a person from the Dominican Republic. Although the trend toward political correctness has fostered the use of terms such as African-American over Black, some Americans of African descent prefer to be called Black because black is what people see, and people may not know whether their ethnicity is Caribbean, African, Hispanic, or American. Chapters 2, 3, and 4 also make clear that it is far too often overlooked that those falling into categories such as Black, Hispanic, and Asian come from vastly different backgrounds, ancestors, skin colors, and origins. A better understanding and appreciation of the differences existing within racial and ethnic groups is a major part of understanding them.

Chapters 5 and 6 examine the special concerns of two groups of native peoples, Native Americans and Native Hawaiians. Chapter 6 is unique in both content and style because a native Hawaiian in typical native Hawaiian style writes it. As with other ethnic and racial minorities, we often find it difficult to decide whether someone is a Native American, an American Indian, or a Native Hawaiian. Native peoples have a long history in America, and they continue to play a significant role in our society. Although most of us are aware of some part of their history, we do not really try to understand it from their viewpoint.

Chapter 7 focuses on the history of interracial relations in America and the legal and societal problems faced by multiracial people. According to the 2000 Census, mixed race dating and marriage are on the rise—the number of interracial couples has more than quadrupled—so, not surprisingly, the number of children belonging to more than one race is also increasing. According to an article in the 13 March 2001 *Washington Post*, children are the most diverse segment of the population. In 2000, nearly 7 million Americans—2.4%—described themselves as belonging to more than one race. Multiracial children must contend with a lot of problems in today's society, as they must be conscious of both their physical appearance and their mixed ethnic/racial heritage and must deal with the difficulty mixed heritage brings to issues of self-identity.

As mentioned earlier, invisible factors are very important in our daily interactions and can particularly affect our decisions about people concerning employment status and benefits. Chapters 8 through 11 address invisible factors, that is, age, sexual orientation, religion, and disability status. Of American homes, 4%—nearly 4 million—house at least four generations. In such environments, families must learn to live together despite their different lifestyles and perspectives. The same challenge, interacting efficiently with people of disparate ages, faces everyone in the workforce, albeit on a smaller scale. Although disabilities, whether physical or mental, are not always visible, when we deal with them and when we talk about them, we are perhaps most carelessly insensitive to disabled people.

The final chapter discusses how opinions of others that we form both consciously and unconsciously guide our daily interactions. As noted earlier, through contact and discussion, people develop more positive feelings about others and become more accepting of those who differ from them. Without contact and discussion, however, people develop misconceptions and harbor resentment about those who differ from them. Each person and each group has a certain reality. Our ability to function in an environment filled with different people depends on our making a concerted effort to communicate. In our interactions with others, both as individuals and as groups, we need to ask more questions. We also need to try to understand their experiences from the context in which they function and from their point of view, which may be very different from our own. Although we cannot expect to be completely successful in every interaction, we should keep in mind that incremental successes are very important, and that trying to see from another person's point of view is an experience that will broaden our knowledge of others and ourselves. Unfortunately, the fear of offending people we are trying to get to know and work with, the fear of violating norms of political correctness, and the desire to avoid what is not comfortable often prevent us from asking questions of others, which further exacerbates entrenched problems. We sometimes feel that it is impolite to ask someone about their country of origin, their race, their disability status, or what they prefer to be called. Yet, how else will we know their preferences if we do not ask? Although we all know these factors do matter and that they affect our interactions with others, we are hesitant to ask about differences. If we appreciate others making an effort to understand our unique characteristics, why can't we see that others value our concern for theirs?

This book is not a collection of academic articles on individual differences but is designed to serve as a guide to assist in understanding our diverse population. We have assembled some of the brightest and the best minds to aid us in this journey. In writing it, our aim was to write in the most accessible and relaxed style, making the concepts understandable and the prose readable, in order to foster open and frank discussion of the issues surrounding diversity. This book can be used as a tool for human-relations training, as well as an introductory textbook for the study of individual differences. Our population is becoming increasingly diverse, so we will increasingly face problems brought about by differences. This book is about communications; about crossing the divide that cultures and society sometimes widens rather than lessens. We hope this book will teach you how not to be afraid to talk to each other and to understand our uniqueness. We believe that only through frank and honest discussions can we become fully aware of the differences that make us unique. Only then can we really enjoy the beauty and richness of the multicultural artwork that is the human tapestry of America.

References

Bugg, S. (2001, May 24). The American buffet. *Washington Metro Weekly*, 12.

Diversity in Human Interactions

BEVERLY GREENE

What Difference Does a Difference Make?

Societal Privilege, Disadvantage, and Discord in Human Relationships

The chapters in this volume are concerned essentially with differences between people and groups that Western culture deem salient and descriptions of those differences. These descriptions help us to organize the information that we have about these groups and our understanding of them, just as descriptive information helps us to organize what we know about the world, in general. However, Bruce Blaine (2000) argues that while such categorization helps to simplify things, it often leads to seeing individuals as members of groups they belong to rather than as individuals. This oversimplification is often a less accurate description of a given individual and can be most problematic in the delivery of human services, particularly but not exclusive to mental health services.

Diversity is a socially constructed concept that indicates the mere presence of differences. However, when we discuss diversity in this volume, we are concerned with a great deal more than just the presence of differences. Any serious discussion of differences leads to a range of other questions. Human beings differ from one another along a range of dimensions and in innumerable ways. The groups that the authors discuss are clearly different from one another on many dimensions just as they are similar on other dimensions. When placed on a spectrum, some of those differences are highly visible at one extreme, while others are completely invisible at the other extreme. However, aside from describing the groups, what makes these differences important? It is clear that some differences are deemed extremely salient while other kinds of differences, even though highly visible, are deemed so inconsequential that we hardly notice them and do not devote much, if any, time or attention to their presence or description. The question we are left to grapple with if we are to understand the tension that often occurs when we directly experience or anticipate differences between ourselves and others, is what difference does difference really make and why. Why are some characteristics, beliefs, or behaviors of people given so much importance while others are not. Simply stated, why do differences matter, to whom do they matter, and who decides which differences make a difference?

The authors in this volume specifically explore the human dimensions of race/ethnicity, gender, religion, age, sexual orientation, socioeconomic class, and disability. In Western culture these dimensions are deemed of great importance, and they are often the focus of, as well as the explanation for, discord between individuals and groups. Is it the difference per se that explains that discord or is it something that the differences are socially endowed with that creates social tension? I contend that it is the latter. Race and ethnicity, gender, sexual orientation, disability, age, socioeconomic class, religious and spiritual orientations have little meaning in and of themselves. It is the social context in which these dimensions are perceived, experienced, understood, and defined that makes them salient. Their salience is determined by how much of a difference these differences actually make in peoples lives, at a given time, and what they mean. Differences in and of themselves do not have meaning outside of a social context and social context helps to define those distinctions thus giving them meaning. What does it mean to share group membership? What does it mean when individuals do not share that membership? We are charged with making sense of these questions as well as appreciating the complexity of these issues in the training of human services professionals.

Allan Johnson (2001) argues that fear of the unknown is usually given as the reason that people fear and distrust those who are not like them, therefore, despite our good intentions this fear is *natural*. However, Johnson argues to the contrary that our fears are not based on what we do not know, rather, they are based on what we *think* we *do* know. When we directly encounter someone from a different ethnic group, someone who is lesbian, gay, or bisexual, someone from a different religion, or a person with a disability for the first time, it is really not the first encounter. It is the culmination of a series of previous symbolic encounters that takes place every single time a piece of information is formally or informally communicated about those group members or when they are conspicuously omitted as if they were invisible. These symbolic encounters occur when we watch movies, television, or overhear conversations of adults as children. Such encounters are perhaps most insidious when they are not accompanied by words or conversations. When adults have a visceral negative reaction to the mention or presence of some group or its member, a child may experience a level of discomfort that casts a pall over the interaction and that comes to be associated with members of that group. These negative associations may linger into adulthood when the presence of the different group members elicits discomfort for reasons that you would be hard pressed to explain other than as a "feeling." They occur when we read newspapers, watch, or hear the news and its contents reveal who and what is considered important, productive, trustworthy and in danger, as well as who and what is considered disposable, unproductive, dangerous, and to be feared. Our information may come directly from peers, as well as loved and trusted figures who tell us what they *know* about members of different groups, based on information that they may have garnered only secondhand at best. Such encounters include our passing and informal observations of people who are different, particularly if we only encounter them when they are in roles that are subservient to ours, when we are dominant and they are subordinate as well as its corollary. What do we think explains someone else's position in the social hierarchy relative to our own and what does that tell us about ourselves? This collection of impressions serves as the body of what we *think* we *know* about people who we may have never really encountered directly before. The information communicated about them and the impressions formed of them are shaped by many complex sociopolitical and economic variables that may have little to do with the reality of who "those" people really are. Descriptions of "them" are not necessarily designed to accurately describe "them" and inform us, rather they may be designed and used to serve other purposes in a larger system of dominant and subordinate relationships. Distortions of groups often represent the way that it has become convenient or comfortable to see or perceive them. All these things constitute what we *think* we know about people who are different long before we ever actually have direct relationships with them.

Those things that we *think* we know about the unknown or about people who are different are learned ideas. We are not simply born in fear of the unknown or the different, we are carefully taught to be afraid. Differences facilitate what Rachel Siegel (1995) and Paul Wachtel (1996) describe as the processes of distortion and projection. It is easier to distance ourselves from people or groups who are different from us than those who are similar. We can view the different group as "other" or "not me" and, of course, view the "other" as capable of all that we do not want to see in ourselves. All human beings share a common pool of potential feelings and behaviors. Despite this, when we use differences to deem people who are different some kind of "other" and not like us, unwanted feelings and behaviors of our own may be easily projected onto "them," experienced as if they represent some kind of flaw in the "other" group or individual and have nothing to do with ourselves. Siegel views fear as a necessary component in this process and observes:

Fear is the glue that maintains existing biases. . . . When people are catego-
rized as *we* or *they*, fear becomes part of the process of projecting onto those
whom we see as unlike ourselves all of the attributes that we would like to
deny in ourselves. *We* are the good self. *They* are the bad self. All players must
be maintained in that position and must deny that this is going on. Socially
unacceptable traits can thus remain invisible to the self while we stereotype
those whom *we* call *they* or *other* and imbue *them* with negative traits. (1995,
p. 297; emphasis added)

Blaine (2000) observes that we explain the behaviors of other people very
differently than we do our own behavior. He uses Allport's concept of ultimate attribution error, described by Thomas Pettigrew (1979), to explain this
phenomena. We tend to explain our own behavior as a function of situational
or environmental factors, while we explain the behavior of those who differ
from us, more harshly and as a function of their personality or internal traits.
This suggests that people who are not like us are seen as less likely to change.
Their behavior is ultimately attributed to some kind of basic flaw in the person's
character rather than some aspect of their circumstances. Furthermore, if their
failing is their own fault, they do not deserve our help, and they may even be
undeserving of the opportunities that they are denied. We may even rationalize the harm they endure as deserved. Moreover, we need not question why
some people have many opportunities and others do not, the explanation is
self-evident.

A clear example of this phenomenon may be observed when it is applied to
analyses of socioeconomic class. John Hartigan (1997) and Annalee Newitz
and Matt Wray (1997), in their work on poor white Americans, observe that
Americans, love to hate the poor. They observe that being labeled "poor" hardly
elicits sympathy, rather it elicits hostility and disgust and can often leave poor
people feeling ashamed of themselves. Being poor is often associated with
negative personality and character traits such as having inadequate values,
being inept, lazy, or simply stupid. Poor people are also viewed as if they refuse
to work (rather than that they are often unable to find work or living wages),
live in female-headed households, live in inner-city ghettos, are primarily people
of color, and are undeservedly on welfare. Even if it were not for these direct negative characterizations, our feelings about the poor are reflected in
our language in the definitions of values and descriptions of behaviors that
are associated with different class status and even the word "class" itself. The
Merriam-Webster's Dictionary defines "class" as high social rank, elegance,
high quality, a rating based on grade or quality. Karen Wyche (1996) tells us
that when we say that someone has "no class" we really do not mean that they
do not belong to a socioeconomic strata. But what do we mean? We are usually suggesting that people with "no class" have lower- or working–class values;

that they are behaving like poor or working-class people, with the clear infer-
ence that such behavior is deficient in some way. The demeaning implication
is clear that to have lower-class values or behavior is the same as having no
"class" at all. Consistent with Webster's definition, being lower class is to possess low quality or low social rank or lack them altogether. Our feelings about
class distinctions are also reflected in our language. People who have "middle-
class values" are viewed as hard working, valuing an education, saving their
money, capable of delaying gratification, and always trying to improve their
lot in life. By defining middle-class values in this manner, the implication is
that people who are middle class acquired that status because they have the
correct values and good moral character. This fails to address in any significant
way the critical role of social systems in the maintenance of class differences.
Such differences are often a function of differential access to opportunities, such
as education, at one time, trade union membership, as well as many jobs or
careers that were completely closed to out LGB (lesbian/gay/bisexual) people,
physically challenged individuals, people of color, women, older workers, and
so on. Simply put, differential opportunity and social injustice often block access
to middle-class status as access is not always merit based. The person, in this
case, the poor person is blamed for their circumstances with the assumption
that they did not do enough to better their circumstances. Blaming the poor
for their plight serves to further obscure the reality of an invisible system of
class oppression in this society. Poverty, like other differences in status, is explained as a function of personal deficits, while situational and systemic barriers go unexplored and remain invisible.

In another example, an openly gay man or lesbian who is the target of a
physical assault or other bias crime may be seen as having brought such treatment on themselves by allowing their sexual orientation to be known, for
example, flaunting behavior. Their difference is seen as the problem rather than
the response to their difference. The victim is blamed rather than the victim-
izer. This kind of thinking facilitates the avoidance of any analysis of the role
of social justice or injustice in someone's dilemma or in their treatment. The
meaning of the characteristic that distinguishes the person or makes them *different* from the observer, that is, their poverty, sexual orientation, ethnicity/
skin color, religion, and so on is defined by a distortion of what it really is and
what it really means as if it were the problem. The person's difference is then
used to explain their ill treatment or place in the social hierarchy. In this analysis,
an individual or group's failings can be attributed to their personal defect. The
role of the social system, and the identities of the players who benefit from
that system, can thus be avoided.

Blaine (2000) and Johnson (2001) both argue that a cultural mythology has
been developed to explain the way many aspects of the human differences
discussed in this volume are responded to. In that mythology, fears or appre-

hensions about differences are deemed *natural*. Since this fear is deemed *natural*, the avoidance of that which is different leads us to inevitably distance ourselves from and fear individuals and groups who are not like us. It is deemed only *natural* that we do this. Johnson (2001) suggests that this myth is designed to keep those who we consider outsiders on the outside of opportunities for social advancement and power and to rationalize mistreating them, if they happen to make it to the inside and actually acquire some of those opportunities. Some groups are deemed presumptuous and are even mistreated for simply advocating that they have equal access to social opportunities. Examples include African Americans and women who had to fight to secure the right to vote; lesbians and gay men who demand the right to work in any occupation, marry, and adopt children; people with disabilities who demand to have equal access to public facilities, as well as educational and occupational opportunities; and members of religious groups that demand the freedom to practice their religions without being discriminated against.

Johnson (2001) observes that historically people have not *naturally* avoided the unknown. To the contrary, many people find mystery in difference and experience the unknown as something compelling that draws them to it as a function of their human curiosity. Children display a natural curiosity about the unknown that reveals a *natural* ignorance about realistic dangers. They must be taught to discriminate between what and who is dangerous and what and who is not. For example, if you observe children in department stores or other public places, they more often than not readily approach each other unless they are discouraged by adults. When they do this and they are discouraged, it sends them an insidious message about difference. The message may be that something is wrong with them, that something is wrong with the other child, or that something is wrong about approaching anyone who is different. However, as long as the prevailing cultural myth about naturally fearing difference is accepted, we can avoid examining the role of social injustice in both creating and maintaining discrepancies in social power, as well as our own personal stake and role in them. Discrepancies in social power may be understood as representations of social privilege and social disadvantage. It is the need to deny the existence and meaning of those power differentials that is often a key ingredient in the discord observed between many individuals and groups who differ along the dimensions discussed in this volume.

While most human services professionals agree in principle that exploring and understanding the role of culture, sexual orientation, ethnicity, gender, race, class, age, and other variables is important in a range of arenas, in practice, people often report that they experience great discomfort when confronted with the need to discuss these issues and even greater discomfort when the discussion leads to an examination of the social inequities that are associated with membership in certain groups, essentially, examining social injustice. It is important to consider the discomfort often present when addressing these differences and its origins.

Materializing the Role of Social Privilege and Disadvantage in Negative Responses to Human Differences

What do we mean when we refer to social privilege? The Merriam-Webster's dictionary defines privilege as a special advantage, immunity benefit granted to or enjoyed by an individual, class, or caste, that people come to feel they have a right to hold. What is noteworthy is that while the benefit or privilege is given regardless of merit, once people have it, they experience it as something they have a right to have and that perhaps others who are not like them do not have an equal right to. Social privilege is usually something that facilitates the optimal development of an individual, increases access to societal opportunities, or simply makes life easier but is not acquired by virtue of merit or personal effort. It is gained simply by being a member of the group that is privileged. It is important to understand the nature of privilege as something that is not merit-based to fully grasp the reluctance of many people to acknowledge that they may have it. The dimensions discussed in this volume represent human dimensions that may be a locus of privilege or a locus of disadvantage, depending on the group you belong to and the current context.

Stephanie Wildman (1996), Peggy McIntosh (1988), and Allan Johnson (2001) analyze white skin privilege as one form of social advantage, and each discusses the ways that they and other White Americans benefit from having white skin in a racist society. In its essence having white skin privilege makes life easier. In her examination of race privilege, Stephanie Wildman (1996) defines key elements of privilege as the systemic conferral of benefit and advantage. She argues that the characteristics of people who are members of privileged groups come to define societal norms and not surprisingly to the benefit of the people who establish the norms. Members of other groups are measured against the characteristics that are held by the privileged, usually the most dominant members of a society, and found to be wanting in some way. The privileged characteristic is legitimized as the norm and those who stand outside of it are considered deviant, deficient, or defective. These are important concepts in mental health. Overall, "they" are seen as deserving of their lot in life.

There is a connection between the need to establish clear boundaries between ethnic, class, sexual, and other groups in our society and the existence of privilege and social disadvantage. The need for socially constructed boundaries between heterosexuals and lesbians and gay men, men and women, lower and upper socioeconomic classes, people of color and White Americans and other groups is not to provide accurate descriptive information about them.

These boundaries are in place to maintain and justify the system of social privilege and disadvantage associated with those characteristics. The ultimate goal is to make sure that the privileged maintain their privileged access and that others do not have similar access.

Achievements by members of privileged groups are usually attributed to individual efforts and rewards for those efforts are seen as having been earned and deserved. Judith Jordan (1997) observes that a myth of "earned power" and "meritocracy" was developed by the members of the dominant culture to justify their right to discriminate against and limit social opportunities for people who were different. When these myths are accepted, people are viewed as getting whatever they deserve. People who are in positions of power are seen as deserving of privilege. People who are powerless, disadvantaged, vulnerable, and who are exploited are presumed to be getting what they deserve as well, which includes blame, punishment, and contempt for their condition. Members of socially disadvantaged groups would not simply go along with this arrangement, unless they were convinced that the social system distributed opportunities fairly. When they accept the myth of meritocracy, they may even blame themselves. This form of self-blame is expressed in *internalized* racism, sexism, abilism, classism, heterosexism, and so on. The person of color who *believes* that White people are superior has internalized racism. Believing the negative stereotypes about some aspect of your identity is a form of internalized oppression. Hence, the systemic determinants of social privilege and disadvantage are usually invisible and if materialized are denied by those who are in power and who benefit from them. Needless to say, members of both socially privileged and socially disadvantaged groups will have feelings about their relative status that will affect the way they feel about encounters with one another.

Social disadvantage stands on the opposite end of the conceptual continuum of privilege. Marilyn Frye (1996) observes that it is important to make a distinction between societal disadvantage and human misery. In her analysis of social oppression she observes that people can suffer, experience pain, and be miserable without being socially disadvantaged. Conversely, privileged status does not always protect one from the experience of human suffering or failure. However, to be socially disadvantaged is to have your life "confined and shaped by forces and barriers which are not accidental or occasional and hence avoidable, but are systematically related to each other in such a way as to catch one between and among them and restrict or penalize motion in any direction" (Frye, 1996, p. 165).

Nancy Boyd-Franklin (1993) writes that in the course of her work training clinical psychologists and family therapists, she finds that it is usually acceptable and sometimes even welcome to discuss cultural differences between various societal groups. There is general agreement that many people will differ from the human services professional and that it is incumbent on that professional to know something about the values, beliefs, and behaviors that characterize people who are different from us. These discussions about cultural specifics often evoke interest and most people agree that a working knowledge of those differences is crucial to doing culturally sensitive work with clients from culturally diverse groups. However, when the discussion shifts to explore the systemic realities of belonging to certain groups, racism, as opposed to race; heterosexism, as opposed to lesbian or gay sexual orientation; classism, as opposed to class status; abilism, ageism, and so on, the mood changes. Members of the audience, who had been previously receptive, polite, and accepting become defensive, angry, attacking, and sometimes absorbed in their own guilt. This response can serve as a metaphor for what people who are members of socially disadvantaged groups report as a part of their experience, when they attempt to talk about the ways they face societal discrimination or to express their anger and pain about it. Their comments evoke reactions that are often hostile. Blaine (2000) observes that color blindness, the belief that everyone has experienced some form of oppression, making everyone the same, and other forms of denial of differences are designed to avoid confronting the reality of social injustice. Johnson (2001) argues that privilege is not only a problem for those who do not have it but is also for those who have it because of its relational nature. When someone is unfairly disadvantaged by social systems and fails to get something they deserve, someone else is unfairly privileged and gains something they do not deserve.

The ego ideal is defined as the collection of ideal characteristics that we would like to see in ourselves. The reality of who we are always falls short of our ideal because by definition the ideal is perfection and therefore unattainable. It is our ideal self, the way we would like to be and sometimes the way we actually experience ourselves. When we are confronted with the ways that we fall short of that ideal, we experience shame. Few people want to acknowledge getting something that they did not deserve or even worse, profiting at someone else's expense, whether deliberate or not. It is not viewed as a positive reflection on ourselves when it occurs, rather it is deemed shameful and makes us uncomfortable about ourselves. To avoid experiencing shame and discomfort, we must deny that we may profit at someone else's expense. This denial becomes difficult if we hold a social privilege and we encounter people who are disadvantaged around that characteristic. The encounter itself can elicit discomfort, even if differences and/or their meaning are never overtly discussed. This often forms the core of the *discord* or discomfort that is experienced between two people or groups that are different. It is not just their difference that is the problem although superficially it is easier to attribute the discord to what is most obviously visible and different about them. It is really the discrepancy in social power as well as the denial of the systemic privilege that both individuals and groups know exists on some level and that elicits discomfort in both. If members of socially disadvantaged groups voice their feelings about this situation or even assert that privilege exists, they may elicit not only discomfort but also anger from privileged group members for many of the reasons previously discussed. For this reason, many members of socially disadvantaged groups will deny any awareness of the role of societal oppression, even if asked directly, out of a realistic fear that the person or group with greater social power will become uncomfortable and use that power against their vulnerable counterparts in various ways. This pretense needed to maintain "harmony" further silences members of socially disadvantaged groups and makes discussions about this issue even more unlikely. The failure to explore the reality of social privilege and social disadvantage maintains the illusion that differences between people per se are the problem rather than what those differences mean in a society that is racist, sexist, heterosexist, ageist, ableist, and so on.

Paula Rothenberg (1988) suggests that identifying institutions and systems that perpetuate the privilege of one group and the subordination of another elicits considerable anger and resistance from members of privileged groups. She attributes their anger and resistance to the need to avoid acknowledging the implications of having privilege, whether intended or not. Among those implications is the challenge to many deeply held beliefs about the inherent fairness of the American dream and the belief in the American value of diversity. When the reality of privilege materializes, it also challenges individuals' personal beliefs about how they became successful and perhaps even more fundamentally, who they really are. This can be particularly troubling to people who need to believe that their *ego ideal* is the reality. Hence, many Americans are invested in believing that sexual orientation, race, gender, and so on represent real and not socially constructed differences, and that those differences justify unequal treatment and limited access to the opportunities that others who are privileged have benefited from. It is unlikely that these issues can be confronted in a client without scrutinizing and challenging one's own sense of self as a health service provider. This task can be a painful and difficult but necessary undertaking.

Clare Holzman (1995) suggests that when people are confronted with the power and privilege differentials between themselves and others, guilt can be an immediate and powerful reaction, and one that they would like to avoid as quickly as possible. She argues that its most unproductive form is one that is misdirected or produces immobilizing shame. By contrast, guilt can be productive when it motivates a person to understand and change their behavior and attitudes. She warns us, however, that when guilt is used to elicit sympathy or ward off anticipated attack, people who belong to socially disadvantaged groups often feel that they are expected to forgive, soothe, or assuage the privileged person's discomfort. When these feelings of discomfort are used to shift the focus away from examining the social locus of disadvantage to taking care of the privileged person's guilt or shame, a healthy transformation cannot occur. Furthermore, this places an unfair, additional imposition on already burdened socially disadvantaged group members. When privileged group members engage in this behavior, it may exemplify an exercise of their privilege as well as a subtle way of silencing the disadvantaged person or persons. Members of privileged groups who experience such emotions often project them onto disadvantaged group members rather than experience the often painful discrepancy between ways they would like to see themselves, their *ego ideal*, and who they really are.

Most people do not want to be considered racist, heterosexist, classist, or sexist, but they spend more of their time seeking to avoid those *labels*, rather than exploring their behavior and the ways that they benefit from or have participated in systems of interrelated privilege and oppression, intended or not. It is unlikely that in a society that is racist, sexist, classist, and heterosexist and discriminates systemically on other levels that one can have privileged characteristics and not have benefited from them. But what does that mean? In a heterosexist society, a heterosexual person has the social rights that are accorded heterosexual persons and denied to LGB persons. In this example, they do not have to actively do anything to acquire the benefits of heterosexuality. Similarly, in a racist society, individuals who have white skin derive the benefits of white skin privileges simply because they possess that characteristic. What is derived is based on the presence of privileged characteristics, not effort, ability, or merit. The rationales for doing this are built into the rules and institutions of our society. The inability of an individual to point to, remember, or name the specific events or times when they benefited from a privileged characteristic does not determine the degree to which they have benefited in some ways. Hierarchies of privilege and disadvantage exist within privileged and disadvantaged groups just as they exist between them.

One of the difficulties inherent in acknowledging privilege is that it often triggers the feeling that you have done something wrong, followed by a self-defense. All people have more than one identity. Some of their identities may be privileged while others may be disadvantaged. Most, however, are more comfortable expressing the ways they are disadvantaged than the ways they are privileged. We are all, however, responsible for acknowledging the presence of social privilege in our own lives, and the ways we benefit from it. It is impossible to grapple with the complexity of difference if we do not acknowledge the social context of privilege and disadvantage that salient human differences are embedded in. We are not personally responsible for the existence of these systems of privilege and disadvantage, but we move within them all the time in some role or roles. Institutional privilege is conferred by interlocking social systems as a reward for the possession of characteristics valued by those who are dominant. It is indeed good fortune to be born heterosexual in a heterosexist society; white in a racist society; financially well off in a classist society; male in a sexist and patriarchal society; young in an ageist society; and able bodied in an ableist society. Possession of those desired characteristics does not make one a better person, despite the fact that superior value is attributed to them as a rationale for the discrepancy in social power attendant to them, however, possessing those characteristics makes life easier. Membership in those categories is a function of the luck of the draw. People do not control their ethnicity, the presence of a disability, their sex, sexual orientation, age, or the economic status of their parents; they are simply born into those statuses. For that reason, the presence of benefits accrued as a function of these characteristics are privileges.

Frye (1996) observed that the presence of a privilege does not eradicate the struggles an individual encounters when those struggles are defined outside the realm of their locus of privilege. When individuals have multiple identities, some of those identities or characteristics may place them in privileged groups, while simultaneously, others will place them in disparaged groups. Some forms of privilege may mitigate or positively moderate some forms of disadvantage, while other privileges may not mitigate them at all. Similarly, membership in some disadvantaged groups can compound the negative effects of simultaneous membership in another disadvantaged group or groups. For example, a poor woman with a disability, lesbians and gay men of color, poor older men and women, and so on.

We often assume that just being a member of a disadvantaged group or experiencing protracted hardship from social disadvantage makes that person more tolerant or accepting of members of other disadvantaged groups than people who are privileged. This wishful thinking is perhaps more myth than substance. A person's membership in a disadvantaged group does not mean that they are incapable of behaving in oppressive ways to members of some other group if they hold a social privilege that the other group is denied. For example, African Americans and other people of color have a long history of patterned social disadvantage that is based on their race/ethnicity/skin color. Despite this, many people of color do not view the struggles of other disadvantaged groups for social justice as similar to or as deserving as their own. How can we explain this response to a group's difference, by people who have been mistreated on the basis of their own difference from the majority?

In this specific example, the relative visibility of race/ethnicity among African Americans as well as other people of color and the invisibility of lesbian/gay sexual orientation play a significant role in the belief that nontraditional sexual orientation is chosen. It is as if the sexual orientation of lesbians and gay men, including those who are also people of color, are not relevant, because of their invisibility, until they make their "difference" known. People who have these beliefs assert that, unlike for example, African Americans, Asians, and other ethnic "minority" group members, lesbians and gay men have a choice about remaining invisible. If they choose to be visible, they bring problems on themselves. People of color on the other hand are deemed readily identifiable and without "choice." This line of reasoning clearly suggests that lesbians and gay men who choose to be "out" are inviting negative treatment and that perhaps they even deserve it. Among some people of color, any behavior that is routinely acceptable among heterosexual men and women is often regarded as something distasteful among lesbians and gay men (just as it is in the dominant culture), for example, displays of affection in public. The core belief is that nontraditional sexual orientation represents a difference that is a flaw, unlike racial identity, and is something that can and should be concealed. The message is that people who choose not to do so are simply asking for trouble and deserve whatever they get. It is assumed that the problem rests in being known and that there is no cost in remaining silent. This position is a stark representation of heterosexual privilege and homophobia because it is a contradiction to what we know about how African Americans, for example, feel about group members who choose to pass for white. Such behavior is viewed as the ultimate betrayal, not only against yourself but also against your people, your ancestor's struggle, and your African heritage; something that only a person completely lacking personal pride or integrity would do.

Aside from the psychological cost of passing, trying to be invisible, and hiding that is associated with being closeted, the cultural and psychological literature document the negative psychological effects of passing as a long-term mechanism for managing discrimination. Intense levels of stress accompany the constant threat and fear of being discovered. There is also a price to be paid in the form of physical and psychic energy that a person is forced to expend if they live a fraudulent life and if they are forced to conceal and compartmentalize important aspects of their lives and selves, particularly from people who they are closest to. There is also an ongoing level of vigilance and a concomitant lack of spontaneity that has a negative impact on the authenticity required in healthy interpersonal relationships. Furthermore, when a climate of terror gives rise to the kind of silence that is required for people to become and remain invisible, the act of silencing itself represents another form of social oppression. Finally, sexual orientation is not routinely visible in the way that race/ethnicity is readily apparent among most African Americans. However, the assumption that race is always equally visible among African Americans or that they are always identifiable is not valid either. This assumption ignores the presence of African Americans, throughout our history, who chose to pass for white. Most group members feel it is important to claim one's African ancestry with pride. However, the same principle is not applied to sexual orientation and constitutes an example of privilege within a disadvantaged group. In this case, heterosexual African Americans who are heterosexist exercise a kind of heterosexual dominance or privilege by defining being "out" racially and ethnically as healthy and imperative, while being "out" as a lesbian or gay man as a problem. Thus, the difference in sexual orientation, being gay/lesbian, is defined as the problem. Among African Americans, and other ethnoracial groups, when a person is unfairly treated because of their ethnic group membership, racism is clearly defined as the problem, not the person who is harmed. In fact, when a person is discriminated against, based on their ethnicity, and they feel that they deserved maltreatment, we consider it an expression of their *internalized racism* and consider it a problem. However, when a lesbian or gay man is mistreated because of their group membership, it is the victim who is defined as the problem. This kind of behavior is an example of within-group heterosexual privilege, in that the very behavior that is defined as laudable in a dominant or privileged group, in this example heterosexual men and women of color, is deemed a defect in their lesbian and gay counterparts, the disadvantaged group. Heterosexism is not defined as the problem; the person who identifies or makes their "difference" visible is considered the problem. While African Americans and other people of color may be righteously seen as socially disadvantaged groups, these examples inform us that all people of color are not equally disadvantaged within their groups, nor are they immune to behaving in oppressive ways just because they are members of a disadvantaged group. Although I have used ethnoracial groups and sexual orientation in this example, there are many other permutations and combinations that may be observed. We cannot understand the tension that surrounds exploring human differences if we need to deny the existence of a system of privileges and disadvantages that those differences are always embedded in. We must also appreciate how those systems operate between as well as within groups.

Thus far, this discussion has focused on the meaning of human differences and the relationship between the meaning of differences, the existence of power and privilege hierarchies, and the need to avoid acknowledging the presence of those hierarchies by deeming differences themselves as problematic. I have discussed privilege and disadvantage within the same categories of characteristics (race: white American vs. Americans of color, etc.) to simplify this analysis. In reality it is far more complicated as many different identities are engaged in every individual simultaneously. Clearly, no individual or group has just one identity. The collective dimensions that this volume's authors explore all exist in every individual. Every person has an ethnic or cultural identification, is a member of a socioeconomic class, a gender, a sexual orientation, an age cohort, and so on. All those dimensions develop in some kind of dynamic interaction with one another across the life span. Hence, the Japanese-American who is a lesbian, from a lower class background, with a visible mobility disability may experience herself as very different from her Japanese-American counterpart who is heterosexual, able bodied, and upper class. The gay African-American male may experience himself and his African Americanness very differently from his heterosexual counterpart. While they both share an ethnic identity that is different from other ethnic identities, they may not view ethnicity as the most salient aspect of their identity. Other identities in this example will "color" the experience of ethnicity. Similarly, the first Japanese-American woman may feel that she has more in common with another woman with a disability, or another woman who is poor, than another Japanese-American woman with whom she shares no other identities that are important to her. The identity that is most salient to some individuals may be the one that requires the greatest expenditure of time and effort to overcome the social barriers associated with it.

Just as we have a cultural myth about differences being inherently problematic, we have a similar myth about similarities being inherently harmonious. People often presume that if they share some salient group membership or identity with someone that they will be more like one another than not. We also assume that people who share some major aspect of identity or *difference* with us will understand us better and will be more accepting of us than someone who is different along that dimension. There is often the assumption that there is one master identity, usually the one that is most visible or the one that is most disparaged by society, that subsumes all other identities in ways that are often more mythical or fantasied than realistic. The reality is that most people have multiple identities that shift in a kaleidoscopic way, depending on the point in time, social and geographical contexts, and the person's personal history. Members of the same group are not homogeneous. Wildman (1996) and Rothenberg (1988) observe that each of us is embedded in a matrix of categories and contexts, where in some contexts we are privileged with respect to some identities and in others we may be disadvantaged, each interacting with the other. One form of privilege can moderate a form of oppression, simultaneously, just as membership in an oppressed group may negatively moderate a locus of privilege in an individual. No person fits into only one static category, rather, each of us exists at the nexus of many groups or categories. All members of a socially disadvantaged group are not disadvantaged equally. All members of a privileged group are not privileged equally.

The very idea of race, sexual orientation, gender, or any similar characteristic exists only because we give them meaning that changes with time, place, and circumstances. Social hierarchical positioning, whether based on race, sexual orientation, class, gender, or other variables, is maintained in part through an unwritten rule that it cannot be discussed; hence, difference per se is deemed the problem.

Recommendations for Human Services Professionals

In human services contexts, professionals involved in training as well as counseling must assess their own feelings, fears, and fantasies about similarities and differences before engaging in such work. For example, it is important to consider the role of difference, social privilege, and social disadvantage in your own life and its meaning. It is important to know what you are predisposed to do when you encounter people who are different and people who are similar. How does difference/similarity make you feel? What assumptions do you make when someone is like you, for example, ethnicity. Do you gloss over or need to deny differences? Are they anxiety provoking? What did it mean to be different/similar to others as a child? We often presume that difference is a bad thing. For some people, however, for example, individuals from large families, being different may have represented the only way they could get any kind of personal attention from overwhelmed adults because the difference made them stand out in the family "crowd." For others, being different may have resulted in having family members distance themselves from you or threaten to do so. Other individuals may have been forced to remove themselves from the company of a loved one who was different and who the family disapproved of. Was it more important to stand out or fit in and if so, around what characteristics was this the case? What do you use to fill in the blanks when you encounter an unknown? How did you come to *know* what you think you *know* about others?

Consider, of course, that you have many identities. Determine where you are located on the spectrum of social privilege and social disadvantage for each of those identities, as well as the person or persons you will be working with. Consider those identities separately and think about how they come together. For example, when you were first aware of them, where did you get the information you have about what it meant to be identified with that group, how old you were, how did it make you feel about yourself, and did this change over time. When you encounter another person, what is the normative power relationship in society represented by your identities? How might this be recapitulated in your professional relationship with this person? How might it be helpful, as well as not helpful? Is there a discrepancy between your personal subjective identity and your social status? How do you explain and manage the discrepancy internally as well as publically. How do you feel when you are more as well as less socially privileged than the person or persons you are working with? How do you manage those feelings?

Summary

The tendency to universalize human experience should be carefully scrutinized. While it is usually engaged to decrease interpersonal tension, the result is that it generally increases marginalization among members of socially disadvantaged groups. The need to see people as just alike, to deny or fear their differences is used to avoid the difficult tensions that can disrupt the false sense of social harmony and security between different groups as well as within the same group. This is often anxiety provoking. Most people grow up believing in the values of fairness and in the explicit assumption of fairness in our social institutions. When people are confronted with the ways in which their optimal development is or has been enhanced by factors that are not based on a simple function of ability, hard work, or fairness, but rather on things they did not earn, they may need to avoid acknowledging that reality. To acknowledge this reality may appear synonymous with minimizing your personal ability and effort, indeed, your personal integrity. Such denial, however, creates major obstacles in implementing diversity and in some settings, even in discussing it. Failing to acknowledge and understand the broad and divergent role of societal privilege and social disadvantage in people's lives ultimately undermines those initiatives whose goal is to celebrate the richness of human differences.

In considering the complicated nexus of cultural differences and similarities in any individual, we are compelled to ask questions that go beyond our understanding of these variables as mere differences or similarities and speak more directly to their meaning. This chapter has discussed the tendency to avoid examining the meaning of differences, such as race, ethnicity, age, gender, religion, social class, sexual orientation, and other variables, and the attribution at least in part to the discomfort associated with examining the differentials in power and privilege that accompany these human distinctions and give them significance in people's lives.

In *Sister Outsider*, Audre Lorde writes:

Somewhere on the edge of consciousness there is what I call a mythical norm, which each one of us within our hearts knows "that is not me." In America, this norm is usually defined as white, thin, male, young, heterosexual, Christian and financially secure. It is with this mythical norm that the trappings of power reside in this society. Those of us who stand outside that power often identify one way in which we are different, and we assume that to be the primary cause of all oppression, forgetting other distortions around difference, some of which we ourselves may be practicing. (1984, p. 116)

References

Blaine, B. (2000). *The psychology of diversity: Perceiving and experiencing social difference.* Mountain View, CA: Mayfield.

Boyd-Franklin, N. (1993, July/August). Pulling out the arrows. *Family Therapy Networker, 17*(4), 54–56.

Frye, M. (1996). Oppression. In K. E. Rosenblum & T-M. C. Travis (Eds.), *The meaning of difference: Constructions of race, sex and gender, social class, and sexual orientation* (pp. 163–167). New York: McGraw Hill.

Greene, B. (2000a). Beyond heterosexism and across the cultural divide. Developing an inclusive lesbian, gay and bisexual psychology: A look to the future. In B. Greene & G. L. Croom (Eds.), *Education, research and practice in lesbian, gay, bisexual and transgendered psychology: A resource manual* (pp. 1–45). Thousand Oaks, CA: Sage Publications.

Greene, B. (2000b). African American lesbian and bisexual women in Feminist-Psychodynamic Psychotherapies: Surviving and thriving between a rock and a hard place. In L. Jackson & B. Greene (Eds.), *Psychotherapy with African American women: Innovations in psychodynamic perspectives and practice* (pp. 82–125). New York: Guilford.

Hartigan, J. (1997). Name calling: Objectifying "Poor Whites" and "White Trash" in Detroit. In M. Wray & A. Newitz (Eds.), *White trash: Race and class in America* (pp. 41–56). New York: Routledge.

Holzman, C. (1995). Rethinking the role of guilt and shame in white women's anti-racism work. In J. Adleman & G. Enguidanos (Eds.), *Racism in the lives of women: Testimony, theory and guides to practice* (pp. 325–332). New York: Haworth Press.

Johnson, A. G. (2001). *Privilege, power and difference.* Mountain View, CA: Mayfield.

Jordan, J. (1997). Relational therapy in a nonrelational world. Work in Progress, No. 79. Wellesley, MA: Stone Center Working Paper Series.

Lorde, A. (1984). Age, race and class. In A. Lorde, *Sister outsider: Essays and speeches.* Freedom, CA: Crossing Press.

McIntosh, P. (1988). Understanding correspondence between white privilege and male privilege through Women's Studies work. (Working paper #189.) Center for Research on Women, Wellesley College, Wellesley, MA.

Merriam-Webster Inc. (1996). *Merriam-Webster's Collegiate Dictionary. 10th ed.* Dallas, TX: Merriam-Webster Inc. & Zane Publishing Co.

Newitz, A., & Wray, M. (1997). Introduction. In M. Wray & A. Newitz (Eds.), *White trash: Race and class in America* (pp. 1–12). New York: Routledge.

Pettigrew, T. F. (1979). The ultimate attribution error: Extending Allport's cognitive analysis of prejudice. *Personality and Social Psychology Bulletin, 5,* 461–476.

Rothenberg, P. (1988). Integrating the study of race, gender, and class: Some preliminary observations. *Feminist Teacher, 3*(3), 37–42,

Siegel, R. Josefowitz (1995). Overcoming bias through awareness, mutual encouragement, and commitment. In J. Adleman & G. Enguidanos (Eds.), *Racism in the lives of women: Testimony, theory and guides to practice* (pp. 295–301). New York: Haworth Press.

Wachtel, P. (1996). The inner city and the inner life. [Review of the book *The analyst in the inner city: Race, class and culture through a psychoanalytic lens.*] *Tikkun: A Bimonthly Critique of Politics, Culture and Society, 11*(3), 59–61.

Wildman, S. (1996). *Privilege revealed: How invisible preference undermines America.* New York: New York University Press.

Wyche, K. F. (1996). Conceptualizations of social class in African American women: Congruence of client and therapist definitions. *Women & Therapy, 18*(3/4), 35–43.

2

MIGUEL A. YBARRA

Becoming Americano

Has the Sleeping Giant Awakened?

Latinos/Hispanics—Definitions

What is the definition of a Hispanic versus a Latino? Well, for the most part, Hispanic has been traditionally used to refer to all Spanish speakers, including those from Spain. This presents a significant controversy as many Latin Americans do not speak Spanish nor do they claim a Latin-American heritage (e.g., Brazilians.) Furthermore, the term often implies a cultural lineage related to Spain, which is also incorrect, as many Native Americans do not speak Spanish nor do they trace their ancestry to Spain.

Latino most often refers to persons from Latin America and is yet not an appropriate term to describe the Native American populations of the Americas. Furthermore, it is important to discuss the term Latin America before progressing. While many individuals would presume that Latin America is composed of specific countries, it might be more useful to determine the migration and final destinations of a people united by a common language, differences in dialect notwithstanding. With this in mind, Latin America can extend from the South Central/Southwestern United States (Texas, New Mexico, Arizona, and California) into Mexico, Central and South America. Latin America, therefore, comprises many people from many countries with different backgrounds and customs.

However, it appears that the more terms we come up with, the more explaining that is necessary in order to continue a simple dialogue. More often than not, these explanations become methods of distraction rather than distinction because it becomes more difficult, and sometimes more important, to determine how a person should address another rather than addressing the needs of a person, group, or community. Also, due to this "method of distraction," we all too often defer the celebration of diversity to "another place, another time." An important point to remember when working with culturally different individuals (for the purposes of this chapter, "culturally different" will refer to people different from you) is to allow them to self-define. By allowing the person with whom you are engaged to define who they are removes the unnecessary trepidation and irrational fear of *saying the wrong thing*. Attempting to participate in this defining process has led to the phenomena of political correctness.

The term political correctness also deserves some attention. First, this process prevents us from discussing adequately and openly the general and real issues of ethnicity as well as prejudice and discrimination. While I believe that political correctness has occurred for good reasons, such as preventing hurtful speech and allowing people to reclaim a collective dignity, I also believe that it has transformed itself into an insidious and uncontrollable beast that focuses our dialogue on the terms we use to describe each other rather than on the content of the dialogue itself. While each of us should be able to self-identify, we should be careful that the real dialogue isn't in the terms I use to define myself, but in what each of us needs in order to fully participate in a country that claims to have removed glass ceilings and glass floors. For me, that means the freedom to call myself Chicano, Mexican-American, Hispanic, or Latino and to use that identity in addressing matters of substance concerning interethnic relations.

At times, it seems that we use present-day political correctness actively as a method to talk about anything but the issues. And, given the issues of our time, how can we accept the fact that we do not talk about them at length and with a strong desire to arrive at a solution (i.e., a poor process of an exchange of ideas and communication between people of color and the white America, a poor process of an exchange of ideas and communication between and among people of color, global economies, lightning-fast communication, affirmative action, relationships between people with different backgrounds, inequitable funding for our children from one school district to another or from one state to another, the fact that there are *any* violent and hate-filled crimes in our schools, children who remain poor and undereducated in the United States, and an increase in the number of hate-groups in this country). As we continue to ignore these and other issues, history has, if nothing else, demonstrated that they will either remain equally volatile or increase in intensity until they burst with much added pain and suffering.

So how do we go about working with each other and using the differences in our background as an advantage? First, we must understand that people of color in the United States have learned to become bicultural and multicultural out of necessity. They must know not only how to be in the context of their cultural roots and community but must also learn how to be when working in a setting in which the dominant white culture prevails. Furthermore, it is important to understand that this is a process with no real beginning or clear end.

Let us consider *biculturalism*. This means to be able to function proficiently in at least two cultures. Those of us who claim a hyphenated identity (Mexican-American, for example) understand very well how we can be, and need to be, bicultural. It is important to continue to function as a member of my community (Mexican-American). It is equally important to understand and to know how to function efficiently within the dominant society (white culture). There's no way, no matter where in the United States I live, that I can go an entire day without coming into contact with persons from the dominant (white) culture who are in positions of power. This contact can occur at the local mall where I can expect the manager of any given store to be white. Or I can be at the local school, college, or university where I can expect the principal or the president of the institution to be white.

The important issue here is to understand not only the fact that people can become bicultural, but also that there is a need for all of us to develop these general skills of a more intimate interaction. Being bicultural is certainly an advantage because it allows each individual who develops these skills to work efficiently and effectively in another culture while maintaining one's own identity. In biculturalism, there is typically no sense of loss of self because the person retains competency in his/her own culture/ethnic group.

Multiculturalism, on the other hand, is a *process* of working, from a competent foundation, with people from other groups. A great portion of the Hispanic/Latino community has learned and actively engaged in the process of multiculturalism. The differences between the groups or cultures of which we speak can be based on ethnicity or they can be based on other factors, including gender, age, sexual orientation, geographical region, or some other cluster of issues that when seen as a whole define a culture. Multiculturalism is when an individual is able to recognize that a process exists in order to work well with people from different backgrounds. The concept of multiculturalism has become more important over the last 20 to 30 years because of the rising number of people from various cultures that are entering this country and the American workforce. As corporate America gains (higher profits, better products), we also gain by introducing this unique diversity into the workplace. While it would be unreasonable to know all that exists about the specific background and nuances of a particular community of people, we can learn how to deal with diversity, as it currently exists, and incorporate this model into our method of daily interaction.

Another process from which we would benefit is *cross-cultural competency*. This concept, at some point in your life, will enable you to engage in social interaction and work with people from other cultures from a competent, learned, and holistic place. A person can become cross-culturally competent when he/she is able to tap into, understand, and use the culture of the other person throughout the process of the interaction. In other words, cross-cultural competency occurs when you are able to address an individual more through their perspective than your own. This new insight about a person or a group of people amplifies the impact of his/her background on current issues. For example, a counselor or manager would be able to use her/his knowledge of cultural subtleties and his/her command of ethnic traditions and customs in a more effective and useful application of therapeutic or human resources techniques.

There is one important word of caution as we immerse ourselves in the process of learning multiculturalism and cross-cultural competence and attempt to understand the Latino/Hispanic communities in the United States; we must remember that because an individual is a member of a culturally/ethnically different group does not mean that that person is cross-culturally competent. Furthermore, simply because a person is from the same ethnic/cultural group in which you are interested (i.e., Chicano) does not mean that (1) this person knows all issues facing all Chicanos in the United States, (2) that she/he can speak on behalf of all Chicanos, (3) that he/she knows the problems being faced by Chicanos in the Northeast as opposed to the West Coast, and perhaps more important, (4) that this person would *want* to be responsible for any of the above!

The difference between multiculturalism and cross-cultural competence lies in the relationship. To be multicultural is to be in a process that affirms and maintains an equal relationship with people from different cultures, much as you would with your friends and acquaintances within your own culture/ethnic group. To be cross-culturally competent means that you can function professionally (or socially) with people from different cultures and backgrounds because of your knowledge and acceptance of their culture.

These concepts are more important than we may think. For example, it has been reported that Spanish is the primary language for the majority (73%) of first generation immigrants. However, for second generation children, it drops to 40%, and more impressively down to 1% for third generation grandchildren. The impact that this may have is that we are increasing our opportunities to communicate and experience others' diversity in our ever-changing society, so it makes sense that the quality of the communication and exchange must improve.

Of greater importance is the concept of Hispanics wanting to become a part of the American tradition without losing their cultural/ethnic identity. For 84% of the Latinos surveyed by the *Washington Post*, it is important for Latinos to blend into the larger society. However, 89% also felt that it was important for Latinos to maintain their distinct cultures. The changing demographics and direction of the Hispanic population and the changing face of America are impressive.

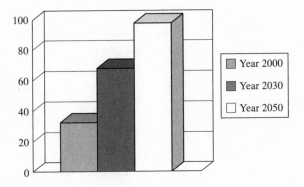

The Latino Population in Millions

The Journey over the Bering Strait

The men and women who traveled over the Bering Strait into the Americas from Asia were the individuals who settled the land long before Columbus arrived and *discovered* the New World. These individuals populated and cared for this land themselves and made decisions based on the impact on future generations that were to follow. This concept becomes especially important as we begin to see patterns of behavior and values between groups of people in the United States. These Native Americans, of Asian decent, were then "taken" by the Europeans who began to settle the land and their progeny became the Latino populations of the Americas.

This sometimes violent history makes more clear the incredible range in skin tone and general features that exist even among people of the same culture and ethnic background. In fact, skin tone plays an important role in the lives of Hispanics/Latinos today. The lighter the skin tone of a newborn, the happier the family seems to be, most often because of a perceived advantage. The darker the child, the more perceived the hardship the child will have to endure. While these generalizations are never 100% correct, they are seated in a grain of truth that can be seen historically. Clearly, this knowledge about other cultures can help us become more culturally competent and improve our communication and exchanges with diverse communities.

Latinos/Hispanics in the United States

As we begin to understand the processes involved in social and professional interactions between people from different cultures in our society, the question becomes, "What does it mean to be Latino/Hispanic in the United

States?" This is a particularly important question because I believe it means different things to different people. For those of us who identify as people of color (a less offensive term than ethnic minority and yet has the added bonus of being politically correct by today's standards), living in the United States means that we have to face a majority of people, who as a whole would systematically negate the experiences as well as the contributions of any group of people that do not look, sound, or act like them. In other words, there is very little recognition of the fact that expansion to the Pacific (Manifest Destiny or "Go west, young man") actually meant to once again (as it did to the Native American population in New England) take land that belonged to other people. While many of these people were American Indian/Native American, others were Mexican/Latino/Hispanic. White settlers consequently occupied Mexican states and territories. The new population then viewed the original residents as trespassers. The original landowners were not seen as part of the legitimate structure and were removed from whatever power they held and relegated to a condition: the condition of existing as less than the new residents and as a ruthless and savage people. Manifest Destiny became a symbol of righteousness to white America, an illustration of progress that made its way into the popular culture of the United States, without the recognition of the reality that lives and families were destroyed in the expansion and construction of this country.

There are many stories (my own included) of Latino/Hispanic children rooting for the white cowboy (with a white hat) while disparaging those dirty "bandidos" during the Saturday afternoon matinee. Many people have been conditioned by Hollywood to think that only the white man could be the good guy. I, myself, bought into the notion that every other person of color was bad and was not to be trusted. Individuals from different ethnic groups have reported being leery and afraid of Blacks because one never knew the extent to which they would go to get what they wanted. They have reported being envious of Asians because they had it made in terms of education, jobs, and great salaries. People of color have reported being disappointed in the Cubans and Puerto Ricans and Chicanos because all they ever did was fight (and usually with each other.)

To be Hispanic/Latino in the United States means that we are constantly exposed to the idea of what it means to be an American. More often than not, to say that you are an American is the same as saying that you are white. The fact that the Mexican people were in Texas before it became a republic and then the 34th state in the union was nowhere to be seen in my history books (grades 1–12). These selective history texts perpetuate the institutional racism that only one group of people, the white people, have made this country what it is today.

What people of color learn about the involvement of their ancestors' contributions to the United States must come from an outside source. It must come from additional learning. This extra effort is a developmental necessity in order to facilitate the self-worth of people of color. In other words, an American of Mexican descent must actively seek out the contributions made to the United States by others like him or her in order to appreciate those contributions and consequently feel the same pride and ownership about this country that is often reserved for families who keep meticulous records about family history! This process happens naturally and appropriately for white students. History texts relate the stories of how their ancestors made a difference in the creation of this country and the world. No culture or society was considered "civilized" until the White man arrived. There can be no feelings of inadequacy when everyone you read about while you are in school looks like you, sounds like you, and whose actions you can relate to. In other words, white kids can relate to the wanting to succeed from the very beginning because that's all there is that they are exposed to throughout their school experiences.

On the other hand, Hispanic/Latino students in the United States must fight for their identity every day of their life. They must determine how they will recognize and be recognized for the gifts that they can offer and have given to others. They must figure out how to prove to themselves and others that they have a place at the table. They also accept the disappointment and anger over the fact that they have to prove something that a person of the dominant culture doesn't, simply because of the color of his/her skin.

To Be Mexican–American in the United States—Loyal Countrymen with No Country

We've talked about what it means to be culturally different and Hispanic/Latino in the United States. There's more to the story. To be Mexican-American in the United States means that you are in a country where your ancestors lived but where you feel that you are no longer valued as a citizen. Geographical and political lines that have been drawn to identify boundaries and ownership do not take into account the human factor of why those lines need to be drawn in the first place. Mexicans who became Americans became Mexican-Americans (as did their children) and not simply Americans. To accept a singular American identity is to deny a spectacular and rich ethnic/cultural background. On the other hand, they do not identify as Mexican because they were not born in Mexico. The difficulty in finding an identity in either one of these countries is compounded by the fact that there is no sense of protection or belonging offered by either country.

Many Mexican-Americans often feel that they have to prove themselves as being as capable as their white contemporaries when it comes to language, and as accomplished when it comes to assertiveness and motivation. When they travel to various parts of the United States, they report feeling challenged to speak Spanish according to the expectations of those living in that area (despite regional differences and dialects that exist within Mexico, Central and South America). Furthermore, there is a perception of being inappropriately challenged when attempting to claim this country's heritage and equally challenged when they do not from both within and beyond our communities. To be Mexican-American in the United States can mean that there is less feeling of belonging to this country, which can also be true of those whose origins are other Spanish-speaking countries.

To Be Puerto Rican in the United States

The perspective of Puerto Ricans in the United States is just as varied and complex as my experiences as a Mexican-American. Puerto Ricans still feel the raw bite of being colonized by the United States, very often not being given due process, not accorded full citizenship, and thus not recognized as a contributing group among the masses brought into and established in this country. In the 1930s, there were less than 55,000 Puerto Ricans in the United States. Today, there are more that 2 million Puerto Ricans living in the mainland.

During the colonization of Puerto Rico, the Spanish deliberately established the concept of community around an interrelated life. To that end, there was usually a plaza in the center of the community, with the main building being the church (Catholic) building. It was in this way that a socioreligious life became a defining highlight of the Puerto Rican people. African religious rites, brought by Black slaves, were often intermingled with the Catholic rites and ceremonies. Today, there is a widespread subscription to a folk system of uncovering the causes of illness, called "espiritismo." There is also a strong emphasis in the use of folk medicine. The participation of the folk healer (curandero/a) is a central part of this (and the Mexican) culture. Botanicas can be found in just about every neighborhood or barrio at which herbs, prayers, potions, and other instruments can be purchased in order to diagnose and treat physical and psychological illnesses.

This sense of community and familiarity is not easy on Main Street, USA. In fact, this pattern of interaction is regarded as intrusive by the dominant culture. While the plaza in the center of the city can be most paralleled by parks in the center of neighborhoods and suburban communities, the plazas did not have neighborhood security to make certain that residents of the small community had preferences and privileges before all others. How does this change in interaction and community affect the person trying to become at a minimum culturally competent? An awareness and understanding of this struggle is necessary in order to identify and maintain a relationship based on equality and acceptance.

To Be Cuban in the United States

The Cuban experience in the United States is similar to that of other Hispanic/ Latinos. The greater perception of the Cuban people in the United States is that they are all criminals because of the Marielle boatlift in the early 1980s. While it is true that Fidel Castro emptied his prisons and mental institutions when thousands fled to the United States, it is hardly fair, nor is it accurate, to define a group of people by this event. Furthermore, it would be inappropriate to take out of context the unreasonable laws and struggle to survive within a small communist country.

The colonization of Cuba was very similar to that of other islands in the West Indies. The island was settled by the Spanish, who searched the land for the treasures it had to offer, after which there was a decline in the native population followed by the importation of Black African slaves. Since the island was an incredible place of beauty, there were many American business interests throughout the island. With American interests in hand, the dictator Fulgencio Batista took control of the country until the revolution led by Fidel Castro. The first groups of Cuban exiles fled the island for the United States after that revolution in 1959. They were mostly middle- to upper-class politicians and professionals. The majority of Cubans in the United States live in the Miami area but have also found opportunities and have established neighborhoods and enclaves in the Northeast and in Chicago.

The struggle for this group is also in coming to a country with very different customs and expectations. However, we must add the burden of losing most of what had been earned and accumulated in Cuba, only to arrive in a country whose society values material success and wealth.

Central and South Americans in the United States

There has recently been an increase in the numbers of Central and South Americans immigrating to the United States. This comes on the heels of difficult times for many people, both politically and economically. As this country has often promised opportunity to all who would come, is it any wonder that this country is still seen as a safe bastion to the rest of the world. Central and South Americans have difficulty with the language, even with the Spanish language as it is spoken here, depending on where they go. The socialization processes in the United States, conflicts between cultural norms and practices, and expected behavior within the family by government groups (Children and Family Services, etc.) is different.

The American Dream and the American Reality: The Process of Acquiring the American Identity

While it is very often stated that this land is the land of opportunity, the "land of milk and honey," it can also be said that opportunity only comes to those in the know. In other words, it is not enough to be a member of this country, to "want" to be a member of this country, or to serve this country. There are still limitations to what can be achieved by certain people in this country. There still exists a glass ceiling as well as a glass floor. The glass ceiling phenomena is bad enough, because you can see those ahead of you with equal training and education and experiences. Another phenomena for people of color is the glass floor, through which you can see those behind you with perhaps equal training, education, and experiences.

And yet these harsh realities do not stop people from attempting to achieve the American dream of having a family (in whatever way that is defined), a home, and living in a safe environment while pursuing happiness and professional success. These attempts at reaching this goal are filled with hopes and hard work. However, there is still an additional component associated with the concept of wanting the American dream: people of color who succeed in the dominant (white) culture are often seen as sell-outs to their original ethnic/culture group.

Political Awareness and Changes in Identity

The majority of people of color living in the United States feel an incredible amount of loyalty to this country. Yet, this country in return has not offered them the same protections, the same rewards, or even the same responsibilities for the sacrifices they have made. Consequently, there has been a push for more political awareness and actions by these groups of people through the organization of political and social groups. A few of these groups include the political party "La Raza"; the Mexican American Legal Defense and Education Fund (MALDEF); and the League for United Latin American Citizens (LULAC), which has taken advocacy issues before the courts and legislatures. Furthermore, the term "Chicano" is now used by younger and more politically aware and involved Mexican-Americans. It is important to note that this

was a pejorative term in the early part of the twentieth century and is consequently rejected by older Mexican-Americans.

In general, efforts to mobilize Latino/Hispanic communities in the political arena have been successful. There appears to be a higher rate of activism
and involvement among all groups within the Latino/Hispanic umbrella in order
to achieve the American dream and provide better opportunities for those that
follow. The close family ties, the collective perspective, and the cooperative
spirit from which Latinos/Hispanics draw compel each of us to work not only
for the individual but also for the community at large. This strength, while
often exploited in the past, is nevertheless an influence that defines and drives
this unique population. The sleeping giant awakens!

3

A. TOY CALDWELL-COLBERT
JESSICA HENDERSON-DANIEL
G. RITA DUDLEY-GRANT

The African Diaspora

This overview of the rich and diverse African-American culture presents important historical and cultural issues to help human services professionals in all fields in their interactions with and understanding of Black Americans. The authors offer suggestions for working with a very diverse Black population with the goal of improving the quality and effectiveness of services and interpersonal interactions. Throughout this chapter, the term "helping situation" captures numerous types of human resource/interpersonal encounters with African Americans and then allows you to fit your unique helping profession to that situation.

This chapter focuses on people of color in America who are descendants of African slaves brought to America and are not primarily considered part of another ethnic group. Usually identified by their skin color or tone, this population has numerous titles, with many differences in meaning. People may be identified as Blacks, Black Americans, African Americans, or Americans of African descent. Unless a distinction is needed, these terms will be used interchangeably. The authors also consider special circumstances of racial identity for Black adolescents and Blacks from Central and South America, Africa, and the Caribbean.

Stereotypes and preconceived notions about Black Americans cause the African American help-seeker to feel that he will not be treated fairly, heard, or understood. Helpers, no matter what the situation or circumstance, must have some insight into the impact of stereotypes if they are truly going to provide meaningful assistance when interacting with African Americans. This is particularly important if the helper is of a different ethnic background. Moreover, these same concerns can apply even when the professional helper is African American because the help-seeking dyad creates issues of authority and power.

Currently, Americans of African descent are the largest ethnic group in the United States, representing about 34.7 million people or 12.3% of the 281 million people who live in this country. The African American or Black American population is the second fastest growing ethnic group, with the Hispanic population the fastest. Population projections suggest that by the middle of the twenty-first century, Black Americans will constitute 53 million and Hispanics 97 million of a total U.S. population projected to be 394 million.

Data from the U.S. Bureau of the Census (2000) show that only 47.8% of African American families were made up of married couples. Between 1984 and 1995, there was a 56% decline in African American families headed by married couples. In 1995, the percentage of single parent, lower income African American families headed by women was 70%. Sixty percent of the births in America were by unmarried black American women, with the largest portion of that percentage being teenagers. African American men were disproportionately represented in the U.S. penal system and on death row. Blacks resided in all regions of the United States, with large pockets of them concentrated in larger cities and urban areas on both east and west coasts, as well as in the South and in specific areas of the Midwest such as Kansas City, Missouri; Chicago, Illinois; and Gary, Indiana. These are but a few of the demographics that help characterize the population of African Americans who reside in the United States. These trends continue into the new century.

Influences of the African Diaspora

Understanding Black Americans and their interactions in contemporary society requires a brief examination of the African Diaspora, as well as African influences that affect cultural characteristics and patterns of behaviors. The Black population is heterogeneous like Native American, Hispanic/Latino, and Asian American groups that reside in the United States. As a result of the transatlantic slave trade from the fifteenth to the nineteenth centuries, people of African descent were dispersed throughout the Americas. The United States is but one country that welcomed the slave trade that transported Africans against their will to reside and work its land as early as the 1600s. Therefore, the African Diaspora includes Spanish-speaking Blacks from Puerto Rico, Cuba, and Panama, other groups from the Caribbean Islands, black Brazilians who speak Portuguese, European blacks, and even Black American Indians (a comingling of Africans and Native Americans during the early expeditions and settlement of this country).

Family Ties

Contemporary behavior and lifestyles of Black Americans continue to reflect African cultural influences. In working with Black Americans, it is important to understand and appreciate the importance of the group and the interdependence and connectedness of individuals within the group. Western cultures emphasize the importance of the individual and deem individuals as independent, autonomous, and self-contained. African cultures, in contrast, are oriented toward the group. For most African Americans, the group is considered as important as the self. Consequently, they tend to use references of "we" rather than "I" when expressing themselves. A strong sense of communalism and collectiveness among African Americans illustrates their feelings about the importance of support, confirmation of behavior, and personal validation through their African American family and friends.

A Black American family is typically an extended family, made up of immediate relatives and significant persons, who are often affectionately referred to as "aunt" or "uncle" but are not immediate relatives. This usage of "aunt" is a custom borrowed from African heritage that is still practiced today in African families. Understanding this concept of the extended family and the important role it plays can be key in working and interacting effectively with African Americans. The strength of the family, the influences of its members, and their survival means the family will always come first, and sacrifices will be made to support the family unit at all costs. The goal is to keep it as a cohesive group despite geographic distances, lifestyle issues, and varying career paths, no matter what the circumstances or socioeconomic status of its members. Consequently, immediate blood relatives and extended family membership are a major resource for African Americans seeking support when problems emerge. When there is a problem, everyone tries to pitch in and help. The cultural traditions resulting in the strength of family bonds make this a logical source of support.

The Impact of Racial Oppression on the Help-Seeking Patterns of African Americans

Centuries of discrimination and blatant segregation have caused African Americans to distrust most American institutions. African American slaves were bred like animals and relegated to a position of inferiority. Even with the passing of Title VII of the Civil Rights Act of 1964, Black Americans continued to suffer discrimination in America because of long-standing Jim Crow practices and attitudes. This inferior status and lack of respect for the human dignity of Black people was also evidenced as psychologists, researchers, health care researchers, and social scientists used African Americans as human guinea pigs.

One of the most blatant examples of human experimentation in contemporary times was the conducting of the syphilis studies that took place at Tuskegee Institute in Alabama. The studies started in 1932 and lasted until 1972. The research question centered around whether or not the course of syphilis differed in Blacks and Whites. Those targeted for the study were poor rural African American men who were infected by the disease then left untreated so scientists could research the long-term effects of syphilis on the body. Four hundred African-American men unknowingly participated. Doctors told these men and their families that they were receiving medication to treat the illness when, in fact, they were receiving nonmedicated tablets or a placebo pill. Physicians were fully aware of the treatment protocols and did not intervene. Even after scientists discovered a drug to effectively treat the disease, the Black American men in this study were denied the medication because it would have interfered with research results. Other efforts were made to assure that these men would not be treated, for example, they were not drafted into the armed forces, where they would have received treatment, during World War II. Scientists offered elaborate explanations for this research protocol. The study persisted despite the focus on informed consent generated by the Nuremberg Trials and the Civil Rights movement of the 1960s. Also, they prolonged the experiment while the federal government supported their efforts.

In 1998, the gross injustices of the syphilis studies, were publicly acknowledged by President William Clinton in an apology he offered on behalf of the United States government. While reparations were made to the victims and their families, the unethical, immoral, and indefensible nature of such human experimentation has caused Black Americans to distrust established health facilities and consequently avoid seeking help from such institutions. Other actions labeled "valid scientific practices" have resulted in some African American women who thought they were having their appendix removed actually being sterilized. This was done especially if they were thought to be developmentally delayed or, in the parlance of the time, "mentally retarded." The current practice of racial profiling in the justice system also fosters oppression that mirrors earlier forms of mistreatment and racial discrimination. Who, then, are the established systems of protection designed to protect?

Discriminatory practices toward African Americans have decreased the frequency of Black clients seeking help and influenced the ways helping professionals in psychology and counseling treat patients. As a result, African Americans have been subject to a high degree of misdiagnosis and overdiagnosis of symptoms and disease. Moreover, they have been institutionalized or incarcerated and subjected to drug interventions in lieu of preventive treatment or rehabilitation. They have not been offered the same psychotherapy interventions that have been available to White individuals. As a result of these experiences, African Americans perceive themselves, and rightfully so, as at considerable risk when contemplating seeking help outside the African American community—especially if the helping professional is not African American.

This highlights another aspect of this group's help-seeking behavior. Due to past limitations in educational and employment opportunities for African Americans, the majority of people in the helping professions including human resources professionals, historically have been White. Thus, the lack of African American helping professionals has further hampered help-seeking among African Americans.

Another complicating cultural factor is the existence of biased attitudes in testing and assessment. Related studies have been designed to support and prove inferiority in African Americans on a variety of dimensions and scales. Controversies about IQ and other forms of intelligence testing continue to loom in public debates. These types of biases, coupled with the small number of ethnic minorities prepared to work in the field, as well as the limited training of White professionals and social and personnel service workers to interact effectively with African Americans, have forced African Americans to choose alternative routes to help-seeking. Moreover, because the Eurocentric perspective emphasizes helping-encounters as "color blind," the importance of race and ethnicity are ignored. Everyone is considered the same regardless of their race, and the manifestations of their behavior are considered the same because of their existence as a common group. Such attitudes and philosophies create even more obstacles because the acknowledgement of underlying problems of racism and ethnicity are central to understanding and ultimately helping the individual seeking assistance.

Alternative Support from Church and Family

Instead of turning to helping professionals, African Americans rely on the church and extended family members for support. For Black Americans, the minister and the elders in the church are among the best caregivers, although human service professionals are available in schools, clinics, and hospitals. Because of the church's basic understanding of the African American family and its ability to provide emotional—and in some cases financial—support, individuals find solace in this environment.

As a result of these support networks and strong cultural traditions, African Americans typically view their problems as spiritual and sometimes medical rather than mental or emotional. These attitudes in help seeking thus lead to counseling via the church minister, as well as the use of traditional remedies like herbs and certain foods. This latter practice stems from skepticism and negative attitudes toward medications prescribed by physicians. A positive cultural attitude toward the "wisdom of the ages" finds individuals seeking guidance and home remedies from elders or older members of the family, within the church or the community.

Crisis and Traditional Helping Resources

After relying on and at the same time exhausting family and church sources of support in the African American community, some Blacks often do not emerge in professional helping situations until they are in crisis, in need of immediate assistance, or drastic, comprehensive care. Other African Americans who decide to engage outside assistance will do so as a result of a referral from a friend or family member rather than through personal solicitation using a phone book. In contrast, there are those Black Americans who engage in help seeking on their own, without a personal referral. These individuals often have a higher educational background and their approach to help seeking could be very different.

Many African Americans, upon first reaching a helping agent, may mask their problem or not be receptive to long-term interventions and insight therapy. If in crisis, their needs will center on problem solving and immediate help, not outcomes experienced through traditional forms of help seeking.

Professionals working with Black Americans should also understand that they might not state the real nature of their problem right away for many reasons. One reason may be lack of trust, another may be the inability to talk about the problem because the individual does not understand the nature of the problem or the help-seeking process; or the problem could be hiding another form of behavior. For example, depression could be evidenced as anger or overeating rather than what helpers are used to looking for: lack of interest in food and extreme weight loss. Waiting until a crisis often means that help is initially sought through emergency services, which may result in a higher likelihood of hospitalization. African Americans may be ready to reengage in long-term helping encounters, following resolution of the crisis at hand, and when they are functioning at a much higher level outside the hospital.

Informal Sources of Support

In addition to the church and religious circles, Black women turn to social settings like the beauty shop and "sister circles," which function like informal support groups. Angela Neal-Barnett and J. H. Crowther, psychologists who treat women with anxiety disorders, have found that middle-class African American women appear less likely to seek help through community health agencies but prefer private sources once they do seek therapy (Neal-Barnett and Crowther, 2000). Fears of being labeled "crazy" have prevented some

African American women from seeking outside help for problems of anxiety. There seems to be a coping style of "survivor" and an espoused myth of "being a strong Black woman" among some middle-class African American women. Both attitudes lead to an acceptance of a situation or problem as just a part of life—with which they have to cope. Some of these women will probably talk about "seeking refuge in the Lord and letting Him take control of the situation."

Other African American women from this same socioeconomic group cope by not acknowledging anxiety-related cognitions, fearing admittance of other forms of negative feelings and emotions. A common response for women falling into this last category might be "I just can't think about that right now." These are behaviors to look for in African American women that might serve to inform the helper of issues that impact help seeking, especially if the seeker is middle class. Overall, Neal-Barnett's work reveals that some African American women don't feel that they need outside help with certain problems. This attitude could impact their acknowledgment of the issues and affect levels of trust of helping professionals.

This is by no means a complete list of help-seeking patterns or reasons why African Americans may or may not seek assistance from helping professionals, but it offers a helpful cultural framework when working with African Americans in a wide variety of settings. The next sections of this chapter will present issues affecting segments of the Black population that present particular considerations for working with Black adolescents and people from nations outside of the United States.

Black Adolescents in the United States

Adolescence is a time when individuals experience physical and psychological changes as they move from childhood to adulthood. Exploration, experimentation, increased connections to peers, and changes in relationships—especially with parents—mark this stage of human development. A major task is to focus on one's identity in all its complexity. For Black adolescents in the United States, the reality of racism and discrimination makes this transition even more complex. Like the rest of the Black population, Black adolescents are confronted by negative stereotypes, which cloud the visions of those who view Blacks as inferior or not fitting into all levels of American society.

Immigration and Black Adolescents

Immigration is an important variable in the lives of some adolescents of African descent. Some Black adolescents are the first generation in the United States. Patterns of immigration vary across the groups. In some Caribbean families, the parents come to the United States first, while their children remain with relatives in the islands. They immigrate to improve the financial well-being of their families, sending money back to the islands and saving to bring children and other relatives to the United States.

The years of separation can range from months to years, sometimes as many as 12 years. Parents and children can become strangers, as meager finances can lead to limited physical contact between parents and their offspring. Even in later adolescence and early adulthood, the "children" may still be struggling with feelings about the years they were separated from their parents and the difficult parent–child relationships when they were finally reunited. The separation coupled with negotiating living in two cultural worlds may be a lifelong challenge for these individuals.

Generally, first-generation and immigrant Black adolescents more quickly adapt to U.S. culture than their parents, who may seek to maintain their culture by using child-rearing strategies they recall from their formative years in their countries of origin. One consequence is often conflict between parents and adolescents around issues such as dating, choice of friends, mobility without supervision, and participation in family and cultural community activities.

Economic and Class Issues

In the United States, poor and working-class Blacks tend to live in urban areas that have limited resources. Black adolescents who live in economically depressed neighborhoods are subject to schools that may offer them a substandard education, inadequate public services, communities with high crime rates, and social stigma as a function of calling that neighborhood home. Schools remain substandard because they are supported by property taxes. Inner-city neighborhoods have lower property values.

Additionally, these adolescents may be limited in their job opportunities, often working at local fast food restaurants that offer little or no job mobility. Many businesses have left the inner city, taking with them employment opportunities that are not accessible by public transportation. Poor and working poor persons often cannot afford the costs of owning a car, that is, the car itself, insurance, and maintenance. High unemployment in the inner-city Black community is a major problem.

A largely unseen group of working-class Blacks are those employed by the utility companies (electricity and gas), a few industries such as Polaroid and Gillette in the Northeast, and the federal government in Washington, D.C. These individuals exemplify the American work ethic. They retire after 25–30 years of service. They are often high school educated and form two-income households. They model a work ethic for their adolescents and often encourage them to go to college. These working-class families live in urban and suburban areas. While they are economically working class, they share the values of the middle class. The adolescent children in these families are often in a position to move to the middle class by attending college and professional schools and by acquiring interpersonal and life skills, as modeled by parents who belong to various organizations such as the Black church, the Masons, and Eastern Star.

Middle-class Black adolescents are a variable group. With the changes in educational and employment opportunities for Blacks, there is now a larger Black middle class. Some Blacks have been members of the educated middle class for several generations. Their families have legacies at historically Black colleges and universities. Others are first generation college educated. Middle-class status has also been obtained by businessmen in the Black community, as represented by the funeral home directors and owners of dry-cleaning establishments, hair salons, and grocery stores. Some families have experienced generational upward mobility, with entire sibling groups and generations advancing together. For others, a few siblings have been the only ones to advance to the middle class. When this occurs, those who advance economically and socially may feel responsible for supporting siblings and creating opportunities for the education of their nieces and nephews so that generation can move ahead.

The Impact of Black Residential Patterns on Adolescents

While the majority of Blacks live in segregated areas of the inner city, some Blacks also reside in rural and suburban areas of the country. In the case of the latter, their children are likely to be one of very few Black children and adolescents living in their communities. The decision to reside in these predominantly White neighborhoods may be influenced by different factors. For those with children, one reason may be access to better schools which will potentially provide them with the skills to compete in the job market. For others, it may be that the neighborhood is closer to their employment. It can also be because they like the neighborhood in terms of location and types of homes. The experiences in this context are quite variable. Some adolescents have made friendships across racial lines; others have spent years in social isolation.

What It Means to Be Black

A critical question for some Black persons, especially adolescents, is "Who is Black?" For some, that designation is reserved for inner-city persons, equating poverty with being Black. These are in fact the "media Blacks." This leaves the suburban adolescent's identity as suspect or, even worse, considered more White than Black. Degrees of Blackness can be points of controversy. The indicators of being Black may vary from region to region, as noted by language, dress, and hairstyle, as well as political stance. The latter may be interpreted as the willingness to take a stand against racism and discrimination.

Among some Black adolescents, high academic achievement has been associated with "acting White." Such thinking is completely at odds with traditions associated with the founding and maintenance of historically Black colleges and universities after the Civil War and efforts to receive "equal education," as argued in the 1954 *Brown v. Board of Education* decision. Having a critical mass of high-achieving Black adolescents along with Black adult role models can provide the structure to sustain their academic development and counter the perception that academic achievement is the domain of Whites only in this country.

Being Black may also be expressed by sitting at the Black table during the lunch hour at the high school. While one may have White friends, the Black table in the middle of the day represents an oasis in an environment that may not affirm Black adolescents. In that setting, they do not have to explain and justify. They sit with those who understand them.

Media Images and Stereotypes

One media image of the Black male adolescent emerges from sports and the entertainment industries. Black males have excelled in football, basketball, and track to the point that many Black boys and adolescents strive to become professional athletes. The reality is that the chances of their becoming the next Michael Jordan in basketball are less than those of their becoming a neurosurgeon.

Black adolescents also seek to enter the entertainment industry primarily as "rappers" or singers. The former is related to the "hip-hop" culture. This music form began as a way to describe and protest life in the inner city. More recently it has been associated with violence and negative portrayals of women.

The second media image of Black adolescent males has been associated with the criminal justice system and poor school achievement. Studies indicate that the police treat Black males differently from other groups of men in this country. "Driving while Black" has come to stand for the harassment of Black men by the police when they are driving. The police stopping them and subsequently treating them as though they were criminals has nothing to do with their violating the law. Their color alone makes them suspicious characters or potentially guilty of some crime. With so many Black males involved negatively with the criminal justice system, employment opportunities for this group have diminished. Employers are not likely to employ those who have criminal records. As a consequence, this fast-growing marginal group in the United States cannot expect abundant gainful employment opportunities.

In addition, the combination of access to primarily substandard schools, limited exposure to out-of-school enrichment experiences, teachers who subscribe to the notion of intellectual inferiority, and few models of academic accomplishment are just some of the factors that may contribute to poor school achievement and the perpetuation of this media image.

Another prominent stereotype inspires fear of Black adolescent males, especially those who are large and/or dark-skinned. Their presence may be experienced as threatening even when there is no reason for these feelings. Such reactions cause a range of responses in Black males. Some consciously try to make people comfortable with their presence, some become angry and vocalize their displeasure with the negative reactions, and still others assume a menacing posture, acting out the stereotype.

Images of Black girls in the media are equally as problematic. They are seen as pregnant, gang-involved, unintelligent, unsophisticated, and sexually loose females. Music videos, print, and electronic media reinforce these images. They are seen as the sources of the children who are unteachable and unruly in the public schools who later as adolescents terrorize the good people. This is the image that Black girls have to fight against. Unfortunately, some girls internalize these stereotypes and begin to display behaviors that compromise their chances for success.

Positive Socialization and Role Models

In stark contrast to the stereotypes described above, Black parents of adolescents have been and continue to be engaged in positive socialization of their children, which fights against the negative racial stereotypes. It is important to emphasize the particularly vital role played by the Black family, the church and other Black organizations in the raising of healthy Black adolescents. Black churches and other Black institutions support parents in their efforts to raise resistors, that is, those who refuse to take in the stereotypes that are self-defeating. Adolescents are taught to recognize racism and to understand the impact of racist behavior on their feelings and behavior. They also are provided models of how to manage racism, which they are likely to encounter in this society. They are advised to pick their battles and to plan to emerge victorious when they raise their voices against racism.

The Black church provides important opportunities that help adolescents develop skills that will help them be successful in school and civic and workplace settings. Teaching children to speak before the congregation, to prepare secretary and treasurer reports, to organize events and programs, to raise funds, and to participate in the worship service are all an integral part of the Black church experience. In this setting, adolescents have role models of achievement.

Many Black fraternal organizations with memberships representing the spectrum of socioeconomic classes have youth-based organizations. Often they provide opportunities to travel to conferences and conventions where they meet other Black adolescents from around the country. As with the Black church, the focus is on skill acquisition, values, and encouragement to succeed despite the odds. They also can practice these skills and receive feedback and reinforcement.

In formal and informal groups, Black adults have long provided role models, financial support, and inspiration for Black adolescents. Even without the benefits of training in child development, the leaders have developed age-appropriate experiences that have contributed to the lives of many Black adolescents.

It is noteworthy that the critical role models in the lives of Black adolescents are most often their parents and other relatives, teachers, and ministers. They are persons with whom they have "real" as opposed to "virtual" contact. While many of these persons may never be in the colleges, universities, or places of employment that these soon-to-be-young adults will find themselves, their influence based on encounters during adolescence can continue to have an impact.

Many Black adolescents make it through this period of development without encounters with the juvenile justice system or unwanted pregnancies. Note that while 20% of Black girls become pregnant as teenagers, some 80% do not. It is critical that the latter group become the emblematic Black female teen. In terms of the Black male population, understanding patterns of arrest and sentencing by the justice system can alter the perception of the Black male as a presumed criminal. Information about Black adolescents can and should reduce the impact of stereotypes on how they are perceived and treated.

Biracial Adolescents

Some adolescents have one Black parent and one non-Black parent. Their physical appearance may determine how they see themselves and how others see them in terms of racial identity. Messages from their parents will also be sources of their identity or identities. Some parents will tell them that they are Black with relatives who are not Black, others that they are biracial, and still others that they are just human beings. Adolescents then have to make meaning of these messages. Given that a large percentage of Black people are racially mixed, these adolescents may not appear to differ in physical appearance from Black adolescents who have two Black parents.

Adolescence is a time to focus on identification. At times, biracial adolescents may feel that they are being forced to reject one of their identities and consequently one of their parents. Those who look like their non-Black parent may opt to identify with that racial group. Given the perception that Blacks have less power, some adolescents may identify with the more powerful parent. As Black culture is a dominant culture in the lives of adolescents, many will identify with being Black. The meaning of this identity will vary, depending on their past experiences with Blacks and their contacts with their Black relatives and other Black networks. For some, the media, including films, television sitcoms, news programs, and music video programs, define the Black community. Contact with Black extended family and friends will help them experience the heterogeneity in the Black community. They can develop a level of comfort and ease with Blacks, especially if they live in an all-White community and have limited daily contacts with Blacks. Awareness of the contributions of Black persons to all facets of American life and culture will contribute to a pride in that part of their heritage.

Diversity and Black Americans

Diversity is a term that refers not only to intergroup or interracial distinctions but to intraracial differences as well. There are recognizable cultural contrasts between Blacks, Whites, Asians, Hispanics, and others. Within the community of Blacks in America, such diversities also exist. Even subtle differences in Black subcultures can be prevalent forces in determining the interactive patterns of individuals, their values, attitudes, and all of the distinguishing characteristics that make up larger cultural diversity issues.

As previously stated, while Black Americans comprise the largest percentage of Blacks in the United States, there are Blacks from other geographic locations and cultures who also feature prominently in the Black community. Immigrants from the Caribbean, Africa, and Central and South America make up a substantial portion of the total American Black population but have not necessarily been identified as distinct within the larger group.

In more recent times, people recognize that the Hispanic culture contains both those who identify as "Black" and those who identify as "White," distinctions which have just begun to be reflected in the census. However, Blacks from the "African Diaspora" are grouped into a singular unit, ignoring distinct values, cultural patterns, and attitudes.

Taking the next step in the journey toward a true appreciation and respect for diversity, one must move beyond gross racial generalities to a deeper appreciation for the complexity that exists within each of the cultural groups. While it is virtually impossible to learn about subcultures without encountering many stereotypes, some of the stereotypes have been unjustly created. Therefore, when engaging in dialogue as part of a working relationship with someone from a different culture than one's own, helping professionals should try not to project onto the help-seeker labels and attitudes that are based on information gained from assumptions or written documents. Being open to the interchange and willing to learn from that individual is perhaps one of the most important attitudes in attempting to build an environment that truly welcomes diversity.

The Contemporary Diaspora

Recent changes in the immigration laws have meant that persons of African descent from around the world, but predominantly from the continents of Africa and Europe, as well as the Caribbean region, have been permitted to enter the United States in larger numbers. Individuals from Africa and the Caribbean often strongly identify with particular countries and in some cases for persons from Africa, even tribes. Given the lack of familiarity with geography in this country, some immigrants will state that they are from a region and continent, that is, the Caribbean or Africa. More often than not they identify themselves as coming from specific nations such as Haiti, Liberia, or Nigeria.

A Variety of Languages and Accents

As a consequence of the above, persons who present as having sub-Sahara African ancestry may speak a language other than English. First languages may be other European languages consistent with the nations that colonized their countries, for example, Spanish for the Dominicans and French for the Haitians, who reside on the same Caribbean Island. They may speak English with an "accent" influenced by the various African languages and dialects. They may also be fluent in various tribal languages. Others are Black Latinos from Puerto Rico, the Dominican Republic, and Central America.

A Wide Range of Skin Colors

Skin color has been a variable in the lives of many Black persons. Some light-skinned Blacks have received preferential treatment from both Whites and Blacks in deference to their appearances being closer to those of the perceived power brokers in the society, that is, White persons. In contrast, some dark-skinned persons have been subjected to mistreatment based on their skin tone. Many of the outstanding Blacks in the past have been light-skinned persons, as a consequence of being more advantaged. It is noteworthy that the premier high school for Colored and Negro adolescents in the Washington, D.C., area during the first half of the last century had an enrollment that was predominantly light-skinned in appearance. Some local and national organizations in the Black community have also practiced this discrimination based on color.

For Black females, skin color may be associated with social desirability and can impact their relationships with Black males. Some of the latter may find light-skinned Black females to be more attractive than dark-skinned Black females. The darker the Black male, the more dangerous he may be perceived. This is in contrast to light-skinned Black males who more easily blend into predominantly White settings. The impact of colorism on self-esteem and access to opportunities is noteworthy for both genders.

Many successful Blacks who live in the United States are bicultural, that is, they feel comfortable in a predominantly Black context as well as in a predominantly White context. Language patterns, food, and topics of conversation often differ between the two groups. For the immigrant Black groups, it may be a matter of being tricultural, being able to function within their own ethnic group, with African Americans, and in predominantly White settings.

Three Major Subcultural Groups
Within the Larger Black Community

This section examines some of the characteristics of the three major subcultural groups within the larger Black community—Caribbean Blacks, Blacks of Hispanic descent, and Blacks of African descent. There is a subset of the African American culture that has deep roots in the Caribbean.

Research shows that West Indian Blacks in America appear to be able to achieve great success, particularly economic and academic success (Kalmijin, 1996). Some of the most prominent American Blacks with Caribbean roots include Congresswoman Shirley Chisholm, Democrat from New York City, the first woman and first Black to run for president; the Honorable William Hastie, the first Black judge on the Third U.S. Circuit Court of Appeals; and General Colin Powell, former chairman of the Joint Chiefs of Staff and present secretary of state. The experiences of these high achievers suggest that while the process of immigration can be quite traumatic, there is a self-confidence that results from having grown up in the Caribbean, where racism is much more muted.

Contrasting Features of Slavery in the Caribbean
and the United States

As we explained earlier, Blacks came to the Caribbean and to the United States as slaves to serve as the primary workforce. However, Caribbean slavery's character, implementation, and psychological impact on the Black psyche differed greatly from the practice of American slavery. According to Eric Williams, slavery, while just as physically brutal and debilitating to Blacks in the Caribbean as in other places, took a different psychological toll on the Caribbean Black's self-image and sense of empowerment than on the Blacks in the United States (Williams, 1984). Many factors played a role in this difference;

however, chief among them was the sheer disparity in numbers between the two geographic locations. On plantations and in towns around the antebellum lands in America, Blacks were consistently in the minority. However, throughout the Caribbean, then as now, Blacks made up the vast majority of the population. Thus, the White overseers had to maintain some measure of harmony with the large Black population. A "divide and conquer" strategy was implemented. Slaveholders created a "middle class" of Blacks (more aligned with the masters) to keep order on the plantations. Scholars note that these middle-class Caribbean Blacks had more power than even the "house slaves" of the American plantations. These individuals, who were often the children of slave owners, and usually had lighter complexions, became the first "white collar" workers of the preemancipation era. They were often slightly more educated and moved into clerkships and other government positions, working subordinate to but in concert with the plantation owners and overseers. This complexion differential served as a basis of intraracial prejudice, which exists within the Caribbean culture to the present day.

There was a much smoother transition from slavery to freedom in the Caribbean. While slaves were still technically considered "chattel," that status was not enforced to any great extent. In the Catholic Caribbean countries, such as the Dominican Republic, Puerto Rico, and Cuba, it was ecumenically forbidden to consider slaves anything other than full human beings. Since the church was focused on converting the slaves to Catholicism and adding to its "flock," consequently, it prohibited consideration of any person, free or not, as anything other than a "child of God." Slaves were permitted to save money to buy their freedom and did so with great regularity. Moreover, some families were not broken apart as in the United States, primarily because of the geographic location and the multination status of neighboring islands.

Caribbean Blacks' Perceptions of and Responses to Racism

The Caribbean Black is not always suspicious of racism or on guard, since racism is much more subtle within the Caribbean culture (Mintz, 1974). While this openness can be harmful, it can also be liberating in that the Caribbean Black is often slightly more willing to take risks and to accept offers of assistance from Whites, whereas the American Black might mistrust the White person based on historical and/or personal experiences. Caribbean Blacks are also willing to take the most menial jobs, a common practice among immigrants, as there is a strong belief that the job does not define the person. This psychological distinction is much more easily made when one has not grown up with constant images and experiences of prejudice and discrimination.

Many Caribbean Blacks will argue heatedly that racism does not exist in their country and that their strategy for dealing with it in America is to ignore it as long as possible. Thus, it appears that racism is experienced by Caribbean Blacks as an evil that is outside of them, which does not define who they are or how they must operate in the world. This attitude may alleviate some of the stress placed on psychological functioning, which is experienced by Blacks raised in America. There is one group of Blacks in America who can claim a similar experience, and that is those who have been raised in a virtually all Black environment, such as the small or midsized Black towns found frequently in the South and parts of the Midwest. With adequate role models and a safe environment, the Blacks who grow up under these circumstances often feel more empowered and less burdened by the need for the "protective paranoia," which is a frequent characterization of the psychology of Blacks in America. It is important to qualify that none of these statements imply that Caribbean Blacks are any less prone to encountering racism once in America. While one can be caught off guard and unwittingly become the victim of racism, the decreased sensitivity can also serve as a protective factor for one's self-image and "psychic energy."

Conversely, Blacks who have emigrated from the Caribbean face a unique set of challenges, in addition to those experienced by anyone of immigrant status (Gopaul-McNicol, 1993). Black Americans who see Caribbean Blacks as receiving benefits from the majority society, such as jobs and education which rightfully belong to the native Black American, perceive them with a certain level of mistrust and even anger. They are also at times ridiculed, considered to be more primitive due to coming from a less well-developed culture. Their accent can be difficult to understand, and the generally slower pace of the Caribbean can give the impression of impaired intelligence and/or motivation. They are often put back a grade in school, as they frequently come from an English- or European-based educational system of forms and standards rather than grades and are generally perceived as coming from an inferior educational system. Thus, the Caribbean Black has to work harder to prove academic ability.

Social and Economic Realities of Dual Cultures

First-generation Caribbean Blacks strive to maintain dual identities, usually feeling that they will one day return home, even if they have lived in the United States for more than 30 or 40 years and have borne all their children in the United States. Frequent movement between the United States and the Caribbean is common. Family ties to the West Indies are particularly strong, and often money is sent home to take care of children and parents left behind. The

Caribbean Black can often be seen as frugal to the point of appearing miserly, with an extremely strong work ethic.

Seeking one's fortune, while an admirable goal, can also create an inordinate stress on the family system. As was discussed in the section on Black adolescents, children are separated from parents and raised most often by a grandmother or a series of aunts. Parents are then reunited with teenagers whom they have not raised. The adolescents are often sent to them to complete school or due to their unmanageable behavior. The immigrant parents, in turn, often experience high levels of frustration and inadequacy. They find it very difficult to parent children who are virtual strangers and who often bear resentment toward them for having been abandoned at a young age. Despite these multiple challenges, Caribbean Blacks have continued to thrive in America and have made many important contributions to the culture. From Reggae to Rastafari, in music, art, literature, and science, Caribbean Blacks make a profound impact on America, Black and White.

Black Hispanics

Intermingled with the Caribbean Blacks are those who share a dual heritage. These are the dark-complexioned Hispanics who hail from the Spanish Caribbean countries such as the Dominican Republic and Puerto Rico, as well as Central and South America. Black Hispanics or Latinos often identify with both the Latin and Black cultures. While the primary identification is Latin, they often experience more of the racism and prejudice exhibited toward Blacks than the "White" Latinos do and therefore are more identified with the struggle for racial equality. At the same time, they may also experience the difficulties of being a linguistic minority and can feel alienated from both cultures. Sometimes considered the "invisible minority," the Black Latino often feels a sense of being overlooked by the majority and minority cultures. A poignant example occurred during the 1999–2000 controversy over Elian Gonzales, a six-year-old Cuban boy whose father successfully struggled to regain custody after Elian's mother had drowned while escaping with her child to America. Black Cubans were never depicted as a part of the community, despite heavy media coverage. Thus, the Blacks from these countries can feel overlooked and their contributions ignored. Yet, Black Latinos also bring a rich heritage to America that far exceeds the rice and beans contribution that is a hallmark of Latin cuisine.

Styles of music and dance are unique and recognizable, as is "Spanglish" (a mixture of Spanish and English), which has gained increasing prominence in America. Spanish is the second most prevalent language spoken in America, and the cultural and intellectual contributions are gaining increasing prominence and recognition. As the Hispanic subgroup has continued to grow within the United States, their influence also has burgeoned. The "Black" Latino, while benefiting from an ever-improving status, still has to confront the special brand of prejudice and racism reserved for the Black-complected and/or Black-identified people of America. Thus, racial identity can be a source of tension within this vibrant and rich cultural group.

Contemporary Africans

Another major group of Blacks besides the indigenous Black Americans are the Blacks from Africa and other sub-Saharan countries. Africans have been treated differentially by Whites during the time of slavery, postslavery, and into the present. During the Jim Crow era of segregation, for instance, Africans were allowed into White facilities when Black Americans were not. This intraracial disparity in treatment by Whites has engendered resentment among American Blacks toward their African brothers, who also were sometimes treated with disdain and characterized with stereotypes by American Blacks. For example, there has been a perception that Africans are "arrogant," which appears to be a reflection of their cultural experience, heavily influenced by European colonization. In addition, Africans in America are most frequently students or come from families who had the resources to fund the expensive trip to this country. Thus, there is frequently a class distinction between Africans living in America and the general Black population, which can contribute to the perception of arrogance.

African and Caribbean Blacks share many characteristics that are engendered by their immigrant status. Africans are also noted for their work ethic and commitment to excelling. While family ties are quite strong, the frequent return visits made by Caribbean Blacks are not as feasible for Africans, thus they are forced to choose between settling in the United States and returning home.

The African culture is recognized as a very patriarchal society. The chauvinistic orientation of many African men can be especially noticeable and distasteful to the more liberal males and females in America. Their interpersonal style is also often more formal, reflecting the European influence on their culture.

During the sixties, with the assertion of Black Power and Black Pride in the American Black community, a connection to African heritage became a source of pride. There are now ongoing efforts for the Black American community to share its considerable resources with Africa to assist in its growth and economic development. Thus, fear and mistrust have increasingly been replaced with collaboration and cooperation. Hopefully, the diversity within the community of Blacks in America will continue to serve as a source of creativity, strength, and understanding. The potential for economic, academic, and social excellence is within reach, as long as the challenge continues to be met.

The Effect of Current Racial Prejudice

The unfortunate "tie that binds" all persons in the Black community in America together is their common experience of racism. Despite intracultural differences, when interacting with the larger society, all peoples of African descent face the increasingly subverted but still quite prevalent prejudice that is the unique hallmark of this country. Racism seems to "reinvent" itself continually so that it takes new forms. One example is Richard Lowry's "Yuppie Racism," where younger Americans believe that issues of racism and prejudice have been eradicated in America, and that the problems experienced by Blacks are problems of class and economic stratification. Another even more deadly form of racism is the internalized racism that can be observed in Black persons such as Justice Clarence Thomas, who repeatedly attempted to undermine those statutes that have been put in place to address the long-term effects of institutional racism.

The common experience of battling racism and prejudice can be both divisive and joining. The hope remains that the community of Blacks in America will continue their quest for heightened unity, as it is this unity in diversity that will ultimately result in Blacks attaining long sought after and still elusive equality. And it is this equality, not only of opportunity but also of respect, appreciation, and acceptance, that will bring about true freedom for all Americans regardless of racial or cultural origin.

Ultimately, then, where a person comes from and their life experiences there informs his or her consciousness and behavior. The helper must keep origin (as well as many other factors) in mind when relating to a help-seeker.

The Issues, Challenges, and Roles of Helpers

Help-seeking situations can range from a job interview, to an interview for a merit or achievement award, to admission into the military, to a work conflict or problem, to a police custody or arrest situation, to an appointment with a physician about a medical problem, to a talk with a teacher about an academic concern, to an intake interview with a counselor or psychologist about a personal problem.

While it is acknowledged, as previously stated, that having a counselor of a different race or culture can be a barrier to care, studies show that African Americans generally consider counseling situations helpful, regardless of whether the facilitator is a White or Black American. However, African American men and women seek different qualities in a counselor. For example, African American women are slightly more comfortable with White counselors, whereas African American males are slightly more comfortable with African American counselors. These preferences may correspond to other types of help-seeking situations and should be considered when choosing a professional helper for a client. *Counseling the Culturally Different* (Sue and Sue, 1999) is an excellent resource for more information in this area.

Helpers as Guides and Educators

The first role of the helper should be that of *guide*. For many African Americans, arriving at the point of seeking help outside the immediate family or community support network may be a new experience. They may be unfamiliar with the setting or surroundings, the prescribed protocol, the actual experience they will be involved in, and, depending on the nature of the situation, the expected outcome. In addition, if all resources have been exhausted, the individual is probably in crisis, which further contributes to the problem at hand. Giving the appearance that you as the helper are a resource and an advocate to assist in steering the person through the situation will help lower anxieties and create opportunities for opening up to the interpersonal exchange that is about to take place.

The function of guide gives rise to the role of *educator*. African Americans in their first helping situation will find the educational aspect of the interpersonal encounter key to their ability to become empowered and to better navigate the situation as it unfolds. This educational role should be used to outline what will take place during the encounter, what the individual should expect, how the information will be protected (confidentiality), and the prescribed function of the professional helper in the situation. Opportunities for questions should be offered and questions answered, no matter how trivial they may appear, to increase understanding about the helping situation at hand and to enhance feelings of trust in the interpersonal exchange. Apprehensions may result in an African American's asking no questions. In this instance, the helper might want to have a few questions readily available to pose as examples of frequent issues of inquiry. It is not necessary to belabor this line of inquiry, but to be open to the fact that questions may emerge during the course of the interaction. In playing the role of educator and guide, the questions should be addressed, even if they appear to interrupt the flow of what is taking place at the time.

Building Trust Between Help-Seekers and Helpers

For African Americans in help-seeking situations, not responding is often seen as a sign of resistance when in fact it is not. It is more than likely a case of testing the trustworthiness of the helper. This testing will probably continue during the early stages of interpersonal interactions and should be viewed as an individual seeker's attempt to test the relationship and to challenge the helper's values and qualifications.

It is important also to point out that for African American men, involvement in a helping situation is often seen as a sign of weakness, powerlessness, and unmanliness. Requests to self-disclose further threaten a manly image and may result in a limited exchange until some level of trust is established. Interaction with a White helper may exacerbate the situation, in that self-disclosure may give rise to increased fears of a helper's (perceived) racist intentions. Exercising patience in developing rapport and a level of trust in the relationship is necessary for a helper to develop and maintain an effective interpersonal relationship with African American help-seeking men.

For African Americans, the "expert" is considered an educator and guide. When working with Blacks, interpersonal interaction can be enhanced if the helper's approach is supportive and not controlling. Allowing the African American help-seeker to engage in the helping process by also sharing knowledge and information produces a greater opportunity for exchange and decreases concerns about being dominated.

Cultural Framework

Much of what has been described thus far is fundamental to any helping relationship, with additional considerations for working with African Americans. Now let's focus on shaping an effective helping relationship for African Americans.

The helper must understand the individual's *cultural framework*. As pointed out in other sections of this chapter, African Americans are a heterogeneous group. Depending on the life experiences of an African American, an interpersonal relationship—either Black and Black or Black and White—will be heavily influenced by variables such as level of acculturation and identification with African culture and tradition, context of racial socialization, attitudes, expressions, and expectations.

Culturally Sensitive Models of Helping

Most models of helping are rooted in a Eurocentric perspective, with White middle-class standards as the norm for appropriate and expected behavior. What may constitute normal and adaptive forms of behavior for this ethnic group cannot be based on White middle-class norms but must be understood from a cultural context. For example, Afro hairstyles such as cornrows and braids are part of African culture and are worn as expressions of pride in one's heritage.

They should not be misread as signs of radical practice or militant behavior. Yet another example is that African Americans have strong religious values, strong church participation, and faith in spiritual healing, stemming from an African heritage that stressed collectivism, community, and being one with nature. African Americans who are overcome by a religious experience and begin speaking in tongues or who seek refuge through intensive praying and reading of the Bible should not be considered in poor mental health or out of touch with reality. Instead, this should be understood as a coping style that provides the individual the means to endure serious hardship, while it provides inner strength and peace of mind to persevere. Talking about praying and the need to pray for the answer to a problem should not be seen as negative or a lack of adjustment when working with African Americans.

Responsiveness to Ethnic Identity

To be effective in a helping encounter, it is crucial for the helper to understand and be responsive to the African American's ethnic identity and the impact it may have on the interpersonal relationship. Ethnic identity is also reflected in preferences for a referent title. While some ethnic classification title preferences are generational, others connote stronger elements of ethnic pride for individuals who, in this chapter, have been referred to most often as either African American or Black. Preferences among African Americans may range from Colored, to Negro, to Black, to Afro-American, to African American. For individuals of Caribbean descent, choices will vary even more. An individual who is interracial may have yet another preference but probably will not prefer "mulatto," which is often considered a derogatory term associated with slavery. A helper should determine the referent title that the individual seeking help prefers, and then use that term whenever referring to him or her in a cultural context.

Skin Color and Ethnic Background

Be careful not to fall into the trap of "judging a book by its cover" when trying to determine the ethnic background of African Americans. Skin color alone, as well as facial features (e.g., wide lips, wide nose, etc.), may not be enough to assign an individual to a certain ethnic group. Do not assume that everyone who has a dark complexion and kinky hair is of African descent. It is better to inquire about ethnic background than to make a determination based on face value.

Cultural Differences and Strengths

Other culturally distinguishing variables that may characterize African Americans is the value and role of elders, a holistic worldview, belief in traditional folk healing methods, emphasis on oral tradition, flexibility in assuming and adopting multiple roles within the family, single parenthood, perceptions of time, and use of non-Standard English (rapping and jiving) or Black lingo.

Avoid Stereotypes

In keeping with earlier comments about the heterogeneity of this group, an important caution for those who assume they have an understanding of the African American cultural framework is to avoid overgeneralizing and stereotyping all Black Americans as the same. It is important to engage in an interpersonal encounter by treating the seeker as an individual in a unique situation with a unique set of concerns, influenced by a particular worldview and heritage. Considering culture in the helping relationship means there is no clearcut answer for an approach to resolving the problem. The helper should look for balance when considering the cultural influences and the individual's unique set of concerns.

Cultural Responsiveness

It is important for the helper to be *culturally responsive*. Just as it is critical to understand the preferred referent title for Black American, it is important to welcome and encourage discussions related to feelings surrounding experiences of racism that either the individual or the family have encountered. When African Americans address issues of racism, it may give rise to defensive attitudes/behaviors on the part of helpers and be dismissed as irrelevant due to their own anxieties and vulnerability to attack. The inability to engage in discussions centered on racism (or the tendency to dismiss racism as unimportant) in the context of the helping relationship is not being "culturally responsive" to the cultural framework of an African American.

Current practices and attitudes fostering "political correctness" may instead foster stereotypical beliefs and may create suspicion in African Americans. Helpers should be cautious in adopting today's "politically correct" practices, lest the attitudes be perceived as disingenuous.

Issues of Bias and Prejudice

The helper must understand his own *issues of bias and prejudice*. For a White person to be most effective in a helping encounter with a Black American requires self-exploration and examination of one's personal biases and ethnocentric attitudes. In the same way, self-exploration may be helpful in dealing with African Americans who are highly educated and acculturated, from wealthy backgrounds, and who have different values and worldviews than African Americans from low income, poorly educated families. Both situations can foster attitudes and perceptions of superiority on the part of the helper. Not engaging in such self-exploration may result in stereotypical thinking about Blacks (especially toward Blacks from a socioeconomic level different from your own) and may serve to perpetuate issues of superiority and inferiority that will block opportunities for forming a trusting alliance. For many Americans of African descent, it is important to form an egalitarian relationship before any true form of problem solving or help seeking can begin. Such an expectation further supports the notion of self-understanding before one can begin to understand and productively work and interact with someone culturally and/or ethnically different from oneself.

It is the White experience that permeates our theory and thinking about interpersonal behavior patterns. Even African American human resource professionals have training rooted in White techniques and White approaches to creating effective interpersonal change and growth. Therefore, an effective helper, either Black or White, needs to examine ideas about behavior and applications for modifying that behavior for its value in an African American context, with related cultural nuances and utility as a helping approach with African Americans. A case in point, as mentioned earlier: White therapists may have difficulty understanding successful coping styles that do not fit White middle-class norms. However, that does not negate the effectiveness of such strategies and they should be considered seriously in a helping encounter for an African American. This type of exploration and modification of technique to fit the African American perspective requires additional work and insight and can make all the difference in creating the most effective outcome in a helping encounter.

Training Techniques and the Black Experience

It has been only recently that new scholarship on the African American experience and other ethnic groups has been introduced into training curriculums. *Assertive Black, Puzzled White* by Donald Cheek is a helpful resource for at least three reasons. First, the book provides a firsthand account of how assertive behavior therapy can be redesigned from a White training technique into a modified strategy helpful for African Americans, who are expected to interact in dual communities—the Black community, as well as the broader dominant White community. Second, it offers a wealth of background on the Black experience in America, which helps in establishing a basic understanding for creating a cultural frame of reference for any human resource professional working with African Americans. Third, it presents helpful information about the benefits of assertiveness for African Americans (Cheek, 1976).

The Importance of Flexibility

One final point before leaving the topic of modifying strategies is the importance of being flexible in the helping encounter. If the helper is too rigid and fixed on theoretically based models and ideas, this will interfere with insights that may facilitate the helping relationship. When working with African Americans, it is important to maintain a level of openness and flexibility and the personal capacity to accept new perspectives from the seeker, who brings to the situation a rich cultural heritage and ethnic background. This can be a significant factor in creating more effective helping strategies that may require modifying existing strategies for the benefit of the help-seeker.

Black Vernacular and Effective Communication Between Help-Seekers and Helpers

The helper must become aware of the *Black vernacular* and differences in the *meaning of words and the word usage* of African Americans. Not all African Americans speak Standard English. Some use Black English or "Ebonics," the more contemporary term derived from the words "ebony" and "phonics." This rich African American speech pattern is rooted in West Africa and is characterized by the dropping of final consonants from words, lack of verb/noun agreement, double negatives, absence of third-person present tense, and word patterns of not conjugating the verb "to be" or dropping it entirely, for example, "she be home." Also characteristic of Black English and Ebonics is black slang, shucking and jiving, when words have opposite meaning to that of Standard English or unique meaning in the African American community, for example, "bad" really means "good" and can be used in extending a compliment—"That is a really bad coat." Or in this example by William Clark, creator of the term Ebonics, "The hawk don't be jiving in St. Louis" in Standard English means that "in St. Louis, the wind is very cold."

Someone unfamiliar with Ebonics who is hearing it for the first time might think that the individual is illiterate or poorly educated, when this may not be the case. In fact, he or she is speaking in a language familiar to his or her environment, which for some may not be seen as any different from a foreigner speaking his or her native language. Introducing Ebonics into this chapter is not an attempt to resolve the debate of its validity as a legitimate language and the existence of bilingualism in African Americans, but to express concern about negative reactions on the part of the helper to non-Standard English. Negative reactions may point to underlying prejudices and forms of discrimination against African Americans and lack of acceptance of their style of communication, presentation, and behavior. Use of Ebonics will require close listening on the part of the professional helper, along with some skillful parroting and paraphrasing, to make sure there is mutual understanding of the person with whom you are interacting.

The help-seeker's use of Black slang, on the other hand, presents yet another skill set for the helper to understand in a helping relationship. It is also an opportunity to express cultural responsiveness to the communicator. An African American can use far fewer words to express the same idea spoken in Standard English. For example, to inquire about the details and information surrounding a situation can be stated in Black vernacular by saying, "give me the 411" or "what's the 411?" Many times, persons who use slang may use terms that are couched in Standard English that may go unnoticed. This style of communication is important for survival and effective interpersonal interactions in the Black community and should not be seen as negative. Interactions involving Black slang when the helper is not familiar with the discourse will require breaks in communication, as the helper seeks clarity in understanding the context of words used.

Being upfront about any lack of understanding presents an opportunity for learning and appropriate self-disclosure on the part of the helper. In turn, the Black American becomes empowered as a contributor in the helping relationship, which enhances trust and genuineness in the interpersonal exchange. Lack of clarity creates confusion for both parties, resulting in ineffectiveness in the helping encounter. Other forms of linguistic differences among African Americans can be seen in Black French Creoles, who reside predominantly in New Orleans and South Carolina, and Gullah Geechee, African American communities in the sea islands and coastal districts of South Carolina and Georgia. Each group has its unique intonation and word usage, which may sound very foreign even though for African Americans they are common forms of communication. Helpers should be careful not to inappropriately stereotype African Americans just because their language is different from standard forms of communication used by the majority.

Understanding Nonverbal Behavior

The helper should not be opposed to seeking outside assistance and consultation to gain greater understanding about African American communication patterns and styles. Of particular importance is the body of knowledge surrounding nonverbal behaviors and their influence on interpersonal interactions. African American nonverbal behavior has a very expressive quality. Use of hand gestures, voice quality and intonation, eye contact patterns when talking and listening, and body posture for some African Americans is greatly contrasted to White nonverbal behavior patterns. "Cool posing," for example, is a form of posturing evidenced in some African American men that is often misunderstood. It is reflected in a certain form of slow rhythmic walking and sliding of the leg, positioning of one hand to hold the crotch and cocking the head to the side. This posturing when paired with baggy pants worn off the hips, an oversized shirt, and a cap pulled down over the eyes can be imposing for people who do not understand that it is a way of expressing Blackness and manliness. "Cool posing" is often perceived as threatening because of its association with behaviors and characteristics of gang members and may result in a helper inappropriately rushing to judgment because of his or her lack of understanding and awareness of its acceptability as a form of expression in African American culture.

Engaging the Family and Extended Networks in the Helping Process

As a helper you may have to seek outside *assistance from family and extended networks*. Because of the closeness of the African American family, you may have to engage others in gaining helpful information and in assisting with the helping encounter. As was mentioned earlier, the family serves a strong support function, and gaining their support and involvement may help with persistence on the part of the help-seeker. It may also be a way for the helper to gain compliance when carrying out tasks outside the immediate helping dyad and to reinforce notions addressed in the helping encounter.

Invaluable insights can be obtained from observing interactions with family members and support networks about what is valued in the context of the family's interpersonal relationships and group dynamics. What role does the help-seeker play in the family that can be translated or generalized to other types of interpersonal relationships? Working with the family can also be a mechanism for enhancing trust. If the family "buys into" what is offered, then they will reinforce the helper's role and validate his or her actions in the eyes of the help-seeker.

The support system of the African American community offers many opportunities for acceptable resolution that may not have readily come to mind to the counselor or to the client, who is probably so overcome with anxiety that he or she sees no helpful outlet. Consider, for example, a counseling situation in which a client has suddenly been laid off the job and has become homeless. The family support may be critical for addressing a person in need of concrete assistance rather than in need of insight therapy. Especially in a crisis situation, the family may need to be engaged until the individual can regain his or her footing and begin assuming regular patterns of daily living. Once that takes place, the counseling can reemerge with a focus on the presenting problem.

To summarize, when interacting with Americans of African descent, the effective helper serves as guide and educator, is culturally responsive, and understands the cultural framework of the individual. He or she is aware of personal prejudices and ethnocentric attitudes and their impact on the helping relationship, is prepared to modify strategies to address cultural factors, has some basic understanding of Black vernacular, and incorporates the family and extended networks into the working alliance with the client.

References

Cheek, D. K. (1976). *Assertive black, puzzled white: A Black perspective on assertive behavior.* San Luis Obispo, CA: Impact.

Dudley-Grant, G. R. (1991). Critical issues affecting ethnic minority communities. Proceedings of an Open Forum, conducted at the 99th annual convention of the American Psychological Association. San Francisco, CA.

Gopaul-McNicol, S. (1993). *Working with West Indian families.* New York: Guilford.

Kalmijn, M. (1996). The socioeconomic assimilation of Caribbean American Blacks. *Social Forces, 74,* 910–930.

Liat Islander. (1999). The magazine of Liat Airlines. Antigua, West Indies: Ft. Caribbean (BVI). Issue 46, 73.

Mintz, S. W. (1974). The Caribbean region. In J. F. Ade Ajayi and S. Mintz (Eds.), *Slavery, colonialism and racism.* New York: Norton.

Neal-Barnett, A. M., and Crowther, J. H. (2000). To be female, middle class, anxious and Black. *Psychology of Women Quarterly, 24,* 129–136.

Sue, D. W., and Sue, D. (1999). *Counseling the culturally different: Theory and practice* (3rd ed.). New York: Wiley.

U.S. Census Bureau. (2000). "Population of the United States: 2000" (Internet Release).

Williams, E. (1984). *From Columbus to Castro: The history of the Caribbean 1492–1969.* New York: Vintage.

4

ASUNCION MITERIA AUSTRIA

People of Asian Descent

Beyond Myths and Stereotypes

Asian Americans are one of the fastest growing segments of the U.S. population and include people whose ancestors are from countries such as China, Japan, Korea, the Philippines, India, Pakistan, Sri Lanka, Bangladesh, Indonesia, Burma, Thailand, Malaysia, Vietnam, Laos, and Cambodia. Samoans, Guamanians, and Native Hawaiians and Tahitians of the Pacific Islands are also included. There are at least 60 distinct Asian groups in the United States. They are called Asians because of the geographical area from which they come and their similarity in cultural values. Unlike the Hispanics/Latinos, they have no common world language. Each group has its own language and dialects, religious traditions, and political and cultural history. They are otherwise referred to as Asian/Pacific Islander Americans (APIA), Asian Pacific Americans (APA), or Asian Pacific Islanders (API). In 2000, the Asian/Pacific Islander American population accounted for approximately 10.9 million people or 4% of the total U.S. population, according to the U.S. Census Bureau. Ranked by size, the largest subgroup within the Asian American population is Chinese (numbering 2.4 million), followed by persons of Filipino, Japanese, Asian Indian, and Korean ancestry. Vietnamese Americans and Laotian Americans also showed large population increases (U.S. Bureau of the Census, 2000). Experts believe that the technological boom in the 1990s was a primary factor in the increase in the Asian American population. The 2000 Census marked the first time that the "multiracial" category was used. Because of the creation of the multiracial category, ethnic minority advocacy groups feared that this resulted in a loss of a large portion of their constituency.

The majority of Asian Americans are immigrants. More than 90% of them reside in metropolitan areas. Filipinos and Vietnamese tend to settle in the West with the largest concentration in California (Asian Americans constitute about 9.6% of the population of California). Japanese tend to be concentrated in Hawaii and California. New York ranks second to California in preferred area of settlement for Chinese, Koreans, and Asian Indian Americans. The states with the largest share of Asian Americans are California, Hawaii, and Washington. Other preferred states are New Jersey, Illinois, and Texas. The Midwest has the lowest percentage of Asian and Pacific Islanders. Just like the earlier European immigrants, Chinese and Korean immigrants, and lately Indo-Chinese immigrants, established ethnic enclaves. Filipinos and Asian Indian immigrants, however, tend to be scattered in the suburbs. Because of their relatively higher educational and occupational backgrounds, as well as their fluency in English as a function of their having been colonized by the United States and Britain, Filipinos and Asian Indians tend not to establish ethnic enclaves.

Perceived in American society as one homogenous group, Asian Americans are a diverse group with different languages, religions, and political and cultural history. Three Asian groups that are physically and culturally similar to one another are the Chinese, Koreans, and Japanese. Two groups that differ physically and culturally are the East Indians and the Filipinos.

A Brief History of Asian Americans in the United States

Asian immigration started in the 1800s with the decline of black slave labor. Chinese men were recruited as cheap contract laborers to work in mining, construction, and to build the transcontinental railroad from California to the Rocky Mountains. However, the Chinese encountered growing resentment and discrimination. Laws and ordinances were passed that were inimical to the Chinese, including the Chinese Exclusion Act passed in 1882, which prohibited further immigrants from China. This ban remained in effect until 1943. The Japanese came to Hawaii and to the mainland as skilled farmers and were also discriminated against. The Koreans followed in the 1900s. More than 80% of all Korean immigrants were foreign born. Many of the Korean immigrants came to the United States as families, and most were well educated.

The second largest Asian American ethnic group is the Filipino American, next to Chinese Americans. The history of the Filipinos in the United States is different from that of all other Asian ethnic groups. This history was a direct result of America's colonization following the Spanish American War, when the Philippines was ceded to the United States in 1898. The earliest Filipinos in this country (1903–1910) came as students sponsored by the U.S. government. They enrolled at the University of Illinois and Purdue University to study engineering, agriculture, and medicine. Then from 1920 to the early 1930s, the second wave of Filipino immigrants arrived consisting of farm laborers and grape pickers. In 1924, the U.S. government passed the immigration control laws ending all Asian immigration. During this time, there was discrimination against these groups, including segregation in schools. The 1924 act was revoked in 1965, when the Immigration Act of 1965 was passed. The 1965 Immigration Act, which abolished Asiatic exclusion, was considered the most liberal immigration law. This enabled the third wave of Filipinos to arrive in the 1960s, comprised of highly educated upwardly mobile professionals, mostly nurses and physicians. Because the Philippines was an American colony for almost half a century, the Filipinos are generally considered to be more Americanized than the other groups. There was an accelerated immigration from Asia in the '60s and '70s, especially of refugees from war-torn Vietnam and Cambodia. The earlier waves of refugees were better educated and wealthier than later immigrants, many of whom, especially the Hmongs and the Laotians, were poor, illiterate, and unaccustomed to Western culture at the time of their resettlement.

Cultural Characteristics of Asian Americans

There are a number of characteristics shared by Asian Americans. These characteristics include the following:

1. Asian Americans see the family as the most important social unit. The family is closely knit and the bonds are continuous. Relatives tend to live close to one another. Important family decisions are likely to involve all family members, and at times, extended family members. The family is also seen as a key element behind the success and achievement of an Asian American. There is a widely held belief that one's behavior is viewed as a reflection on the family.

2. Asian Americans emphasize obedience to parents, authority figures, and to tradition. Obedience is coupled with family loyalty and filial piety and responsibility. It is not uncommon for Asian Americans, who have long left the country, to provide financial support to their parents and relatives. Children are expected to obey their parents and comply with their parents' expectations of them.

3. Asian Americans emphasize respect, politeness, and deference to elders and authority figures. The elders are valued and exert considerable authority, even over adult married children. Respect and deference to elders and authority figures is exhibited in polite and formal communication with them. One does not call an older person by his/her first name, including one's in-laws. One's in-law is addressed just as the spouse addresses his/her family members, for example, a daughter- or son-in-law calls the mother-in-law " Mom" and father-

in-law "Dad." Older siblings are also not addressed by their first names. They are addressed with a title that connotes their birth order (i.e., first-born, second-born, or third-born). Only the last-born does not have a title. Respect and deference to authority is also exemplified by a nonquestioning cognitive style toward authority figures, exhibited both at school and at work. The ritual of showing respect in speech and behavior for one's authority and status becomes an important area of socialization. Among Filipinos, for example, titles are used such as "attorney," "engineer," or "architect" in addressing persons holding these educational degrees (Austria, 1990). Moreover, an Asian American may simply smile when scolded or criticized by a person of authority, as a sign of submission.

4. Asian Americans value high achievement orientation, industriousness, and perseverance. Asian American's superior educational achievement, aspirations, and attainment are well established. Parents expect and demand high levels of educational and occupational achievement in their children. Kao (1998) reported that 43% of Asian American students aspired to postgraduate education, compared to 25% of White students. In addition, she reported that 47% of Asian American parents wanted their children to pursue postgraduate education, as compared to 20% of White parents.

5. Asian Americans put great emphasis on smooth interpersonal relations or harmony. Free emotional exchange is inhibited in the presence of strangers. Filipinos as well as other Asian Americans use indirect styles of communication. Confrontations, which can lead to disagreements, are avoided. One is socialized to have peaceful and harmonious relationships with others at home and at work. Disruptive and conflictual situations reflect noncaring behaviors and are to be avoided. In conflict situations, third-party intermediaries are often used for the resolution of conflicts.

6. Nonassertiveness, passivity, stoicism, and modesty are Asian attributes. Asians are generally viewed as quiet, passive, socially introverted, and non-expressive. This is the traditional Asian reticence, self-effacement, and modesty. Self-effacement and modesty are well depicted in a famous Asian saying "the nail that sticks out is hammered back in." In Filipino culture, for example, one is admonished "Not to lift one's own seat/stool." Low level assertion behavior among Filipinos, for example, is reflected in their difficulty to say "no"; instead, they say "maybe," or "perhaps," or "I'll see" (Austria, 1990). American values of openness, self-disclosure, directness, and public displays of affection are considered rude, boastful, and inappropriate. In addition, Asian Americans are not given to provide appropriate credit for another family member's good work or success. For example, a Filipino husband would not compliment his spouse for food that she prepared, or a parent would not reinforce a child for school success. A Filipino mother once consulted with this author regarding the problems she was having with her teenage daughter. The

mother indicated that her daughter had complained that her parents are taking her for granted. That not once had she heard her mother or father tell her "I love you." The mother was dumbfounded because she claimed that they had done all that they could to provide for the needs and wants of their children. As she put it, "We have made much sacrifice to make their life better for them." A Filipino parent's love is shown through sacrifices one makes (Austria, 2000). The word "love" in Filipino and other Asian languages is not verbalized. The word "love" is used between lovers. In fact, once married, a husband and wife no longer speak of love, especially in public. In addition, "love" could have an erotic connotation in the Japanese language; hence, it would not be used to describe the affect that a parent has for her/his child (Goetz, 2000).

7. Pride and shame play a major role in maintaining equilibrium. Achievement promotes family pride while failure results in shame. Shame and guilt are powerful measures of control, that is, "What will relatives say?" This feeling of shame is well illustrated by an Asian American woman whose husband was having an affair with her cousin who lives with them. She could not "kick" her cousin out of the house nor could she separate from her husband "because all the relatives would know about the affair and the reputation of the family would be tarnished." In addition, the husband who had a propensity for womanizing refused to see a mental health professional because he "does not have a problem, and if he has, he will solve it on his own." This example is consistent with studies that show the differences in self-disclosure between Western and Eastern cultures, where there is greater reticence to disclose by members of Eastern culture (Toukmanian & Brouwers, 1998), and the need for Asian males to self-conceal or to "save face" and "keep a good name"(Cepeda-Benito & Short, 1998).

Meanwhile, Filipinos, who are predominantly Catholics, show characteristics including:

1. Religiosity. The authoritarian nature of the social structure and family situation is well reflected in one's attitude toward God and to the church. The tendency to withdraw from taking an active role in controlling one's life may, in part, be due to a belief that life events are God's will. One accepts whatever life trials are encountered as God-given (Austria, 1999). One turns to church and to prayer to cope with life stresses, as the current president of the Philippines, Gloria Macapagal, is fond of saying, "do what is right, do your best, and let God take care of the rest."

2. Cooperation versus competition is emphasized in Filipino culture. Cooperation and compromise are important factors in interpersonal relations among Filipinos, well illustrated by the terms "pakikisama," which means the ability to go along with the wishes of the group; and "kapwa," referring to consideration accorded to someone. Group-oriented words are also used, for example, "kami" (we) versus "ako" (I), thus avoiding impressions of boastful-

ness or selfishness. Kinship bonds are stressed, together with spirits of reciprocity, cooperation, and a sense of community. This trait is well depicted in neighborly assistance provided to a friend in need in the spirit of "bayanihan" or cooperation (Austria, 1990).

3. Generosity/hospitality. Filipinos are known for their proverbial warm hospitality and generosity. One is offered the best accommodations, in the use of the master bedroom for the houseguest, and the best food that one can afford. When one invites a friend to lunch, it is assumed that the friend will not pay. "Dutch treat" and "potlucks" are recent practices borrowed from Western culture.

4. "Utang na loob" means debt of prime obligation that is not payable. It connotes a system of lifelong reciprocal moral obligation and behavioral expectations, based on receipt of service rather than goods. This is also seen in the system of interdependence and obligatory relationship between a child and a parent. In Japanese and Filipino cultures, parents make undue sacrifices to send their children to school. In return, the children are obligated to take care of their parents in sickness or in old age or their siblings, as a gesture of their gratitude.

It is in light of these cultural characteristics that we can gain a better understanding of Filipino values and attributions. Some of the traits, such as assertion behavior, seen in Asian Americans are situation-specific, that is, Asian Americans are assertive with people they are familiar with such as friends and members of their own groups. Asian American writers also believe that these traits could have been brought about or exacerbated as coping mechanisms against the continuing onslaught of racism and discrimination.

Socioeconomic Status

Asian Americans who emigrated in the mid- to late '60s are highly educated and are mostly professionals. Asian immigrants are reported to surpass the U.S. general population by a large margin in educational levels. For example, Asian Indian and Filipino immigrants who came in the '70s have a high proportion of college graduates, and a large number of them were medical professionals, such as physicians, surgeons, pharmacists, and nurses. The educational achievements of Asian Americans surpass the educational achievements of Euro-Americans (Wong, 1998). Additionally, a greater proportion of Asian Americans (44%) obtained at least a bachelor's degree than did the Euro-Americans (28.1%) (U.S. Bureau of the Census, 2000).

The high educational attainment of Asian Americans (Japanese, Chinese, and Filipinos) is reflected in their slightly higher socioeconomic status (12% of Asian Americans have incomes of $75,000 or more compared to 10.9% of Euro-

Americans). However, Filipino males completing more years of education and having almost double the proportion of college graduates compared to that of Europ-Americans, had lower average economic status than Euro-Americans did. A number of authors (Min, 1995; Cabezas & Kawaguchi, 1998) have argued that Asian Americans' incomes are not comparable to their attained level of education. That is, Asian workers receive smaller economic rewards for their education than their White counterparts. In addition, the median salary of Asian American families cannot provide a good index of their socioeconomic position, as the income is actually a consolidation of more than one wage earner in the family (Lee, 1998). More telling, is the percentage of Asian American families living in poverty. The U.S. Census (2000) recorded the poverty rates of Asian Americans at 10.7 % compared with Euro-Americans at 7.7%. Lee indicated that the poverty rates of Asian American groups differ from one another, with the Japanese (3%) and Filipinos (5%) poverty rates much lower than those of American subgroups. That is, the staggering poverty rates of Southeast Asians (Laotians, Cambodians, and Hmongs) are as much as 30% to 60%.

Myth of the Model Minority

Asian Americans are considered to be the most educated ethnic minority group, most successful, most middle-class, and most respected of all non-Caucasian groups in the United States. They are perceived as the "model minority" (Kitano & Sue, 1973). Asian American scholars, however, argue that the successful minority belief is based mainly on observations of well-educated and high-achieving members of the group. Lee indicated that the model minority stereotype occurred at the height of the civil rights movement, and the "uncomplaining Chinese" were used as a model in comparison with other "recalcitrant minorities" (Lee, 1998, p.11). Could it be that the stereotype was a means to undermine the civil rights movement (Lee, 1998)?

Some writers viewed the "model minority" image as an attempt to demonstrate that the U.S. social system does work for ethnic minorities. It is this perpetuation of the model minority that has caused Asian Americans to be excluded in discussions of racial and ethnic relations and affirmative action programs. It is further believed that the success image ignored and trivialized the real concerns, health problems, and social service needs of Asian Americans. Some scholars have alluded to the unique cultural values and norms (such as family unity, respect for elders, respect for authority, industry, and high achievement orientation) as traits that have served the Asians well in helping them succeed. Other attributes included in the "model minority" characterization of Asian Americans are hardworking, industriousness, perseverance, and law-abiding. Writers have noted, however, that these Asian American virtues are extolled to disparage other groups for their lack of hard work and failure to take advantage of the opportunities available in this society (Kivel, 1996).

It is this "myth of the model minority," where Asian American students outperformed the White students, which resulted in quotas imposed on the number of school admissions available to Asian American students. In sum, many scholars and researchers have countered the notion of the "model minority" as inaccurate and misleading (Sue & Sue, 1985).

Concerns and Issues

Asian cultural values that emphasize restraint of strong feelings, obedience, dependence on the family, and formality in interpersonal relations are in sharp contrast to the Western emphasis on assertiveness and informality. This has led to serious psychological problems for Asian Americans.

Racism and Discrimination

Asian Americans, especially native born, may think and act "American," but their color precedes them. Because race is a salient variable, they can never be American. Asian Americans also face challenges, including discrimination. A Filipino young man (mistaken for a Vietnamese) was told, "Why don't you go back where you belong, they would have killed you there" (Anonymous, personal communication, 1995). In a study of 20 ethnic minority female psychologists comprised of African Americans, Latinas, and Asian Americans, race stood out as a salient variable (Austria, 1993). In this study, one Asian American psychologist stated, "My Asianness and femaleness interact with each other. Though I had the experience and competency to be the director of a child guidance clinic, I was made just a co-director. The other co-director was a white male. Because it was difficult putting someone in a director position who was female and Asian, the organizational structure was changed to co-directorship."

Asian Americans also fall prey to negative stereotyping and subtle and blatant racist remarks. In the study cited above, one ethnic minority female psychologist who was new at her school, which serves a predominantly white student population, said, "Students referred to me as either Dr. Jappo, or Dr. Chinks, at times, right to my face." Another respondent said that because of her short stature, she was not appointed to an executive position and one of the reasons given was that she was "young and was just a kid." A clinical psychologist consulting at a hospital claimed that "people reject my services because of my accent and how I look." Still another Asian American psychologist claimed that "my contributions in group discussions are not considered. Yet the very statements I made when repeated by a white colleague are favorably responded to by the group" (Austria, 1993). More surprising is the report by the Committee of 100, a Chinese American organization, which found that Americans hold a host of negative stereotypes about them, even compared with other racial and ethnic groups: 24% of Americans would not approve of inter-marriage with an Asian American, higher than the disapproval rating for inter-marriage with Hispanics (21%). Additionally, respondents to the survey also expressed negative attitudes about Asians in the workplace, with 7% of them indicating they would not want to work for a CEO of Asian descent but would rather work for an African American CEO. The respondents are also less comfortable with Asians holding power, with 23% expressing discomfort with an Asian American president (American Demographics, 2001).

Cultural Variables and Diagnosis of Psychiatric Disorders

The closely knit family of Asian Americans could very well be misinterpreted as pathological by the dominant culture, where Asian children are seen as "dependent" and their parents "overprotective." The reticence and nonassertiveness of the Asian American may be perceived as noninvolvement or noncommitment and may present a serious hindrance to one's achievement in school or professional career.

Underemployment and Loss of Status, Rank, and Prestige

Many Asian Americans who are unable to communicate in English are not readily employable. When employed, it is often in sweatshop factories with unsafe and unhealthy working conditions. On the other hand, newly arrived Asians, despite their professional education, commonly accept jobs for which they are overqualified. Asian American immigrants who were lawyers, architects, accountants, or dentists are unable to find gainful employment in their profession. Many have become entrepreneurs and owners of small businesses such as food stores. We find teachers as aides or postal clerks, engineers as drafts-men, mechanics, laborers, factory workers, or as cleaning persons (Austria, 1990).

Role Overload

Professionally, ethnic minority female psychologists felt overextended. Generally, they are assigned tasks in areas of their expertise, yet these areas are considered to be of low importance or value. Consider this Asian American psychologist's response, "As an ethnic minority psychologist, I get called upon to make speeches and give talks about being a minority person, whether I want to do these things or not" (Austria, 1993).

Feelings of Social Isolation

Asian Americans not only have to deal with work overload, but they also have to be resilient in warding off feelings of isolation, feelings that one does not belong, or that one is not a member of the social network (Russell, Cutrona, Rose, & Yurko, 1984; Weiss, 1975). As one Asian American female psychologist said in the 1993 study of ethnic minority women psychologists, "At lunch time in the cafeteria, I would eat alone. Once in a while, they eat at the same table but they talk past me"; "You know how people invite each other to do things, or to their homes. I am usually not included in those things" (Austria, 1993).

Glass Ceiling and Other Professional Issues

Despite their relatively high levels of education, there are fewer Asian Americans in management or executive positions compared to African Americans. Very few Asian Americans with impeccable credentials are at the helm of corporations or occupy administrative positions in academia. It is surmised that the stereotyped notions about their lack of leadership skills account for their underrepresentation in leadership positions. Meanwhile, Asian American physicians, known for their "bedside manner," either have solo practices or have group practices with other Asian American physicians. Very few get invited to join group practices of White physicians.

Disparity in Health Care

Asian and Pacific Islander Americans have various socioeconomic and health profiles. For example, Filipinos, Japanese, and Southeast Asian groups in the United States have a prevalence of high blood pressure (hypertension was found to be more of a problem for the Filipino Americans than for the Chinese or Japanese Americans), while obesity and diabetes are also problems among Pacific Islanders, according to a 1998 American Heart Association statistical update. Although cancer is the second leading cause of death for most Americans, cancer has become the number-one cause of death for Asian American and Pacific Islander women (National Center for Health Statistics, 1995).

Between 1980 and 1993, cancer death rates for Asian Americans and Pacific Islanders more than doubled: 290% for males and 240% for females. This figure represents the highest percentage increase for any racial/ethnic group. Contrary to the stereotype that Asian Americans are a model minority with few health problems, and that they have the lowest prevalence of smoking, a survey in California showed that Vietnamese men's smoking rates range from 35% to 56%; Korean males are at 70%; Kampuchean males are at 71%; and Chinese-Vietnamese males are at 55% (Centers for Disease Control and Prevention, 1992). Lung cancer is most common among Filipino and Japanese males. Meanwhile, the incidence of liver cancer among Chinese, Filipino, Japanese, Korean, and Vietnamese groups are 1.7 to 11.3 times higher than the rates among Euro-Americans. Cervical cancer incidence among Vietnamese women age 55 to 69 is nearly five times higher than the rate among Euro-American women. Breast cancer is the leading cancer among Chinese, Filipino, Hawaiian, Japanese, and Korean women (American Cancer Society, 1991). Lack of awareness of available services implicated in the underutilization of mental health services could very well hold true for infrequent use of medical facilities. Asian Americans who are aware of the health services may not use them because they believe that service providers are not responsive to their needs. Lack of financial resources for screening for various types of cancer could also be one of the reasons for underutilization of health services. Low paying jobs without health insurance and lack of knowledge of federally funded programs for health care could be contributing factors for the Asian immigrant's low use of health services. Meanwhile, the tobacco industry has historically targeted ethnic minorities in their aggressive cigarette advertisements (e.g., linking tobacco to betelnut use). Asian American Pacific Islanders are vulnerable to such high-pressured advertising tactics, hence, the high incidence of lung cancer among them. And then again, there are few appropriate tobacco prevention programs due to geographic distance and lack of culturally appropriate models, especially for Pacific Islanders. Other factors that can contribute to disparities in health care include language and cultural barriers, poor living conditions, lack of proper assessment of medical conditions, lack of access to health care and preventive health care. The overriding factor in underutilization of health care services is the lack of culturally responsive health professionals to the health concerns of Asian Americans. Sue and Sue (1985) and Sue and Zane (1987) believed that it is essential for health professionals to acquire knowledge of Asian cultures and to view and understand them as unique individuals.

Lack of Power Base

Since Asian Americans are diverse in class, language, and culture, unity among them is an elusive goal. Differences in foreign-born and American-born, old timers and newcomers, Catholics and Protestants, Christians and Buddhists override a common ethnic identity. Although Asian Americans outindexed other groups in educational attainment and entrepreneurialism, they continue to be perceived as a small minority without purchasing and political power.

In conclusion, we hope that this chapter provides an overview of Asian Americans: who they are, where they came from, and their experiences. Because of their color, Asian Americans fall prey to the narrow confines of stereotypes and hidden assumptions. Some of the assumptions are insidious and hurtful. We need to understand that their cultural traits and traditions have served as adoptive strategies against racism and discrimination. Despite having been objects of pervasive demeaning and devaluing messages, Asian Americans have continued to ward off the onslaught of hostility and racism and have contributed much to the strength of this country. In closing, we hope that we have presented information that will move the readers beyond the oversimplified image of Asian Americans.

References

American Cancer Society. (1991). *Cancer facts and figures for minority Americans*. Atlanta: American Cancer Society.

American Demographics (2001). *The Asian American blind spot*. Washington, DC: Intertec Publishing Corporation.

Austria, A. M. (1990). *Consulting with ethnic minorities: Problems/opportunities for majority/minority consultants*. Invited Address presented at the annual convention of the American Psychological Association, Boston, MA.

Austria, A. M. (1991, Summer). Training psychological consultants to Asian Americans. *The Clinical Psychology of Women*, 7(1), 1991.

Austria, A. M. (1993, Winter). The psychologist as a female, ethnic minority. *The Clinical Psychology of Women*, 9(11), 1993–94.

Austria, A. M. (1999, August). *The psychology of peace in Filipino and Asian cultures*. Paper presented at the annual convention of the American Psychological Association, Boston, MA.

Austria, A. M. (2000, August). Ethnic identity of Asian American youth. In D. Goetz (Chair), *Adolescent development and ethnic minorities*. Symposium conducted at the annual convention of the American Psychological Association, Washington, DC.

Cabezas, A., & Kawaguchi, G. (1998). Empirical evidence for continuing Asian American income inequality: The human capital model and labor market segmentation. In G. Y. Okihiro, S. Hune, A. A. Hansen, & J. M. Liu (Eds.), *Reflections on shattered window: Promises and prospects for Asian American studies* (pp. 144–164). Pullman: Washington State University Press.

Centers for Disease Control and Prevention. (1992). *Cigarette smoking among Chinese, Vietnamese, and Hispanics. MMWR*, 2, 41, 363–367.

Cepeda-Benito, A., & Short, P. (1998). Self-concealment, avoidance of psychological services, and perceived likelihood of seeking professional help. *Journal of Counseling Psychology, 45*(1), 58–64.

Goetz, D. (2000, August). *Adolescent development and ethnic minorities*. Paper presented at the annual convention of the American Psychological Association, Washington, DC.

Kao, G. (1998). Asian Americans as model minorities? A look at the academic performance. *American Journal of Education, 103*, 123–159.

Kitano, H., & Sue, S. (1973). The model minorities. *Journal of Social Issues, 29*, 1–9.

Kivel, P. (1996). *Uprooting racism: How White people work for racial justice*. Philadelphia, PA: New Society Publishers.

Lee, L. C. (1998). An overview. In L. C. Lee & N. W. S. Zane (Eds.), *Handbook of Asian American psychology* (pp. 1–19). Thousand Oaks, CA: Sage Publications.

Min, P. G. (1995). Major issues relating to Asian American experiences. In P. G. Min (Ed.), *Asian Americans: Contemporary trends and issues* (pp. 23–24). Thousand Oaks, CA: Sage Publications.

National Center for Health Statistics. (1995). *Health, United States*, 1995. Hyattsville, MD: Public Health Service, 1996.

Russell, D., Cutrona, C. E., Rose, J., & Yurko, K. (1984). Social and emotional loneliness: An examination of Weiss typology of loneliness. *Journal of Personality and Social Psychology, 46*, 1313–1321.

Sue, D. W., & Sue, D. (1985). Asian Americans. In N. Vance, J. Wittmer, & S. Devaney (Eds.), *Experiencing and counseling multicultural and diverse populations* (pp. 235–262). Muncie, IN: Accelerated Development.

Sue, S., & Zane, N. (1987). The role of culture and cultural techniques in psychotherapy. A critique and reformulation. *American Psychologist, 42*, 1, 37–45.

Toukmanian, S. G., & Brouwers, M. (1998). Cultural aspects of self-disclosure and psychotherapy. In S. S. Kazarian & D. R. Evans (Eds.), *Cultural clinical psychology: Theory, research, and practice* (pp. 106–124). New York: Oxford University Press.

U.S. Bureau of the Census (1990, 1995, 2000). Statistical abstract of the United States. Washington, DC: Government Printing Office.

Weiss, R. S. (1975). *Marital separation*. New York: Basic Books.

Wong, M. (1998). The cost of being Chinese, Japanese, and Filipino in the U.S., 1960, 1970, 1976. In F. Ng (Ed.), *Asian American issues relating to labor, economics, and socioeconomic status* (pp. 177–195). New York: Garland.

5

DIANE J. WILLIS
DOLORES SUBIA BIGFOOT

On Native Soil

The Forgotten Race: American Indians

They call themselves Ojibway, but in the written history books they are called Chippewa. The Dine' people are called Navajo; the Tis-Tsis-Tsas are called Cheyenne; recently the Winnebago returned to their name of Ho-Chunk Nation; and the Papago are recognized by their original name of Tohono O'Odham. Many changes have been thrust on the American Indian and only in recent years have they begun returning to their roots. This chapter on American Indians presents a brief overview of the history of the first Americans and discusses the diversity of American Indians. Sections on family roles and relationships, language, education, health, and values are presented to help the reader understand American Indians. However, in order to understand the American Indian today, one must recognize the trauma and oppression (Duran & Duran, 1995). The reader who wants to know more about the history of the American Indian might read James Wilson's (1998) well-written and well-documented book *The Earth Shall Weep: A History of Native America*.

Understanding Early Historical Oppression

When the first French, Spanish, and English explorers arrived on the soil of what is now known as the United States, Indians were here. The colonists left England and other countries to seek religious freedom, to look for gold and other wealth, and to lay claim to land (Wilson, 1998). Many Indians resided in

northeastern United States (Boston, Baltimore, Providence), where early settlers landed, but the transformation of these coastal Indians into "shadows and
delusions" after the Europeans arrived is little known history today (Wilson,
1998). The early colonists who settled farther down the coast of North Carolina and Virginia spent time looking for gold and other goods, and history
records their near starvation. Indeed, half of them died of diseases and starvation during their first summer in the New World. It was American Indians
who fed these early settlers Indian corn, bread, fish, and meat. Upon arrival in
the New World, the settlers found field after field of crops that Indians had
been growing and cultivating for years. For two decades the settlers traded or
bought corn from American Indians, but recorded journals made by the settlers suggested that they felt dishonored and humiliated at their dependence
on "savages" (Debo, 1989; Wilson, 1998). As the settlers began to realize their
dependence on the Indians' agricultural expertise, they began to treat them
poorly. For example, Captain John Smith developed a system of compulsory
purchase, so that if American Indians would not sell their corn, the English
would take it by force. This resulted in occasional Indian raids on settlers to teach
them a lesson, but this made conditions worse. From the English perspective,
the raids gave them reason to confiscate the land from the "savages." The colonists and their leaders came to this New World to settle, and while the First
Congress tried to work out treaties to protect the Indians from encroachment
by settlers, a large number of settlers were intent on removing the Indians, and
in some instances, killing them. Wilson (1998) reports the following:

> In one incident alone, 200 Indians died when the English concluded a treaty
> with the rebellious Chiskiacks and then gave them poisoned sack to toast the
> two peoples' "eternal friendship." (p. 71)

Between 1630 and 1633, at least 3,000 more settlers arrived at Massachusetts
Bay. Prior to those dates, large areas of land had been cleared by the Indians
for farming, but the diseases and epidemics brought over by the settlers had
decimated the Indian population. By 1630, the cleared land was reverting to
forest. Indeed, the 5 million or so American Indians residing in what is now
known as the United States declined rapidly with the arrival of the Europeans.
The Spanish, French, and English brought Old World diseases that decimated
large numbers of Indians as well as settlers. Small pox, cholera, and other diseases
took their toll, but the battles against the Indian and genocide also contributed
to the decline of the American Indian population. Indeed, the devastation of
the Native people within this New World has been described as a holocaust
that has lasted 500 years (Thornton, 1987). Today, only about 2 million Indians survive in the United States. Many American Indians today still live on
their allotted land and still reside on reservations.

While Europeans came to this country to seek freedom and to make their wealth, they did not recognize that freedom extended to all. The well-advanced civilizations of tribes such as the Cherokee (with their sophisticated system of government and their economic prosperity) made non-Indians covetous of their land. The Europeans reasoned that the Cherokees were savages and biologically inferior, and this provided a rationale for removing them from their own lands (Debo, 1989; Wilson, 1998).

The southeastern Indians, including some of the Five Civilized Tribes, were quite progressive and self-sufficient during these early years, yet were being forced out of their homeland by the settlers and the government. Even when tribes such as the Creeks voted to remain in Alabama and adhere to state law, they were rejected as a people and were forced to leave. White settlers stole their land and their crops, took their homes and livestock, and when Indians tried to retaliate or defend themselves they were killed. President Andrew Jackson rejected all attempts by tribal leaders, such as Chief John Ross or Elia Boudinant of the Cherokees, to assert their right of jurisdiction over lands. History records that President Jackson, a noted Indian fighter, wanted the Indians removed and he did not discourage harassment of the Indians. During this time, treaties were ignored or invalidated by the government and the Indians were forced to leave their lands. Perhaps as many as 8,000 Cherokees died on the "Trail of Tears," as the tribe was removed from their homes and lands to settle in Tahlequah, Oklahoma, now capital of the Cherokee Nation.

Boarding Schools

As the American Indians were removed from their homelands, many were placed on reservations because the government reasoned that the Indians could be watched and monitored better there. It was the agreement that in exchange for land and confinement, the government would provide American Indians rations of food, clothing, and shelter. Some treaties included health care and education. However, confinement to reservations, isolation, and limited resources created a forced dependency on the government that still exists today. Economic viability is limited and the reservation land is all that is left for many tribes, and for many tribes, the land they were given was not conducive to subsistence (e.g., the deserts). Once the American Indians were placed on reservations, their children were forced to leave home to receive education through boarding schools, and this caused considerable damage to the structure and function of tribal societies (BigFoot & Braden, 1998, p. 38). At the boarding schools, sometimes located hundreds of miles from the child's family, the children were forbidden to speak their Native language, their hair was shaved, and they were taught non-Indian ways. Little respect was shown for the children's Native culture because the goal was to make them "nonsavages." In many respects, there was a tremendous loss of culture, language, and spiritual beliefs, in that children, when they returned home, were unable to speak to their parents in their Native tongue. Moreover, the negative messages the children received about Indians and Indian beliefs served to confuse them and create conflict among them and their families and the greater society. Since the 1970s, progress has been made by many tribes to have their own reservation schools so that children are able to be educated "at home." Within many of the schools, tribal languages and traditions are now being taught. Indian boarding schools still exist, but they are more culturally sensitive, offer a better education, and are now voluntary. Even at that, there are about 11,000 American Indian children and youth living in boarding schools.

To understand the modern American Indian and their families, one must understand this early history and the impact it has had on being "Indian." James Wilson (1998) said it best when he wrote the following:

> As well as losing most of the land on which their aboriginal way of life depended, generations of Native Americans have been traumatized by a sustained assault on their social, psychological and spiritual world and a breathtakingly ambitious experiment in social engineering. In the period following the end of the "Indian Wars," native cultural and spiritual practices were outlawed and Indian children were sent in the thousands to boarding schools, where they were kept from their homes sometimes for years at a time and punished—often brutally—for speaking their own languages. The aim was nothing less than to turn them from "Indians" into "Americans": to supplant, almost overnight, a whole people's history and sense of identity with someone else's. At the same time, the United States used its immense power over the defeated tribes to reshape the reservations themselves, punishing "traditionals" who tried to cling to their culture and trying, for much of this century, to destroy tribal status altogether and force Indians to assimilate individually into the American "melting pot."
>
> These experiences, not surprisingly, have left Native Americans one of the most troubled minorities in America. Their communities are plagued with social and health problems: poor housing, diabetes, alcoholism, social breakdown, violence, fatal accidents (the second commonest cause of death), homicide and suicide. (pp. xxv–xxvi)

Yet, after all of these massive upheavals, we find a resurgence of pride and tradition among tribal members today. A new sense of identity is emerging and oral history is being passed down from elders to the young. Also, schools, colleges, and reservations are immersing themselves in tribal languages, and pow-wows and other Indian social events are well attended.

Indian Child Welfare

During the nineteenth century and well into the twentieth century, American Indian children were often taken from their families and adopted into non-Indian homes. It was not until 1978 that the government passed the Indian Child Welfare Act (ICWA). The intent of the act was to curtail the number of Indian children placed in non-Indian homes and to recognize the rights of tribes to have jurisdiction over their tribal members. Primarily, it was to provide minimum federal standards for placement of Indian children, when they were removed from their home due to maltreatment. If Indian children were removed from their homes, the act provided for their placement in homes that reflected their Indian culture. A brief historical overview of other federal policies and events affecting Indian country can be found in BigFoot and Braden (1998).

Stereotypical Images of the American Indians

Stereotypical images of American Indians still exist today and many of these images can be attributed to early reports from colonial leaders, to textbooks, and to films (Trimble, 1998). Early colonial leaders and settlers viewed the Indians as savages, ranging from "noble savages" to "treacherous savages" and "filthy savages" (Beaman, 1969). Trimble (1998) reports that the American Indian Historical Society (AIHS) in San Francisco examined over 300 books dealing with American Indian history and culture. The 32 Indian scholars concluded that "not one (book) could be approved as a dependable source of knowledge about the history and culture of the Indian people in America. Most of the books were . . . derogatory to the Native American. Most contained misinformation, distortions, or omissions of important history" (Costo, 1970, p. 11). In a number of texts, Indians are grouped with fugitives from justice and riffraff, and in others they are referred to as savages and hostile to settlers.

In early films, the Indian is portrayed as bad—raiding and scalping the settlers—while the "good" Indian is generally portrayed as a scout helping the white man. Indians are portrayed as though all Indians are alike rather than being portrayed as Kiowa or Apache or Navajo. This diversity of tribes could not be appreciated through early films (Trimble, 1988). More recently, Hollywood movies portray a more realistic view of the Indian through such films as *A Man Called Horse* or *Little Big Man*.

As a result of the inaccurate information presented about the American Indian, tribal governments even now are hesitant to disclose traditions to outsiders or to permit researchers to study their customs or their people for fear they will be misinterpreted, inaccurately portrayed, negatively portrayed, or even federally abolished or outlawed again (e.g., the sun dance). This is one of the reasons that much less research is reported out of Indian country today. All these negative portrayals of American Indians have, to some extent, impacted their self-confidence and self-esteem.

American Indians Today

Who are the Native people of today? They exist as tribal members, as citizens of the United States, and as citizens of their tribe; they exist as individuals who are as varied and as diverse as the tribes to which they lay claim. The very name "Indian" came from Christopher Columbus when he landed in the Bahamas in 1492. He thought the island was India so he called the inhabitants Indians and this name became forever attached to the American Indian (Berkhofer, 1978; Joe & Malch, 1998).

The term "American Indian" is used throughout this section, however there are many other names by which Indians are known. Other commonly used terms include Native American, First Americans, First Nations, and Native Peoples. The groups encompassed by these terms have not always been consistent. American Indians, Native Hawaiians, Puerto Ricans, Native Alaskans, Eskimos, and Aleut are now included in the "Native American" umbrella term, although Native Hawaiians are not American Indians (Trimble, 1987; Trimble, 2000). Inclusion of individual groups within the larger category of Native American gains different meanings when this determines which communities can receive federal and state funding.

At one time the term American Indians seemed sufficient to capture the population of Indian tribes, but with increased understanding of the diversity within and among tribal groups, this broad term became increasingly inadequate. It became apparent that Alaskan Natives and Eskimos viewed themselves very differently from the American Indians, but the new terminology of Native Americans became the encompassing label that now includes American Indians, Alaska Natives, Eskimos, Native Hawaiians, and Puerto Ricans (for more on definitions of American Indians and Alaskan Natives, see Thurman, 1999).

Currently, there are about 400 federally recognized tribes, about 200 more tribes (some recognized by states) who are now seeking federal recognition, and residents of about 220 Alaska Native Villages (Snipp, 1996; Trimble, 1987; Trimble, 2000). With this extensive tribal and linguistic diversity, it would be difficult to lump American Indians into a specific personality or category (Trimble, 2000). Federal recognition of a tribe is the status given by the federal government that allows tribes to have a government-to-government relationship and recognizes their sovereign status. Sovereign status allows tribes to enact laws, govern their people, and maintain jurisdiction for their tribal members.

A *tribe* was defined by the U.S. Supreme Court in 1901 as "a body of Indians of the same or similar race, united in community under one leadership or government, and inhabiting a particular though sometimes ill-defined territory." Before the federal government developed official definitions for an Indian tribe, the term was purely ethnologic. A tribe was a group of indigenous people, bound together by blood ties, who were socially, politically, and religiously organized according to the tenets of their own culture, who lived together, occupying a definite territory, and who spoke a common language or dialect.

Language

Currently, there are approximately 250 Native languages still spoken out of hundreds that originally existed. Only 250 Native languages are viable due to the limited number of Native speakers, many of whom are elders. The majority of Native languages disappeared when entire tribes were annihilated by disease or war and by the systematic elimination when boarding schools staff restricted Native languages and punished Native speakers. In some situations, parents wanted their children to be "educated" and wanted to lessen the possibility of the children being punished for their Native language; therefore, parents did not teach children their Native language, resulting in the transition from Native to the English language within one generation. Today, in an attempt to prevent the loss of tribal languages, some tribes have developed language emergence programs in their education systems (Head Start, elementary schools, and tribally controlled colleges), and American Indian programs at selected universities teach one or two tribal languages. Tribes are recognizing that their language is a unique element of their history that serves as a standard for tribal identity and culture. In reality, however, few American Indians can speak their Native tongue.

Tribal Enrollment

Tribal enrollment began in the late 1800s and early 1900s. This was done, in part, because the U.S. government was in the process of selling Indian land and wished to allot the remainder of the Indian land to American Indian families and individuals. Therefore, they needed a procedure for counting Indians. Before this time, tribal identity was an individual and tribal matter. When the census began, families and individuals had to register with the government if they were to be counted as American Indian. With the beginning of tribal enrollment came the designation of blood degree. This somewhat arbitrary designation has continued to the present time, with some tribes requiring a minimum percentage of "Indian blood" as a criterion for tribal membership.

Each tribe has formally established their own enrollment criteria, with no single set of criteria existing for all tribes. Most criteria require one-quarter or more degree tribal blood (blood quantum), with some requiring that a parent be enrolled with the tribe, in addition to the offspring having one-quarter degree blood quantum, whereas other tribes require individuals to provide proof of descent from historic census rolls to be eligible.

It is unfortunate that the degree of Indian blood is a legal determinant for enrollment because the degree of Indian blood is an arbitrary standard that is not measurable. The federal government used the guide from English Horse Breeding of Quarter, Half, Three Quarters, and so on to arbitrarily set a measure on the census rolls. At the time of the census, the agent or census taker made the determination of measure for the degree of Indian blood by physical attributes, either the person was Indian or had parents who were Indian or non-Indian. They did not take into account the family's historical lineage that may have included adoptions or captives or marriages with nontribal individuals. At the time the census was taken, the government agent arbitrarily determined if the person were Indian, half-Indian, or quarter-Indian based on the immediate family lines. In some tribes, all the Indian people were declared full-blooded Indians. For other tribes that had African slaves, all the slaves were declared full-blooded Indians.

Today tribes face a dilemma of maintaining the arbitrary standard for degree of Indian blood. The acceptance of this as the standard has many opponents, since this disallows many children who have hereditary claim as descendants of Native people. Some tribes are reviewing their criteria for enrollment, especially if the criteria were based on prior Bureau of Indian Affairs (BIA) policies. Some tribes who accepted the initial policies established by the BIA have since changed their criteria and are reclassifying their enrollment. Other tribes may have to change their tribal constitution in order to change their criteria for enrollment. The author's own tribe (Willis/Kiowa) just rejected, by vote of tribal members, the reduction of the quantum blood level from one-fourth to one-eighth. The only Indians who qualify as tribal members must have a blood quantum level of one-fourth or more to be voting members of the Kiowa tribe. The Oglala Lakota on Pine Ridge have all but done away with any blood quantum criteria and now place enrollment matters in the hands of a committee who verify ancestral claims. This is a growing practice in many communities; however, the Mountain Ute in southern Utah cling to a three-fourths blood quantum criterion.

Although American Indians are dual citizens of both the United States and a federally recognized tribe, most tribes will not allow dual tribal enrollment. Thus, individuals cannot be enrolled in more than one tribe should they meet the eligibility requirements for more than one tribe. In the nineteenth century, the prevalent opinion was that an Indian could not be both a tribal member and a U.S. citizen; however, this changed in 1924 with the passage of the one-sentence law entitled the "Indian Citizenship Act," whereby U.S. citizenship was granted to the Indian population. For all the reasons mentioned, it is not unusual to interview a person who appears to be white but who identifies as an Indian. Skin color is not necessarily an indication of how "Indian" a person might be. Tribal enrollment and attendance at Indian dances or ceremonies are better indicators of how strongly one identifies as being Indian.

Population

The American Indian population has grown at a faster rate than the U.S. population *as a whole* in the past decade. Between 1990 and 2000, the American Indian population grew by 17.9%, while the total population grew by 10.7% (BigFoot & Braden, 1998).

The average age for U.S. American Indian population is 27.8, which places this population eight years younger than the mean age of the entire U.S. population. Of the 2.4 million people who identified themselves as American Indian/Alaska Native, only 167,000 people were 65 years old or older, and only 22,000 people were 85 years old or older (from U.S. Census Bureau 1992 statistics). Information from the census also indicated that 11.7% of American Indians were younger than 5 years old and 39 percent were younger than 20 years old. In 1990, the American Indian birth rate was 26.6 per 1,000 live births, compared to 15.9 for the general U.S. population. The large number of American Indian minors means that there are numerous children in need of adult supervision. Because American Indian communities traditionally turn to elders for direction and advice, the current age of this segment of the population leaves many young American Indians with relatively few elders who can provide needed guidance and knowledge.

American Indian people live all across the country, however, approximately half of all American Indians live in the western portion of the United States. Several states have substantially larger concentrations of this population: California, Oklahoma, Arizona, New Mexico, and Washington. American Indian people are also distributed across urban and rural areas. Relocation and the general migration from rural to urban areas have placed the majority of the Indian population in urban settings. Roughly half of all American Indians live in urban areas. Numerous families and individuals relocated to urban areas from rural areas in search of work, to flee from poverty, and/or to have access to more educational opportunities. Relocation often separates individual families from larger extended families, leaving many urban families to make frequent trips to homes of origins. In the urban workforce, it is not unusual for the American Indian to request leave to attend special yearly ceremonies back in their home communities.

Education

In general, American Indian individuals have less formal education than the average U.S. population. In 1990, 65.3% of American Indians over age 25 were high school graduates or higher, and this was an increase from 56% ten years earlier. For the general population, 75.2% of people over 25 years of age were high school graduates. Approximately, 9% of American Indians completed a bachelor's degree or higher compared with 20% for the total population. According to the Census Bureau (2000), in the fall of 1996, there were approximately 134,000 American Indians enrolled in the nation's colleges and universities.

American Indian students in the public schools comprise 16% of the total school enrollment compared to 21% for African American students. The American Indian who has attained a college degree or beyond often has had to overcome obstacles both within the community and their family to attain their degree.

Health Conditions

American Indians are plagued with the same health problems that face all Americans; however, some health problems are more prevalent in the American Indian population. American Indians are suffering from tuberculosis 7.4 times more than other groups. Diabetes is seven times more common among American Indians when compared with other U.S. ethnic groups. It has been reported that some American Indian communities are stricken with adult-onset diabetes rates of up to 90% (IHS, 1996).

In other cases, improvements have been made for certain health conditions. Only 10 years ago American Indian infant mortality rates were three times greater than the national rate. Since then, prenatal care for American Indian mothers has improved gradually, and many diseases, including measles and small pox, that were once prevalent are no longer as common. Today, infant mortality rates are 60% lower, although children over age one are now at greater risk for accidental death (IHS, 1996). Despite these advances, American Indians can be described as having the poorest general physical health of any other ethnic minority group in the United States (BigFoot & Braden, 1998).

Alcohol-related illnesses and deaths are also affecting American Indian communities. Some communities report thirty-three times more American Indian children with Fetal Alcohol Syndrome than non-American Indian children. Children with Fetal Alcohol Syndrome are likely to have a variety of health problems, resulting in difficult temperament in infants, developmental delays, and learning problems. Deaths related to alcohol use are approximately 465% greater in the American Indian population than all other U.S. populations (IHS, 1996) and is one of the greatest problems facing American Indians (Sue & Sue, 1990).

Unfortunately, suicides have also affected many American Indian communities. Approximately, 16% of all American Indian adolescents may have attempted suicide. This statistic is substantially higher than the 4% rate of attempted suicide in the general U.S. population. American Indian males in their late teens and early twenties are at greatest risk for suicidal attempts (IHS, 1996). Indeed, American Indians commit suicide at a rate 46% greater than all other races combined in the U.S. population and die from accidents at a 184% greater rate (IHS, 1996). Thus, many American Indians in the workforce have experienced a greater loss of friends and families by death than many other races.

Adding to the health problems facing American Indians, many individuals and families are without health insurance. Approximately 27.1% of American Indians and Alaska Natives were reported to be without insurance between 1997 and 1999. Many American Indians obtain their health care through the Indian Health Service (IHS). The IHS is comprised of 11 regional administrative units called area offices with 144 service units, 76 of which are operated by tribes. The IHS operates 38 hospitals and 61 health centers, while individual tribes operate 11 hospitals, 129 health centers, 73 health clinics, and 167 Alaska village clinics (IHS, 1996). Many of these clinics provide minimal care with no x-ray capabilities. Serious illnesses must be contracted out to regional or state non-Indian hospitals. American Indians with serious illnesses are placed on a list to be reviewed by a committee, and each week referrals may be made to comprehensive centers. It is known that American Indians can die while waiting to be referred from this list.

Economy

Roughly one-quarter of the American Indian population lives in poverty. This is comparable to the estimates for African Americans (25.4%) and Hispanics (25.1%), but significantly higher than the poverty rate for Asians and Pacific Islanders (12.4%) and non-Hispanic whites (8.2%). Overall, a higher percentage of American Indians are living in poverty than any other ethnic group in America (Willis, 2000).

American Indian reservation communities also suffer from an unfortunately high unemployment rate. Statistics from the 1990 U.S. Census indicated that approximately 45% of all adults living on reservations were unemployed, and 75% of those employed were paid less than $7,000 per year. Why are the unemployment numbers so elevated? Possible reasons include the often-isolated nature of reservation life, which limits the job opportunities available to the community members. Much of the monies available to individuals living on reservations are generated from federal funding. Tribes are gradually regaining economic independence and self-sufficiency by making their own financial decisions and establishing profitable businesses such as gaming.

Values

Harmony with Nature

The American Indian values harmony with nature, and many ceremonies and rituals or dances are carried out to ensure harmony with the land as well as with oneself. Table 5.1 presents an overview of value comparisons between Indian and non-Indian cultures (Joe and Malach, 1998). Joe & Malach (1998) report that cultural conflicts sometimes arise among tribal members who want to protect tribal lands while others want to develop the land. By and large though, tribal groups teach respect for the land and believe that one must remain in harmony with it.

Time and Group Orientation

American Indians have a present-time orientation, and in the past they marked the passage of time by seasons (Joe & Malach, 1998). American Indians, particularly those on reservations and those who are more traditional, are not tied to clocks, hours, and minutes like the majority culture. This sometimes makes it difficult for those in the helping professions, for instance, an appointment for Tuesday at 9:00 A.M. may be viewed by the Indian as an appointment for Tuesday at some unspecified time. American Indians residing in urban areas are more socialized to the clock (time).

American Indians also are more group oriented rather than individualistic. Decisions affecting the family or tribe may take hours and even days to make because discussion is ongoing and no movement will necessarily be made until all issues are discussed and group consensus reached. Joe and Malch (1998) report:

> This emphasis on group consensus has some interesting consequences. Native American children, for example, are not likely to want to draw attention

Table 5.1. Overview of Value Comparisons
between Indian and Non-Indian Cultures
(Joe & Malach, 1998)

Pueblo Indians	Non-Indians
Harmony with nature	Mastery over nature
Present-time orientation	Future-time orientation
Cooperation	Competition
Anonymity	Individuality
Submissiveness	Aggressiveness
Work for present needs	Work to "get ahead"
Sharing wealth	Saving for the future
Time is flexible	Time is not flexible

Source: Adapted from Zintz (1963).

to themselves as individuals but usually prefer to be part of a group. Educators often mistake this behavior as evidence that Indian children are passive or do not want to compete for top grades. Conversely, Indian children who display the aggressive or individualistic behaviors common to the mainstream culture are often taunted or teased by their Indian peers. (p. 140)

Family Roles and Relationships

American Indian families are broadly defined to include extended family members, special people, and one's own family (Malach, Segal, & Thomas, 1989). It is not unusual for extended family members such as grandparents to raise their grandchildren. Parents of children often look to their own elders for guidance and assistance and elders tend to be revered. With the high rate of unemployment on reservations, it is not unusual for the adult children to move back in with their parents. In some areas of the reservation, household crowding can be very real and often stressful. In addition, poverty and unemployment contribute to the high incidence of alcoholism among Indian families.

Summary

What can be said about the American Indian population today is that they are a fast growing population. This increase cannot be attributed to birthrate increases alone and is probably also due to improvements in U.S. Census Bureau procedures and increases in the number of individuals now identifying themselves as American Indians. Thus, the tide has turned with more American Indians, Native Alaskans, Eskimos, Aluets, and Inuits viewing themselves as Americans who are proud to list their heritage as Native. While American

Indians are the first Americans, their numbers have been decimated to the point that they are the "forgotten" Americans. When one reads newspaper accounts on various topics such as health care issues, economic problems, alcoholism, suicide, or any other topic, Caucasians, African Americans, Hispanics, and Asians may be mentioned, but American Indians, as a race and a people, have again become a "shadow and a delusion" (Wilson, 1998).

And each spring, as they have done for hundreds of generations, they will come for the green corn dances; they will come for the wild onion dinners; they will come for the sacred arrow renewal; they will enter the stomp dance grounds; they will go into the forest to select the center pole for the sun dance; and they will go to carry the tree that will become the next totem of the village. Native people may be considered "forgotten," but each year American Indians, Native Alaskans, Eskimos, Aluets, Inuits, and others renew and remember the Native traditions and teachings that have been handed down from elder to child. Modern education, technology, and economic advancements are not foreign concepts among the Native people today, but they seek a culture that captures both the traditions of old generations while helping the youth of new generations.

The authors would like to thank Megan Dunlap, a predoctoral student in the Department of Psychology at Oklahoma State University, for her contribution in preparing this chapter.

References

Beaman, K. (1969). American Indians are still called "filthy savages." *New York Times Educational Supplement, 2834*, 20.

Berkhofer, R. F. (1978). *The white man's Indian: Images of the American Indian from Columbus to the present.* New York: Vintage Books.

BigFoot, D. S., & Braden, J. (1998). *Upon the back of a turtle: A cross-cultural training curriculum for federal criminal justice personnel.* Oklahoma City: Center on Child Abuse and Neglect.

Costo, R. (1970). *Textbooks and the American Indian.* San Francisco: Indian Historian Press.

Debo, A. (1989). *A history of the Indians of the United States.* Norman: University of Oklahoma Press.

Duran, E., & Duran, B. (1995). *Native American postcolonial psychology.* Albany: State University of New York Press.

Indian Health Service (IHS). (1996). *1996 trends in Indian health:* Washington, DC: U.S. Department of Health and Human Services.

Joe, J., & Malach, R. S. (1998). Families with Native American roots. In E. W. Lynch & M. J. Hanson (Eds.), *Developing cross-cultural competence* (pp. 127–164). Baltimore, MD: Paul H. Brooks.

Malach, R. S., Segal, N., & Thomas, R. (1989). *Overcoming obstacles and improving outcomes: Early intervention service for Indian children with special needs.* Bernadillo, NM: Southwest Communication Resources.

Remini, R. V. (1999). *Andrew Jackson.* New York: HarperPerennial.

Snipp, C. M. (1989). *American Indians: The first of this land.* New York: Russell Sage Foundation.

Sue, D. W., & Sue, D. (1990). *Counseling the culturally different.* New York: John Wiley & Sons.

Thornton, R. (1987). *American Indian holocaust and survival: A population history since 1492.* Norman: University of Oklahoma Press.

Thurman, P. J. (1999). Alaska Native, American Indian. In J. S. Mio, J. E. Trimble, P. Arrendondo, H. E. Cheatham, & D. Sue (Eds.), *Key words in multicultural intervention: A Dictionary* (pp. 11–12, 15–16). Westport, CT: Greenwood.

Trimble, J. E. (1987). American Indians and interethnic conflict: A theoretical and historical overview. In J. Boucher, D. Landis, & K. Arnold (Eds.), *Ethnic conflict: International perspectives* (pp. 208–229). Beverly Hills, CA: Sage.

Trimble, J. E. (1998). Stereotypical images, American Indians, and prejudice. In P. A. Katz & D. A. Taylor (Eds.), *Eliminating racism* (pp. 181–202). New York: Plenum.

Trimble, J. E. (2000). In A. E. Kazdin (Ed.), *Encyclopedia of psychology.* New York: Oxford University Press and Washington, DC: American Psychological Association.

U.S. Bureau of the Census (1992). Washington, DC: U.S. Government Printing Office.

Willis, D. J. (2000). American Indians: The forgotten race. *Clinical Psychology of Ethnic Minorities Newsletter, 8,* 3.

Wilson, J. (1998). *The earth shall weep: A history of native America.* New York: Grove.

Zintz, M. (1963). *Education across cultures.* Dubuque, IA: William C. Brown.

6

CYNTHIA KANOELANI KENUI

Na Kānaka Maoli

The Indigenous People of Hawai'i

Current concerns and growing awareness for diversity issues have gained considerable recognition in the twenty-first century. An area of increasing interest has been in cross-cultural diversity and the interactions between the minority and dominant mainstream groups. Although there are numerous articles that describe and discuss these interactions, there are far less publications from a within-group perspective, more specifically, from a Native Hawaiian or *Kānaka Maoli* (the indigenous person of Hawai'i) perspective.

Presently, there are several definitions created by the United States to describe the indigenous people of Hawai'i. According to Public Law 103-150, also known as the Apology Bill, the U.S. federal definition of "Native Hawaiians" in Section 2 "means any individual who is a descendent of the aboriginal people who, prior to 1778, occupied and exercised sovereignty in the area that now constitutes the State of Hawai'i" (U.S. Public Law, 1993).

The definition of "Native Hawaiian" is considered a politically correct, racial definition used by America to describe the indigenous people of Hawai'i. This definition was originally created to define and describe the "aboriginal people" of Hawai'i. Currently, from a sociopolitical perspective, this term is now used to classify, divide, and separate the indigenous people of Hawai'i (Wood 1999, p. 3). This classification, division, and separation occurs because it further defines a "Native Hawaiian" as anyone with an aboriginal blood quantum of 50% or more and a "Part Hawaiian" as any person with an aboriginal blood quantum of less than 50% (Boyd, 1998).

Although the diversity of these definitions may appear as merely semantics, this is an example of the complexity of *Na Kānaka Maoli*. According to *na kupuna* (elders), in the past it was unnecessary to use a diverse and complex range of words to differentiate or classify the indigenous people of Hawai'i. The belief among many elders was that as an indigenous person of Hawai'i, if you could trace the genealogy of your ancestors, before contact with *ka po'e haole* (the foreigners), you were Hawaiian and that was enough.

According to the *Hawaiian-English Dictionary* by Mary Kawena Pukui and Samuel H. Elbert (1957), *Kānaka Maoli* is defined as a "true person" or "indigenous person" (Blaisdell in Dougherty 1992, p 182). *Kānaka Maoli* has become a definition widely used in many Native Hawaiian communities today to describe the indigenous people of Hawai'i as they strive for sovereignty and explore and reclaim their cultural identity.

The twenty-first century is a challenging and dynamic time. For the purposes of this chapter the term, "Kānaka Maoli" and "Native Hawaiian" will be used interchangeably to describe the indigenous people of Hawai'i. This chapter attempts to increase awareness and understanding of *Na Kānaka Maoli* (the indigenous people of Hawai'i). First, there is a brief historical overview of Hawai'i and the impact of sociopolitical changes from past to present. Second, an exploration of the diversity of *Na Kānaka Maoli* cultural identity and worldview within a dominant Euro-American society is discussed. How might *Kānaka Maoli* conceptualize their identity of self in modern society? Third, this chapter presents a description of the basic cultural values, beliefs, and traditions of *Kānaka Maoli*. And finally, this chapter will propose recommendations for others to develop cultural sensitivity and appropriateness when working with *Kānaka Maoli*.

Of course, it would take an entire book or dissertation to fully describe the worldview of *Na Kānaka Maoli* in the twenty-first century. Therefore, readers are encouraged to research, study the literature, ask *Kānaka Maoli* critical questions about their personal worldview, and learn the depth and breath of Hawai'i's indigenous people. Use your own critical analysis to examine historical records, from both perspectives: *Na Kānaka Maoli* and Euroamerican. But most important, use your *pu'uwai*, your heart as your guide.

'A'ohe pau ka 'ike i ka hālau ho'okāhi.
All knowledge is not taught in the same school.
One can learn from many sources.

Historical Overview

Important historical events introduced a dramatic transformation that shaped the political, social, and economic arenas in Hawai'i. These developments resulted in Native Hawaiians becoming highly suspicious of Euro-Americans,

who had differing values and customs, thus creating an interference and conflict in relationship building between two varying cultural groups (Wood, 1999).
Understanding the indigenous people of Hawai'i who were, prior to contact
with *ka poe haole* (the foreigners), a sovereign people is a complex topic.

These political events of Hawai'i are briefly described in Public Law 103-
150. The U.S. Congress considered and passed this public law on October 27,
1993 in the Senate and on November 15, 1993 in the House. On November
23, 1993, President William Clinton officially signed the Apology Bill, Public
Law 103-150. In Section 1 of this public law, the U.S. Congress acknowledges and offers an apology to Native Hawaiians for

1. . . . the illegal overthrow of the Kingdom of Hawai'i on January 17, 1893
    . . . which resulted in the suppression of the inherent sovereignty of the
    Native Hawaiian people . . . ;
2. recognizes and commends efforts of reconciliation initiated by the State
    of Hawai'i and the United Church of Christ with Native Hawaiians;
3. apologizes to the Native Hawaiians on behalf of the people of the United
    States for the overthrow of the Kingdom of Hawai'i on January 17, 1893
    with the participation of agents and citizens of the United States, and the
    deprivation of the rights of Native Hawaiians to self-determination;
4. expresses its commitment to acknowledge the ramifications of the over-
    throw of the Kingdom of Hawai'i, in order to provide a proper founda-
    tion for reconciliation between the United States and the Native Hawaiian
    people; and
5. urges the President of the United States to also acknowledge the ramifi-
    cations of the overthrow of the Kingdom of Hawai'i and to support rec-
    onciliation efforts between the United States and the Native Hawaiian
    people. (U.S. Public Law, 1993)

In the late 1970s, a renaissance took hold in the Native Hawaiian community. This revival and resurgence of indigenous cultural traditions and practices spread, like wild fire, throughout Hawai'i's indigenous community, as
Kānaka Maoli began to collectively restore and revive cultural traditions and
practices in an effort to preserve their cultural heritage. *Kānaka Maoli* became
synonymous with this renaissance and the increased interest in cultural practices and traditions such as *'ōlelo Hawai'i* (Hawaiian language), *hula* (dance), *'oli*
(chant), and *mele* (song). In addition, spiritual practices that were once practiced within families and forced to go "underground" during the time of Euro-
american colonization, resurfaced. Some of these practices included *ho'oponopono*
(to set things right), *la'au lapa'au* (herbal medicine), and *lomilomi* (Hawaiian
massage). The renaissance became the catalyst to *huli* (reverse) Hawai'i's Euro-
american influences that negatively impacted *Kanaka Maoli* in their efforts to
reclaim their sovereignty and *'aina* (land) and cultural heritage, traditions, and
practices.

Historical Time Line and the Impact of Sociopolitical Changes

How have past historical events led to the deterioration of *Kanaka Maoli*? First, understanding place and time is an important concept for understanding the worldview of Hawai'i's indigenous people. Therefore, it is appropriate to describe the geographical location of the Hawaiian Islands and then to systematically explore the historical time line of Hawai'i.

Geographically isolated in the middle of the Pacific Ocean, are the Hawaiian Islands, a chain of volcanic islands located in the north central Pacific. Although there are 130 islands that comprise the Hawaiian chain, the eight primary islands consist of Hawai'i, Maui, O'ahu, Kaua'i, Moloka'i, Lāna'i, Ni'ihau, and Kaho'olawe. Because of the isolation of the islands, *ka po'e kanaka* (the people of old) were excellent voyagers, navigators, and astronomers, who sailed large double-hulled canoes with a deck and cabin for long ocean voyages and used smaller single-hulled canoes with outriggers for shorter interisland voyages. *Kanaka Maoli* journeyed throughout the Pacific Ocean from Southeast Asia to South America long before Captain Cook and other foreigners arrived (Bushnell, 1993, and Wood, 1999).

Using the time line in Table 6.1 as a reference point, we begin the journey of exploring the influence of past events and the impact on *Na Kānaka Maoli* today. The influx of foreigners and their social, economic, and political dealings with the Hawaiian indigenous community reflected the Euro-Americans' quest for native Hawaiian land and resources (Kame'eleihiwa, 1998). These dealings created devastating changes that impacted negatively on the indigenous people of Hawai'i. Prior to foreign contact, it was estimated that the Hawaiian Islands were inhabited by approximately 300,000 to 1 million Hawaiians. According to historical records, Hawaiians were "healthy and robust due to a healthful diet, exercise, and a philosophical worldview of cooperation and harmony" (U.S. Public Law, 1993).

Excerpts from the U.S. Apology Bill, Public Law 103-150 offer a further description of Native Hawaiians:

> Whereas, prior to the arrival of the first Europeans in 1778, the Native Hawaiian people lived in a highly organized, self-sufficient, subsistent social system based on communal land tenure with a sophisticated language, culture and religion;
> Whereas, the health and well-being of the Native Hawaiian people is intrinsically tied to their deep feelings and attachment to the land;

The description above provides a basic framework for understanding Native Hawaiians. Their attachment to the *'aina* (land) and the importance of indigenous cultural heritage are noted. It is also important to note that the identity of the indigenous people is closely linked with their *moku* (island) and

Table 6.1

1778	First recorded haole (foreign) arrival in Hawai'i: British Capt. James Cook. Introduction of foreign diseases triggers massive native depopulation.
1795	Kamehameha I unites the island kingdoms. First centralized Hawaiian government is established. Hawai'i becomes a major whaling port.
1804	Ma'i 'ōku'u (cholera) epidemic. Thousands of Hawaiians die, population continues to plummet.
1819	Death of Kamehameha. 'Aikapu (taboo system) abolished, 'Ainoa established. American Calvinists arrive from New England.
1848	Māhele divides lands among maka'āinana (commoners), the government, and the ali'i (royalty). Foreign system of private land ownership promoted by foreigners.
1860	Act to Regulate Names. Required newly married native women to take the surname of their husband and children born in wedlock shall have their father's name as a family name. They shall, besides, have a "Christian name suitable to their sex" (Wood 1999, p. 10).
1893	Queen Lili'uokalani plans to promulgate a new constitution restoring the power to the throne. The "Annexation Club" comprised of nonnative citizens and foreigners becomes the "Committee of Safety." American troops land at Honolulu. Lili'uokalani abdicates the throne to avoid bloodshed. She asks the U.S. government to investigate the actions of U.S. citizens against the Hawaiian monarchy. "Committee of Safety" immediately establishes a provisional government.
1895	Queen Lili'uokalani is arrested by the foreign provisional government for treason. She is imprisoned in 'Iolani Palace. U.S. government admonishes provisional government for its unjust acts.
1896	Republic of Hawai'i bans Hawaiian language from all public and private schools.

Source: Office of Hawaiian Affairs, *Ka Wai Ola o OHA, 15*, no. 9, September 1998.

ahupua'a (land division) of their birth and the place they were raised. Samuel Kamakau, a renowned Hawaiian scholar, described the Hawaiian people as

a religious people, kind, humble, merciful, freely giving away eatables and rainment; they welcome strangers, or call the stranger to sleep in their house, and partake of their food and fish without pay, and wear apparel without compensation. These people are ashamed of giving away things for the sake of gain. (Kamakau, 1992, p. 27)

First Contact   Prior to 1795, the islands and their '*ahupua'a* (land divisions) were ruled by separate and distinct *ali'i* (royalty). In 1795, King Kamehameha I united the islands to form the first centralized Hawaiian government. Uniting the islands under one kingdom was primarily a strategy for Kamehameha to ascend to power and perhaps his response to the increasing influx of foreigners, foreign diseases, and foreign influences. The introduction of foreign diseases such as tuberculosis, smallpox, measles, influenza, sexually transmitted disease (syphilis and gonorrhea), and cholera resulted in the devastating loss of life and a massive decline in population. The indigenous people of Hawai'i had no natural immunities that foreigners had to survive these diseases. As a result, the '*ohana* (family) was threatened as entire families and communities experienced deaths in alarming numbers. Thus, the disintegration of the Hawaiian social system became apparent as the Hawaiian population became fragmented and quickly deteriorated at a rapid rate.

Abolishment of the Kapu System   In 1819, after the death of Kamehameha I, the *kapu* (taboo) system was abolished by the combined efforts of the *ali'i* (royalty): Kamehameha II known as Liholiho, Ka'ahumanu the favored wife of King Kamehameha I, and Kaheiheimalie the aunt of Liholiho (Kamakau, 1992). The *kapu* (taboo) system was a formalized system that regulated the cultural norms of a people. According to Kamakau, the *mana* (spiritual power) that Kamehameha possessed when he conquered and united the Hawaiian Islands occurred because Kamehameha strictly observed the *kapu*. The *maka'ainana* (commoners) were very strong supporters of Kamehameha because they believed that "by faithfully preserving these *kapus* (taboos) a child born into one of these ranks would become like a god (*me ke akua*)" (Kamakau, 1992; Kame'eleihiwa, 1998; Wood, 1999). With the abolishment of the *kapu* system, the deterioration of a social system that kept societal norms stable spread rapidly throughout the Hawaiian community. The social structure of the Hawaiian people collapsed.

Influence of Christianity   As the influx of foreigners steadily increased, a wave of many different Christian religions swept through the Hawaiian Islands. In 1820, the American Calvinists arrived in Hawai'i from New England, along with Catholics, Congregationalists, Protestants, and Mormons, to name a few. Historically, the common goal of many of these religious denominations was to educate and convert the indigenous people of Hawai'i. Yet, the influences of Christianity left a colonization effect that also created a negative impact because the doctrine of many of these Christian religions included the prohibition of hula and indigenous spiritual or religious practices.

Land Tenure   From 1848 to 1850, during the time of the "The Great Mahele," the Hawaiian land tenure system changed dramatically. Land tenure prior to the Great Mahele was communal land that was converted, as a result of foreign influences, to private, individual land ownership. Hawaiians rapidly lost control and ownership of their land, resulting in a devastating loss of sovereignty. For many Hawaiians socialized on "communal land," the concept of "privatization of land" was indeed a foreign concept many had difficulty understanding.

The Overthrow of the Monarchy   In 1893, the Hawaiian monarchy was overthrown by Euro-American businessmen supported by the American government. Consequently, the historical significance of this event resulted in the suppression of the inherent sovereignty of the Hawaiian people. According to historical records, Queen Lili'uokalani so loved her people that she felt compelled to yield to the American military force that occupied Hawai'i. She offered, in 'olelo Hawai'i (Hawaiian language), the following explanation,

> To prevent the shedding of the blood of my people, natives and foreigners alike, I opposed armed interference and quietly submitted to the arbitratement of the Government of the United States the decision of my rights and those of the Hawaiian people. Since then, as it is well known to all, I have pursued the path of peace and diplomatic discussion and not that of internal strife (Allen, 1982, p. 103).

After the overthrow of Hawai'i's monarchy, the dismantling of the Hawaiian culture by Americans in dominant positions was swift. The provisional government, comprised of Euro-American businessmen, actively disputed the use of the Hawaiian language. Hawaiian language schools were discontinued as financial support was withdrawn.

Annexation and Statehood   In 1898, although most American and foreign residents were in favor of annexation, the vast majority of Hawaiians were vehemently opposed. The provisional government, comprised primarily of Euro-Americans, developed a constitution preventing many Hawaiians from voting on annexation. In 1898, Hawai'i became a territory of the United States, without the consent of the indigenous Hawaiian people.

In 1998, after a long struggle to obtain and review critical documents from the federal government, Nalani Minton and Noenoe K. Silva received these documents and compiled "Kū'ē: The Hui Aloha 'Āina Anti-Annexation Petitions 1897–1898" (Minton & Silva, 1998). This compilation provides evidence of the organized opposition and resistance of the Hawaiian people to annexation.

The Apology Bill   The historical time line of Hawaiian history demonstrates the rapid decline in the Native Hawaiian population, the breakdown of societal norms and mores, the disfranchisement of a people to self-govern, and the disintegration of a native people's cultural heritage. On November 23, 1993, William Jefferson Clinton, president of the United States, along with a joint resolution of the U.S. Congress, issued an official apology to Hawaiians on behalf of the United States for the overthrow of the Kingdom of Hawaii (U.S. Public Law, 1993).

Effects of Colonization

The rapid process of colonization of Hawai'i began when Euro-Americans took a firm foothold in the Hawaiian Islands. The process of colonization exterminated, subjugated, oppressed, and assimilated *Kānaka Maoli* through introduction of foreign diseases; privatization of lands; prohibition of cultural practices such as religious ceremonies, hula, chanting, and healing practices; prohibition of naming children with nongender Hawaiian names; the overthrow of Hawai'i's monarchy; and finally, prohibition of *'olelo Hawai'i* (Hawaiian language) in public schools.

The aftermath of colonization has been devastating for Hawai'i's indigenous people. With the decline in population, loss of land, disfranchisement, and cultural decline, a multitude of problems have surfaced. Native Hawaiians have the worst health statistic in the state of Hawai'i with the highest rates of diabetes, cancer, cardiovascular disease, and obesity. Socioeconomically, many are impoverished and live at or below the poverty level; academically, less than 5% of Hawaiians continue on to higher education; and psychologically, in all age ranges, Hawaiians exhibit higher rates of depression and aggression, with many Hawaiian children in public schools receiving therapeutic care.

In the past, colonial practices were more overt, more observable. However, in today's world, *ka po'e haole* (the foreigners) use laws and constitutions devised and legitimized by the United States to continue the practice of colonization. Euro-Americans who migrated to Hawai'i generations ago, and even recently, conveniently define or redefine themselves as "Hawaiians" or "Native Hawaiians." These terms, created by the U.S. Congress, once used to classify and categorize the indigenous people of Hawai'i as a racial group are now being used selectively and conveniently as a "universal" term for all people, native and nonnative. Perhaps this play with semantics or meaning of words is an indication of the inconsistencies of Euro-Americans, who may not have strong roots in their own ethnic culture and have a strong desire for identification with and in Hawai'i's indigenous culture.

Trauma from the multitude of losses experienced by the indigenous people of Hawai'i has yet to be resolved by Euro-Americans. The policies of the U.S. government preach freedom and democracy for all, yet it consistently maintains a policy of oppression. The historical events of Hawai'i have created a mistrust of *ka po'e haole* (the foreigners). Therefore, until satisfactory reparations and restitutions are made, many Hawaiians will continue to mistrust the *po'e haole* because their words are empty, without meaning, and the memories of colonization is still fresh in the memories of *Na Kānaka Maoli*.

Cultural Identity

"How do Hawaiians conceptualize their identity in today's modern society?" Another critical question to explore is, "Could the disintegration of Hawaiian cultural values, beliefs, traditions, and practices be a result of assimilation and acculturation into the dominant American society?" The *kuleana* or responsibility for defining an individual's cultural identity cannot come from outside a cultural group but must come from, collectively, within the cultural group (Rezentes, 1996, p. 15). Individually and collectively, Hawaiians have an inherent right to determine their own self-definition (Blaisdell, 1992).

Hawai'i has been influenced by many different cultural groups. Cultural identification can be described from a number of different dimensions on a continuum that is dependent on the context of the individual's interaction with the world. Various theories have evolved to explain the phenomenon of cultural identification, yet one may speculate that identification with more than one culture simultaneously, or biculturalism, suggests that single-dimension explanations are too simplistic (Fleming, 1992, p. 159).

Acculturation is a process that occurs when two distinct groups with continuous, first-hand contact begin to experience cultural changes (Berry & Kim, 1989). Two common models of acculturation are the linear bipolar model and the bidimensional model (Phinney, 1990). According to the linear model, ethnic identity occurs on a continuum that is variable, ranging from a strong ethnic identification to strong mainstream identification. This model is too simplistic because it polarizes and creates an imbalance with individuals who strongly identify with a primary ethnic group and yet affiliate with the mainstream culture. Contrasting the linear model is the bidimensional model that implies ethnic and mainstream identity as having an independent relationship. This model states that identification with both cultures can be both strong and weak.

A bidirectional acculturation model developed by John W. Berry and Uichol Kim (1987) appears to be a better fit for indigenous people (see table 6.2). While various acculturation measures have been used in Hawai'i to explore the impact of culture on health, the acculturation model that appears to adequately assess the acculturation phenomenon in Hawai'i's indigenous community comes from Berry and Kim. Their two-dimensional model is based on two key issues: (1) The degree of identification with and maintenance of cultural characteristics of one's own ethnic group; and (2) the extent to which one maintains relationships with the dominant mainstream culture and/or other ethnic groups (Rezentes, 1996, p. 73). According to Berry and Kim's Model of Acculturation, there are four separate and distinct modes:

Integration. An individual who identifies as both Hawaiian and American may be considered integrated in both cultural groups. Other terms used to describe individuals in this mode are *bicultural* or *multicultural* because individuals in this mode have the ability to successfully interact with and adapt to two or more cultural groups.

Assimilation. An individual who identifies strongly as an American and no longer identifies himself or herself as Hawaiian. The process of assimilation might result in the individual developing a new cultural identity. Additionally,

Table 6.2. Berry and Kim's Model of
Acculturation (1989)

		Hawaiian	
		Yes	No
American	Yes	Integration	Assimilation
	No	Separation	Marginalization

Source: Rezentes (1996).

assimilation may result in dissonance or an internal conflict because of possible conflicting value systems between two cultural groups: the original ethnic culture and the dominant mainstream culture.

Separation. An individual who identifies strongly as a Hawaiian and separates from the dominant American culture is considered a Separatist. Another term used to describe individuals in this mode is *Traditionalist.* With the renaissance of Hawaiian culture, struggle for sovereignty, and revival of traditional Hawaiian cultural practices, many Hawaiians have placed greater value on their identification as *Kānaka Maoli.*

Marginalization. An individual who does not identify as a Hawaiian or as an American is identified as marginalized. In this mode of acculturation, an individual may experience difficulty with self-identification and identification within their ethnic group, as well as the dominant mainstream group.

A dynamic sociopolitical and demographic change in the Hawaiian Islands has resulted in a diversity of cultural groups. These cultural groups have been, individually and collectively, assimilated, acculturated, separated, and marginalized in the dominant culture of America. For some, this process has resulted in ethnic groups interacting and creating change in values, beliefs, practices, and traditions.

For example, the industrialization of Hawai'i created a plantation community of immigrants from many different cultural groups (Chinese, Japanese, Portuguese). In an effort to communicate and cope with plantation life, a type of creole language was created called "pidgin English." This language was a mixture of all the different cultural group's efforts to socialize and communicate. This is one example of the dynamic process of acculturation in Hawai'i's community.

Conceptualization of the Hawaiian's identity in today's society is an individual and collective effort for self-preservation for Hawai'i's indigenous people. This concept of self may be an identity of being "assimilated" into the dominant culture. A Hawaiian may choose to be fully assimilated into the dominant culture and discard their ethnic identity. It could possibly be an identity of "separation" from the dominant culture to be fully immersed in one's own ethnic culture. A

Hawaiian may choose to be fully immersed in their indigenous identity and discard their identity with the dominant culture. Another concept of self may come from not having a cultural identity or being "marginalized" from one's ethnic group as well as the dominant culture. A Hawaiian may be unable to identify a connection with their ethnic group and the dominant culture. Finally, the concept of self that is "acculturated," whereby identity of self comes from identity both as Hawaiian and with the dominant culture and/or other ethnic groups. This self-identity provides a broader, global sense of self. This Hawaiian is able to "translate" between the indigenous and the dominant. Although understanding the level of acculturation for Native Hawaiians is a difficult task, it is easier if one first has an understanding of their own self-identity.

Basic Cultural Values, Beliefs, and Traditions

> Whereas, the Native Hawaiian people are determined to preserve, develop and transmit to future generations their ancestral territory, and their cultural identity in accordance with their spiritual and traditional belief, customs, practices, language, and social institutions. (U.S. Public Law, 1993)

In general, the value that holds most importance for many Hawaiians is *ho'omana* (spirituality). *Ho'omana* is infused and permeates throughout the cultural values, beliefs, traditions, and practices of Hawaiians. The concept of *lōkahi* (harmony, unity) is another important cultural value. *Lōkahi* is one of the key components whereby an individual is encouraged to live interdependently and harmoniously with *Ke Akua* (God, the Higher Power, Divine), man, and nature. To be in a state of *lōkahi*, one must also be *pono* (righteous, proper behavior) and have *aloha* (love and compassion) in thoughts, actions, and deeds.

Understanding these core values are the foundation blocks from which indigenous Hawaiian cultural beliefs, traditions, and practices are built on. Other values that emphasize both the quality and interdependent nature of relationships include the concept of the *'ohana*, (family, relative, kin group) and *'ohana nui* (extended family, clan) as the fabric by which individuals are valued and are an integral part of the collective whole.

Relationships and the quality of the relationships are vitally important to developing trust and understanding. Developing rapport and trust may begin with an introduction, "Where are you from?" As the relationship begins to unfold over time and both parties become comfortable with each other, a second question might emerge, "What is your family name?" This question helps *Kānaka Maoli* understand "sense of place and time." This question creates a connection, a reciprocity of information that leads to a relationship of higher quality. For example, a person's "family name" helps another Hawaiian understand the *moku* (island), *ahupua'a* (land division), and family group an individual belongs to and how they might communicate and behave. Table 6.3 is an example of how a person's cultural makeup comes from the land. This basic understanding helps to reduce possible conflict and misunderstanding.

Recommendations

Who are Hawaiians and what makes them significantly different from any other cultural group? By definition, Hawaiians are group members whose identity is inseparably tied to shared cultural values, beliefs, traditions, and practices (see table 6.4).

Hawaiians are a highly diverse and complex people. Their diversity emerges from their cultural identity that is intimately linked to the *moku* (island), the *ahupua'a* (land division), and the *'ohana* (family). The interdependent connection with the *'aina* (land) offers Native Hawaiians a sense of place and time. The interdependent connection with *'ohana* (family) is defined and exists in the quality of their personal and familial relationships. Hawaiians are intricately

Table 6.3. Traditional Hawaiian Values (alphabetical)

Value	Definition
Aloha	Love, affection, compassion, mercy, sympathy, pity, kindness, sentiment, grace, charity; greetings, regards; sweetheart, loved one; beloved
Aloha 'Aina	Love of the land or of one's country . . . a deep love of the land
Ha'aha'a	Humble, meek, unpretentious, modest, unassuming
Ho'okipa (Pukui & Elbert, p. 154)	To entertain, treat hospitably; hospitable; hospitality
Ho'omanawanui	Patience, steadfastness, fortitude
Ho'omau (Pukui & Elbert, p. 241)	To continue, keep on, persist, renew, perpetuate, persevere
'Ike	Knowledge, awareness, understanding, recognition; perceptive, visionary; to receive divine revelation
'Kōkua	To help, aid, assist, relieve
Kū'auhau	Genealogy, lineage, pedigree
Kūpono	Honest, decent, proper, reliable, right, just, fair
Laulima	Cooperation, working together
Lokomaika'i	Good will, good disposition, generosity, grace; kind, humane, benevolent, beneficent, obliging
Mana	Spiritual; divine or miraculous power, authority, power
Na'auao	Learned, enlightened, wise, intelligent
'Ohana (Pukui & Elbert, p. 276)	Family, relative, kin group; related
'Ohana nui	Extended family, clan
'Olu'Olu	Pleasant, nice, amiable, satisfied, contented, happy, agreeable, congenial, cordial, gracious
Pa'ahana	Industrious, busy, hard working

Source: Rezentes (1996).

Table 6.4. Cultural Phenomenon

Social organization	Family, group orientation: ranges from egalitarian to hierarchical structure; large, extended family networks both biological and extended; genealogy—connections with the 'aumakua (ancestors) and the spiritual realm.
Self	Primary emphasis is on family or group while the self is secondary.
Spiritual-religious orientation	Cultural traditions and practices; strong religious and/or spiritual affiliations within the community
Language and communication	Ranges from use of pidgin English, English, and 'Olelo Hawai'i (Hawaiian language). Use of nonverbal body language and contextual cues.
Expressive language	Language is high content. Expression is variable: indirect, subjective, creative, intuitive, verbal, and behavioral. Words have power and cause an effect.
Cognitive processing	Process-oriented. Listens carefully and quietly before responding verbally.
Learning styles	Cooperative learning (Napeahi, et al., 1998). Children learn through social learning: observation, instruction, and participation.
Space	May range from close personal space to no boundaries; closer contact and touch.
Time conception and orientation	Less rigid adherence to fixed time schedule; circular or cyclical.
Goals	Primary focus on present orientation with inclusion of past and future goals.
Health and wellness	Holistic view; well-being occurs when there is a harmonious, interdependent relationship between the physical, mental, emotional, and spiritual states.

Source: Adapted from Rezentes (1996); Spector (1992).

bound together by a distinct ideological and highly functional system of values and beliefs that is demonstrated in their lifestyle and behaviors and makes them an identifiable and distinct cultural group.

Generally, the social organization for many Hawaiians places more emphasis on the self as an extension of the group. They are sociocentric in nature. The self is validated by how the individual functions in relationship to and in harmony with the collective whole. The 'ohana (family) is often a large, extended family network that includes both biological and extended family members. Extended family members may be hanai (adopted) into a large family system both informally and formally. The hanai (adopted) person's tie to a family system is often considered as strong as the "blood ties" of a biological family member.

Family connection includes a strong affiliation for spiritual-religious practices. The influence of Christianity has left a definite mark on the identity of many Hawaiians. For the older generation, the survival instinct was strong. Hawaiians believed that assimilation into the dominant mainstream society was more favorable for survival of the entire group. Recently, with the renaissance of indigenous practices, the younger generation has been instrumental in reviving spiritual-religious practices of *na poʻe kapiko* (the people of old). This revival of spiritual-religious practices includes offering prayers and chants to *Ke Akua* (God, goddess, divine) and *Na Aumakua* (ancestors) and visitation to *heiau* (temple).

The Hawaiian renaissance also included a renewed interest in *ʻolelo Hawaiʻi* (Hawaiian language). Although the Hawaiian language was forbidden in many areas when the American government overthrew the monarchy, there were many Hawaiian families who continued speaking their native language in their homes. The influences of assimilation resulted in a diversity of language and communication styles in Hawaiians. These diverse language styles range from English, to pidgin or creole English, and *ʻolelo Hawaiʻi* (Hawaiian language). Their communication style is highly subjective, including use of nonverbal body language and contextual cues. Expressive language is high content, including indirect, subjective, intuitive, creative, verbal, and behavioral expressions.

Although Hawaiians may initially appear to be nonresponsive or reticent to Americans when they are asked direct questions or are participants in group discussions, most Hawaiians are process-oriented. They believe that words have *mana* (power) and cause an effect. They are socialized to listen carefully to the question or statement, then withdraw to quietly process the information by searching for the *kaona* (hidden meaning) of the question, and finally, offer an appropriate answer.

Socialization for many indigenous Hawaiians begins at a very young age. Children learn through cooperative, social learning that requires a keen observation, instruction by a *kumu* (teacher) or *ʻohana* (family) member, and application of practice with close observation and supervision. Another integral part of socialization includes understanding of space and time orientation. As part of the Hawaiian's group orientation, personal space may range from close personal space to no boundaries. Initially, Hawaiians will maintain a slightly distant personal space when they meet someone who is unfamiliar. However, as familiarity and trust evolve, personal boundaries become closer and may sometimes include frequent touching.

Time orientation is also diverse among indigenous Hawaiians. Hawaiians who are more acculturated into the American society have a time orientation that is more rigid and less flexible. However, for most indigenous Hawaiians, time orientation is less rigid and more flexible. Their primary focus is present-oriented and includes both past and future. Time is believed to be more cyclical or circular. The more traditional Hawaiian individual believes everything happens in its own time and more attention is paid to the *hōʻailona* or spiritual sign from nature. This relationship with time comes from understanding the "three *piko* (*umbilical cord*)" (Blaisdell, 1992). The first *piko* is located on the top of the head. At birth, this is the soft, diamond-shaped area at the top of the skull. This connects us to the past. The second *piko* is located in the navel.

Table 6.5. Traits of Maturity and Immaturity

Mature Person	Immature Person
Has friends of both genders.	Is jealous of others.
Evaluates situations and behaviors rather than judging.	Belittles the accomplishments of others.
Is patient and able to practice self-control.	Is impatient and unable to practice self-control.
Appreciates the other person's view.	Lives in a dream world without action.
Accepts responsibility.	Is dependent on parents and others, without accepting responsibility for actions.
Is adaptable.	Rigid, inflexible. Believes that people are against him or her.

Source: Adapted from Napeahi & Pe'a (1996).

This is one's connection to the present. Finally, the third *piko* is located in the genitals. This is our connection to the future, the area of procreation.

Important Concepts for Developing Understanding

Trust. Developing trust involves understanding the historical background and cultural values and beliefs of the indigenous people of Hawai'i. Become familiar and curious with *'ōlelo Hawai'i* (Hawaiian language), pidgin English, and cultural practices and traditions.

Familiarity. Go to Hawaiian *kupuna* (elders) and leaders to ask for advice, then listen carefully to their *mana'o* (knowledge) about what might be the best approaches to use in working with the local community. Do not assert your own agenda or assign your priorities on their community needs. Do not assume expertise in community concerns or cultural traditions and practices. For many indigenous people, expertise comes with an accumulation of wisdom and knowledge over the years.

Genuine curiosity. Demonstrate, through actions, a capacity and willingness to be genuinely curious about Hawaiian culture. Earn the community's trust by patiently learning through respected individuals and groups. Select culturally relevant media and/or materials to educate oneself about Hawaiian culture. Become open receivers and listeners of "culture" and its dynamics in the local community.

Conclusion

The information presented in this chapter is just a snapshot into the worldview of *Na Kānaka Maoli*, the indigenous people of Hawai'i. To gain a basic understanding of the complexity of all Hawaiians, all people are encouraged to search within themselves and to rediscover their relationship with those who came before them, those who stand up with them, and those who will come after them. Understand where you come from, what is your ethnic lineage, and where your ancestors come from, in order to understand your place in the world and your relationship with the world.

> *E kuhikuhi pono i na au iki a me na'au nui o ka 'ike.*
> *Instruct well in the little and the large currents of knowledge.*
> In teaching, do it well, the small details (Pukui, 1983, p. 325)

Kanaka Maoli Acknowledgment

Nothing we do is solely our own. The *'ike* (instinct, birth knowledge) one possesses comes from past, present, and future relationships held close to the *pu'uwai* (heart). It comes from our ancestors and encoded in our *kino* (body), in our DNA. It is part of our cellular makeup, from the memories of *ka po'e kahiko* (the people of old). In the present moment, the *mana'o* (knowledge) each of us possesses comes from the interdependent relationships we have with those who came before us because we stand on their shoulders, those who stand beside us, and those who will come after us. Nothing we do is done individually but collectively, with both the seen and the unseen, with all of our relations.

Working on this chapter filled me with so many different feelings, but mostly ambivalence. Ambivalence because of the *nui kuleana* (great responsibility) placed before me because I am a representative of *Na Kānaka Maoli*. I am entrusted with the responsibility to educate others by sharing *mana'o* in the most comprehensive manner possible. In the *po* (night), when darkness and silence fell, I felt my ancestors' gentle guidance reminding me to be *pono* (righteous) in publishing this chapter.

E mahalo nui loa (Thank you very much) to *Ke Akua, e na 'aumākua, e na kūpuna, e na 'ohana, e na kamali'i, e na ho'aloha, a me na kumu* (The Higher Power, ancestors, elders, families, children, friends, and teachers) for your loving support, guidance, wisdom, and knowledge. *Aloha* and *mahalo nui* to all those who came before me who epitomize the term, "*ho'omau*," to persevere. *Mahalo nui* to John Robinson and Larry James for never giving up and who understood the concept of *ho'omau,* who persevered when I wanted to *huli* (turn) and run in the opposite direction. This is for all people who work tirelessly, ceaselessly, and endlessly to share the knowledge and wisdom with those who seek to understand *Na Kānaka Maoli* (the indigenous people of Hawai'i) past, present, and future.

References

Allen, H. G. (1982). *The betrayal of Liliu'okalani: Last queen of Hawai'i 1838–1917.* Honolulu: Mutual Publishing.

Berry, J. W., & Kim, U. (1989). Acculturation and mental health societies. In P. R. Dasen, J. R. Berry, & N. Sartorius (Eds.), *Health and cross cultural psychology* (148–151). Beverly Hills, CA: Sage Publications.

Blaisdell, R. K. (1992). Afterword in M. Dougherty (1992). *To steal a kingdom.* Waimanalo: Island Style Press.

Boyd, M. (1998). Dispelling the myths. *Ka Wai Ola o OHA, 15*(9), 1, 12–13.

Bushnell, O. A. (1993). *The gifts of civilization: Germs and genocide in Hawai'i.* Honolulu: University of Hawai'i Press.

Davis, W. (1999, August). Vanishing cultures. *National Geographic.*

Deloria, V., Jr. (1988). *Custer died for your sins.* Norman: University of Oklahoma Press.

Dougherty, M. (1992). *To steal a kingdom.* Waimanalo: Island Style Press.

Duran, E., & Duran, B. (1995). *Native American postcolonial psychology.* Albany: State University of New York Press.

Fleming, C. (1992). American Indians and Alaska Natives: Changing societies past and present. In M. A. Orlandi (Series Ed.), & R. Weston & L. G. Epstein (Vol. Eds.), *Cultural competence for evaluators: A guide for alcohol and other drug prevention practitioners working with ethnic/racial communities* (pp. 147–171). (DHHS Publication No. (SAM) 95–3066). Rockville, MD: U.S. Government Printing Office.

Ii, J. P. (1959). *Fragments of Hawaiian history.* Honolulu: Bishop Museum Press.

Ka'imikaua, J. (2000). *A mau a mau: To continue forever* (Cassette Recording 09–30–00). Laie, HI.

Kamakau, S. M. (1992). *Ruling chiefs of Hawai'i.* (Rev. ed.) Honolulu: Kamehameha Schools Press.

Kame'eleihiwa, L. (1998). *Native land and foreign desires: Pehea Lā E Pono Ai?* Honolulu: Bishop Museum Press.

Malo, D. (1903). *Hawaiian antiquities.* Honolulu: Hawaiian Gazette Co.

Meyer, M. A. (1998). *Native Hawaiian epistemology: Contemporary narratives.* Unpublished doctoral dissertation, Harvard University, Cambridge.

Minton, N. (Producer and Composer) & Ka'imikaua, J. (2000). *A mau a mau: To continue forever.* John Ka'imikaua: Cultural and spiritual traditions of Moloka'i. Life giving knowledge of peace. [Video]. (Available from Hālau Hula O Kukunaokalā, 89–314 Lepeka Ave., Nanakuli, Hawai'i 96792.)

Minton, N. & Silva, N. S. (1998). *Kū'ē: The hui aloha 'āina anti-annexation petitions 1897–1898.* Compilation, Kailua, HI.

Mokuau, N., & Tauili'ili, P. (1992). *Developing cross-cultural competence: Families with Native Hawaiian and Pacific Island roots.* Baltimore: Paul Brookes.

Napeahi, J., & Pe'a, T. (1996). Guide through the ho'oponopono process. Honolulu: ALU LIKE.

Orlandi, M. A. (1992). The challenge of evaluating community-based prevention programs: A cross-cultural perspective. In M. A. Orlandi (Series Ed.), & R. Weston & L. G. Epstein (Vol. Eds.), *Cultural competence for evaluators: A guide for alcohol and other drug prevention practitioners working with ethnic/racial communities* (pp. 1–22). (DHHS Publication No. [SAM] 95–3066). Rockville, MD: U.S. Government Printing Office.

Phinney, J. S. (1990). Ethnic identity in adolescents and adults: Review of research. *Psychological Bulletin, 108*(3), 499–514.

Pukui, M. K. (1983). *'Olelo No'eau: Hawaiian proverbs and poetical sayings.* Honolulu: Bishop Museum Press.

Pukui, M. K., & Elbert, S. H. (1986). *Hawaiian-English dictionary* (6th ed.). Honolulu: University of Hawaii Press.

Rezentes, W. (1996). *Kukui Malama Hawaiian psychology: An introduction.* Honolulu: A'ali'i Books.

Spector, R. (1992). Culture, ethnicity, and nursing. In P. Potter & A. Perry (Eds.), *Fundamentals of nursing* (3rd ed., p. 101). St. Louis: Mosby.

U.S. Public Law 103-150 (1993). 103d Congress Joint Resolution 19.

Wood, H. (1999). *Displacing natives: The rhetorical production of Hawai'i.* Lanham, MD: Rowman & Littlefield.

7

DAWN L. CANNON

A Place for God's Children

On Becoming Biracial in America

In a 1988 *Los Angeles Times* article entitled "Mixed-Race Generation Faces Identity Crisis," sociology scholar Dr. Jewelle Taylor Gibbs was quoted as saying that, by the middle of the twenty-first century, "current racial categories in America will become almost meaningless." In describing one of the many dilemmas faced by parents of biracial children, Gibbs remarked that these children are sometimes brought up with "unrealistic attitudes" about who and what they are. Children are told that they are "citizens of the world" or "one of God's children." She reminded us at that time, prior to the 2000 census, that there was "no place on the census for God's children."

Dr. Molefi Kete Asante, who was then chairman of the African American Studies department at Temple University, referred, in the same article, to the "mulatto dilemma" that was gathering force as the biracial children of the post–Civil Rights era came of age. As descendants of the society that produced the "one-drop" rule (such that any fraction of African ancestry made one black), with one black parent and one white parent, they had begun to ask the question, "Who are we?"

In chapter 1 of this book, the concept of difference among people was examined in terms of the positive or negative value placed on certain differences, and the social advantage or disadvantage assigned to individuals based on these differences. Against the historical backdrop of European colonization of Africa and the Americas, the subjugation and internment of the American Indian, the transatlantic slave trade, the appropriation of Hawaii and parts of Mexico, and the various periods of emigration from the countries of Europe and Asia, and later, Africa, South America, and the Caribbean, a country was created that was not merely ethnic but tribal. And while we have, in many ways, attempted to move away from this tribalism, we are constrained by the prejudice and racism that created much of the history alluded to above. It is this legacy that set the stage for the interpersonal and political dynamics around interracial relationships and the children that are born of those relationships.

Biracial children in the United States faced a quandary concerning their legal status. Prior to the 1967 ruling of the U.S. Supreme Court (*Loving v. Virginia*, 388 U.S. 1), interracial marriages were banned in some states in this country, thus bringing into question the "legitimacy" of biracial children. This landmark case struck down state bans on interracial marriages. It took some states over 10 years to enact legislation on the state level to void these laws. Because these marriages were illegal, the children of these marriages were "illegitimate."

Before the *Loving* case, Virginia was 1 of 16 states that prohibited and punished marriages between persons solely on the basis of racial classification. In the 15 years before 1967, 14 other states banned interracial marriages. Some of the states instituted these antimiscegenation statutes, in part, for economic reasons growing out of slavery. The "one drop" rule was used as an economic advantage because, if it could be proven that a child could trace even a fraction of its heritage back to Africa, that child was considered black and was therefore subject to enslavement. After slavery, a number of states kept these laws in order to "preserve the racial integrity of its citizens," to "prevent the corruption of blood," to "prevent a mongrel breed of citizen," to prevent "the obliteration of racial pride," and to perpetuate the doctrine of white supremacy. Interestingly enough, there was no legal restriction imposed if a white person were not involved. Though most of these laws imposed a prohibition against a "white person" marrying other than another "white person," there was one legal exception. The definition of "white person" included whites with "no more than one-sixteenth of the blood of the American Indian," because of "the desire of all to recognize as an integral and honored part of the white race the descendants of John Rolfe and Pocahontas." However, if one was one-quarter or more American Indian, one's status reverted to American Indian. It is unclear what the status was if one were one-eighth American Indian, but what is crystal clear is the bigotry of the entire scheme. Since marriage was traditionally subject to state regulation without federal intervention, these laws were valid until challenged in federal court. Once these laws were overturned, children who were the product of interracial marriages were considered "legitimate" and had all of the rights and privileges afforded them by law. This legal victory, while legitimizing interracial marriage, did virtually nothing to create a safe place in this country for interracial couples and their children. And so the post–Civil Rights era biracial children, and later, those born of more recent interracial marriages, formed a steadily growing nucleus with unknown numbers and uncertain status.

Selected statistics from the 2000 census partially illuminate the issue, because, for the first time since the nationwide count began in 1790, reporting forms allowed respondents to report more than one race. Of the 281.4 million U.S. residents counted in the 2000 census, 6.8 million, or 2.4%, answered to more than one racial category, with the overwhelming majority of these (93%) reporting exactly two races. Forty percent of the nearly 7 million multiracial[1] individuals counted (although the census did not include a "multiracial" check box) lived in the western United States, with more than one million in the state of California alone. Twenty-one percent of the population in the state of Hawaii reported being multiracial. Of the more than 8 million inhabitants of New York City, nearly 5% claim more than one race. A little over 5% of the 3.7 million inhabitants of Los Angeles, California are multiracial. About four in five multiracial residents reported some proportion as white, and unless otherwise specified, nearly half indicated that "some other race" was in the mix, that is, a race outside of black, white, American Indian, Alaskan Native, Asian, Hawaiian Native or other Pacific Islander.

Approximately, one-quarter of multiracial persons claimed some black, one-quarter, Asian, and one-quarter, American Indian or Alaska Native. More than half of the Native Hawaiian or other Pacific Islander population of the United States reported being multiracial. Numerous organizations and websites have sprung up around the political and social agenda of the multiracial population. But what of the personal dimension?

The Language of Superiority: Entryway to Alternative Universes; or, What Are You Mixed With?

While there is clearly no need to review in detail the entire list of well-worn racial slurs and epithets, it is worth discussing some of the more subtle verbal slights and lesser-known affronts to dignity that shape the language of racial domination. It is necessary to consider, for example, that the word minority may mean one thing when used alongside words like "contract," "set-asides," or "entitlement"; it means quite another when one looks at other connotations. The root word *minor* is synonymous with slight, small, inconsequential, insignificant, unimportant, trifling. The word *minority* is synonymous with alternative (as in opinion), which leads us to option, choice, and the special bane of multiracial individuals, *other*. This is important because, while most multiracial people in the United States are partly white, all are, in part, so-called

1. Multiracial is used interchangeably with biracial.

minority. Just as physical appearance informs the world of so-called monoracial minorities, so it does in multiracial individuals. The experience of a biracial person who is identified by others as black can be very different from another who is identified by others as white. The experience of a multiracial person can be further modified by their perception of their own racial designation. Conceptually, consider the experience of a hypothetical biracial individual (black/white in this example) as falling somewhere within the matrix in figure 7.1, shifting from one cell to another according to time and setting, presence or absence of one or the other parent in the home during the formative years, degree of interaction with relatives, friends, and neighbors of both parents, and so on. The "I am . . ." statements reflect the self-perception. The center cells are shaded to emphasize the relatively new (in a historical sense) biracial category and its impact on self-awareness and the perception of others regarding the self.

"I Am Black and Most Others See Me as Black"

Cell number 1: This is an experience common for many black/white multiracial persons, where others view the individual as black. In the past, because the black community was often more accepting of biracial children than the white community, identifying with "the black side" in an attempt to minimize rejection tended to be less acutely painful. There was, and still is, the tendency of many multiracial persons to identify with the "stigmatized" minority within and without. To deny one's black heritage was often seen by blacks as an unforgivable betrayal of the self and of the race. While the lives of many biracial persons continue to be dominated by this experience, the existence of a language that more sensitively describes an individual's background has opened the door for increased flexibility.

"I Am Black but Most Others See Me as Biracial"

Cell number 2: While a biracial person's outward appearance may strongly suggest that they have parents of different races, they may still, for reasons such as the ones given above, identify strongly with black people. Author Lisa Jones (the daughter of black poet Amiri Baraka and Hettie Jones, a first-generation American Jew) puts it this way in her book *Bulletproof Diva—Tales of Race, Sex and Hair:*

> I'm a writer whose work is dedicated to exploring the hybridity of African American culture and of American culture in general. That I don't deny my white forbears, but I call myself African American, which means, to me, a

	Most others see me as black	Most others see me as biracial	Most others see me as white
"I am black"	1	2	3
"I am biracial"	4	5	6
"I am white"	7	8	9

Figure 7.1

person of African and Native American, Latin or European descent. That I feel comfortable and historically grounded in this identity. That I find family there, whereas no white people have embraced me with their culture, have said to me, take this gift, it's yours, and we are yours, no problem. That, by claiming African American and black, I also inherit a right to ask questions about what this identity means. And that chances are, this identity will never be static, which is fine by me. . . . White women in particular have trouble seeing my black identity as anything other than a rebuff of my mother. Deep down I wonder if what they have difficulty picturing is this: not that I could reject, in their minds, my own mother, but that I have no desire to be *them*. (p. 31)

Such a no. 2 person might feel uncomfortable with others calling attention to the fact that one parent is white, especially if the white parent was not a part of the childhood household. Or they may clearly embrace the white parent and feel much like Ms. Jones about the entire matter. In the past, prior to the more common usage of the word biracial, these children were frequently called "mixed," but more often they were called black and experienced scenarios within no. 1. Strangely enough, in this color-obsessed society, many African Americans (who would be hard pressed to locate or admit to any white ancestor) can relate well to this experience. The poorly disguised question posed to many light-skinned, straight and/or light haired, light-eyed black people, "Where are you from (where are your parents from)?" or the more blatant, "What are you mixed with?" are manifestations of this experience. In black families where there are children of biracial marriages, the children of these unions are often quite similar in appearance to cousins with two black parents. Author Danzy Senna, who is biracial but was raised by her parents as black, in "The Mulatto Millennium," sheds further light on this experience:

my sister and I grew up with a disdain for those who identified as mulatto rather than black. Not all mulattos bothered me back then. It was a very particular breed that got under my skin: the kind who answered meekly, "Everything," to that incessant question "What are you?" Populist author Jim Hightower wrote a book called *There's Nothing in the Middle of the Road but Yellow Stripes and Armadillos*. That's what mulattos represented to me back then: yellow stripes and dead armadillos. (p. 17)

"I Am Black but Most Others See Me as White"

Cell number 3: This can be a very difficult situation, as the separation between what others see and the way one sees oneself is wide. Permutations range from people who turn other's perceptions to their "advantage" by "passing" for white, just long enough to expose the prejudices of those around him or her, to those who spend a great deal of time angrily correcting the assumptions of others. At either extreme, positive, long-lasting relationships with whites may be especially difficult. As children, these individuals are sometimes teased by their black cohorts for "looking like a white person." They will often share this suffering with their self-described black counterparts who are very light-skinned and may carry memories of these alienating experiences into later relationships with black people.

"I Am Biracial but Most Others See Me as Black"

Cell number 4: The person who considers himself or herself biracial, but is seen by others as black, faces a potentially trying experience. He or she may want simply to acknowledge the "white side" of the family but will often be viewed by blacks as "trying to escape the race alive." It may be seen as an attempt to elevate oneself to a higher social status within a hierarchy which has historically been rigidly confining. Politically, this type of self-determination among biracial individuals has been seen as anything from social posturing to an attempt to create a caste system akin to apartheid in South Africa, where "coloreds" enjoyed significant advantages based on their mixed heritage. This way of viewing oneself will often offend blacks who are, ironically, often biracial, but whose white ancestor may be impossible to document. Historically, it is believed that most African Americans are biracial as a by-product of the rape and sadistic manipulation of enslaved Africans during slavery. These "hidden" white ancestors often raped and impregnated their female slaves, both in order to increase the number of slaves on the property, as well as to satisfy their own sexual desires. They routinely considered the children of these rapes their own property, to be bought or sold as they saw fit. These are not ancestors that one is anxious to discover or acknowledge.

"I Am Biracial and Most Others See Me as Biracial"

Cell number 5: This would seem to be the experience that allows for the most complete integration of all the parts of the whole. Both races are acknowledged and accepted by the self. Both cultural heritages are explored and honored. Both sides of the family are accepting and accepted, even if, in the out-side world, both races are not as welcoming. This may also be a relatively new experience, since the biracial concept is new, at least in terms of the black/white paradigm. Hence, the gray shading of the matrix in table 7.1, as mentioned previously. Do we now consciously view another as two or more races simultaneously? Or is the interpersonal process fragmented and staccato, ratcheting back and forth between old and new patterns of identification and connection? In the past, when there was awareness of a person as "mixed," they were frequently seen as black for all intents and purposes. Now there is an entire verbal shorthand for biracial people. While much of it tends to feel derogatory, at minimum, it indicates that people are beginning to display awareness of both elements of the biracial heritage.

"I Am Biracial but Most Others See Me as White"

Cell number 6: This experience can be similar to that of no. 3, where the bi-racial person may be affronted by derogatory remarks made about black people in his or her presence. They may also find themselves being excluded from activities with black cohorts because of their apparent whiteness, but suddenly warmly included when these same individuals find that they are biracial and decide to "claim" them as black. Again, black people historically have been more accepting of biracial people than whites. Recent changes, which position biracial people above blacks in the unyielding racial pecking order of this country, have strained this relationship.

"I Am White but Most Others See Me as Black"

Cell number 7: This experience is probably even more difficult than no. 1, and possibly just as rare. An interesting, although somewhat campy example might be found in the experience of the main character in the movie *Imitation of Life* (1959). This type of experience sparked the creation of the term "tragic mulatto."

"I Am White and Most Others See Me as Biracial"

Cell number 8: Any of the experiences where the self-perception of whiteness disagrees with the perception by others is problematic. In the United States, a minority racial designation is often seen by members of the majority as an in-escapable caste or stigma. Members of the minority group will infrequently be accepting of this perception. Individuals experiencing this scenario may be viewed by blacks and whites as trying to elevate themselves to an unattainable station.

"I Am White and Most Others See Me as White"

Cell number 9: This can be the final destination in that experience known as passing for white. Also overlaps with the "tragic mulatto" experience, until a black relative shows up unexpectedly. The individual is then no longer viewed as white and may, at that point, become "just plain black."

Other biracial and multicultural experiences seem to echo the black/white paradigm. The theme of wanting to deny the European contribution to one's heritage is described by David Mura in "Reflections on My Daughter." Here he describes the process of acquainting his young daughter with the history of the U.S. imprisonment of the Japanese during World War II:

> As I read *Baseball Saved Us* to Samantha, I know she didn't feel a strong con-
> nection to the whites in the book—the guards who sit in the rifle tower and
> watch the camp games, the young boy's white teammates, or the opposing
> team and fans who hurl racial insults. I didn't talk to her much about how
> she is both Japanese American and European American. The lessons of the
> camps, their legacy of racism, seemed difficult enough to absorb.
>   As I look back, I see other reasons for my neglect of the "white" side of
> her identity. For one thing, I grew up wanting desperately to emulate the
> white mainstream. By high school, I reached the point where, if a friend said
> to me, "I think of you, David, like a white person," I would consider it a
> compliment. I know how strong the pressures often are to assimilate, to erase
> your own sense of difference. (p. 85)

He also writes of the fluid nature of the self-concept:

> I have a friend whose father is European American and whose mother is a
> Japanese national. She says when you grow up in two cultures, you aren't
> split in half. Instead, there are two distinct beings inside of you. If you're
> separated from one of the cultures, that being dies, at least for a time. It has
> no light to bathe in, no air, no soil. It can, like certain miraculous plants and
> seeds, come back to life, but the longer it dwells in the state of nonbeing, the
> harder it is to revive. (p. 87)

There is at least one additional experience not accounted for by the nine-cell matrix. Sometimes, an individual with a black/white heritage is viewed, however briefly, as belonging to another race or ethnicity entirely. Rebecca Walker, in *Black, White and Jewish* (appropriately subtitled *Autobiography of a Shifting Self*), not only alludes to this experience but also expresses her desire to be claimed by those from both sides of her "family":

> For many years, I tell people whom I think will be shocked about my Slavic, Jewish ancestry. I get a strange, sadistic pleasure from watching their faces contort as they reconsider the woman who was more easily dismissible as Puerto Rican or Arab. On the subway, surrounded by Hassidim crouched xenophobically over their Old Testaments, I have had to sit on my hands and bite my tongue to keep from shouting out, "I know your story!" I don't feel loyalty as much as an irrational, childlike desire to burst their suffocating illusions of purity. (pp. 36–37)

"I Want to be Recognized as Family"

The matrix introduced here, along with brief commentary, is merely over-simplified food for thought. In the case of the multiracial individual, the concept is rendered impossibly complex. So it is, even with the biracial person. Each position on the matrix is, in itself, a chapter, and so a detailed dissection of the experiences is well beyond the scope of this chapter.

Other; or, What's in a Name? The Example of Tiger Woods

Tiger Woods has been designated (mostly by Madison Avenue) the poster child of the multiracial movement. His own father admits that "for marketing purposes" Tiger's multiracial background "goes off the charts." Tiger is a case in point from an interpersonal perspective as well, because he embodies a need of the child of multiple races to acknowledge and pay homage to each part of the whole. *Cablinasian*. According to Tiger, the name was the creation of a young boy who didn't want to deny his white, black, Indian, or Asian ancestors. It is also a declaration of a young man who publicly refuses to acquiesce to the need of the black or Asian population to claim him as their exclusive champion. The African American population is especially quick to "claim as their own" any individual within the African Diaspora, however distant they may be from the genetic pool of the African continent. This proprietary behavior also takes place when public figures that may physically appear to be white let it be known that one parent is a member of a racial minority. In Tiger's case, while Black America may wish to claim him as their own, we may be mistrusting because white people get top billing. We may also feel slighted because he refuses to identify as "just" black. It is this "just" that goes to the heart of the sometimes conflictual social and political dynamics between bi-racial people and "minorities" who have chosen to identify as a single race. Not "just" something, by definition, suggests that one is something more, and the not-so-subtle implication here, in the context of our particular racial hier-archy, is that one is "better than."

By positioning himself at the nexus of each of his racial components, Tiger Woods can tell us how it feels to be told by blacks that, because you don't identify as exclusively black (therefore buying into the one-drop way of think-ing), you're "not black enough." Or what it's like to be regarded by others as black to the exclusion of all else, thereby denying his maternal contribution to the mix. A good measure of the self-esteem we develop as we mature centers around being able to understand and accept each part of ourselves and to iden-tify with any and all of those parts, as we ourselves see fit. For those who see themselves as a monoracial minority, this struggle for self-determination, self-definition, and self-acceptance may include (among other struggles) breaking away from prevailing stereotypes (as perpetuated by the majority and minority populations), reversing negative self-concepts regarding physical characteris-tics that are different from the majority, overcoming institutional racism, and bigotry in interpersonal relationships. Those who are multiracial may struggle with any or all of these as well, depending on how closely he or she identifies with (and is identified with) a racial minority.

Until the year 2000, census forms chose the name multiracial respondents would use—*other*. For some, to check "other" was empowering because it provided an escape from imposed labels and hierarchy. For many, it was insuf-ficient, even offensive, completely nondescriptive, and a cop-out.

Naming inappropriately can be dangerous. Best to let everyone name and define himself or herself, as the Chinese/Asian American author, Lori Tsang, reminds us in "Postcards From 'Home'":

> The Asian American community is something created through sheer will-power—the strength of our own desire. I'm hanging out with my friend, Theo, when some visiting filmmakers from France ask us how we identify ourselves. "I'm Chinese," I answer innocently. But then, Theo frowns and states, "I'm Asian American," claiming the history of Asians in America and asserting the correct pan-Asian solidarity in a very firm voice. But being "Asian American" isn't that easy. A lot of Koreans, Southeast Asians and even Fili-pinos living in America don't call themselves Asian American. Some of them even accuse "Asian Americanism" of being some kind of Chinese/Japanese American hegemony. (pp. 211–212)

The lives of multiracial persons living in the United States, as illustrated in the scenarios in this chapter, are, at once, varied and fluid but share common themes. In the context of a society where differences are often emphasized and always weighed, one against the other (my difference is better than your difference), multiracial people are currently viewed as another "minority" by many, in spite of the strong possibility that a majority of U.S. inhabitants *are* biracial or multiracial. This defines the political and social dynamic in competitive terms (the tribal motif), pitting multiracial persons against other so-called minorities in a contest for acceptability, attention, resources, and a higher rung on the socioeconomic ladder. Will "minorities" organize to *redefine* relationships as cooperative rather than competitive *only* when the differences between us are genetically erased? Will racism be left intact while a new "colored caste" reaps economic and social benefits by asserting itself as somehow "better than" so-called (monoracial) minorities? Or will those in the multiracial movement use their political voices to do more than merely eliminate labels and instead begin a process of inclusion and help create a language and a culture that ultimately turns racism (which spawned the labels in the first place) upside down?

References

Jones, L. (1994). *Bulletproof diva—Tales of race, sex and hair.* New York: Doubleday.

Mura, D. (1998). Reflections on my daughter. In C. C. O'Hearn (Ed.), *Half and half: Writers on growing up biracial and bicultural.* New York: Pantheon.

Senna, D. (1998). The mulatto millenium. In C. C. O'Hearn (Ed.), *Half and half: Writers on growing up biracial and bicultural.* New York: Pantheon.

Tsang, L. (1998). Postcards from "home." In C. C. O'Hearn (Ed.), *Half and half: Writers on growing up biracial and bicultural.* New York: Pantheon.

Walker, R. (2001). *Black, white and Jewish.* New York: Riverhead.

8

WILLIAM E. HALEY
CLAIRE ROBB
YURI JANG
BETH HAN

The Wisdom of Years

Understanding the Journey of Life

Aging is viewed by many Americans as being a process of loss and decay, and late life is often seen as a time of life characterized by dependency and despair. News reports about aging tend to emphasize economic problems, such as the threats posed to Medicare and Social Security by an aging population, or age-related diseases, such as Alzheimer's disease. In response to prejudicial views of older persons that pervaded the youth-oriented society in the 1960s, Robert Butler coined the term *ageism* to reflect the similarity of these prejudices to racism and sexism. Like racism and sexism, Butler perceived ageism as a way of "pigeonholing" people and denying older adults the opportunity of being individuals capable of unique ways of living their lives. Ageism can lead to ill effects such as job discrimination, poor medical care, and even helpless attitudes by older adults themselves.

Gerontologists increasingly view aging as a life-long process that affects us physically, psychologically, and socially. Older adults are increasingly recognized not only as drains on society but also as potential resources. We are increasingly learning that the effects of aging are not as negative as is widely thought to be the case, and that individuals and society can take important steps to promote successful aging and to deal effectively with common problems accompanying aging. Aging can be a journey that is profoundly different, depending on one's generation and one's lifestyle during earlier years.

The present chapter will review important facts about the aging of America; present information on what each of can expect in terms of physical and psychological changes with normal aging; and discuss ways to promote successful aging. We will also review the implications of aging for continued involvement in such roles as work and family activities. Finally, we will review common medical and mental disorders of late life, and what we know about the best ways to manage common disorders of aging.

Demographic Issues

Growth of the Older Population

According to the U.S. Census Bureau, 12.4% of the U.S population was age 65 and older in 2000. In the beginning of twentieth century, this age group made up only 4% of the total population, and it is projected that in the year 2050, one in five Americans will be in this group. A major portion of this increase is expected to occur from 2010 to 2030, as the baby boom generation (those born between 1946 and 1964) reaches age 65. The number of Americans age 55 and older has increased from 13.1 million in 1950 to 59.2 million in 2000, and it is expected that this group will more than double to 138 million by 2025. Among age groups, the "oldest-old," which refers to those over the age of 85, is the fastest growing. This group, numbering approximately 3.1 million in 1990, was 4.4 million for the year 2000 (or a 41% increase for the decade based on census 2000 figures).

The dramatic increase in number and proportion of older adults, especially oldest-old, has great social implications since this age group will require both public and private policies on education, health, recreation, employment and retirement, health and long-term care, and social services to be modified.

Life Expectancy

Life expectancy in the United States has consistently increased during the past century due to reduced infant mortality, health care advances, and improved nutrition and public health measures. In 1900, the average individuals could expect to live about 47 years. However, overall life expectancy in 1998 was approximately 76.7 years, and this number is expected to increase to 82 by the year 2050. White Americans and women have higher life expectancies than racial/ethnic subgroups, but all demographic groups have shown remarkable increases in life expectancy over the past century. For example, life expectancy in 1900 was only 48.7 for White females and 33.5 for Black females; this increased to 79.9 for White females and 75.0 for Black females by 1998.

Often unappreciated is the fact that life expectancy for individuals who have reached advanced age has also been steadily increasing. For example, in 1900, among individuals who had survived to age 65, the age-specific life expectancy for additional years was 11.5 years for White males and 10.4 years for Black males. In 1998, these figures had increased to 16.1 for White males and 14.4 for Black males. Table 8.1 shows detailed figures for life expectancies at birth and age 65, for White and Black Americans in 1900, 1990, and 1998.

Educational and Economic Status

In 1960, fewer than 20% of Americans over age 65 had finished high school, but this increased to 68.1% by the end of 1998. Because of discrimination and other factors, older African Americans and Hispanics are particularly likely to have lower educational attainment. Future generations of older people, including those from racial or ethnic minority groups, will be have higher educational attainment than their grandparents have today. This shift has great implications, considering education affects income, employability, access to information on political issues, knowledge of benefits and services available, and a host of other factors that influence quality of life.

Although the economic status of the elderly population has improved over the past several decades, in particular due to Social Security, over 10.5 percent of the older population still fall below the poverty level. Poverty is even more problematic for women, ethnic minorities, those living alone, and the oldest old. It is of note that, despite the general improvements in the economic status of elders, older Hispanics and African Americans have poverty rates of 21 percent and 26.4 percent, respectively. Figure 8.1 shows the distribution of older Americans with incomes below poverty in 1998.

The primary source of income for the older population remains Social Security (40%), with additional income from assets and investments (23%), private pension (18%), savings (17%), and earnings (17%). For the older population, consideration of financial status should also include attention to assets. Net worth becomes more important since financial assets can be used to retain one's stan-

Table 8.1. Life Expectancy at Birth and Age 65, Over Time by Ethnicity

	White female	Black female	White male	Black male
At birth				
1900	48.7	33.5	46.6	32.5
1990	79.4	73.6	72.7	64.5
1998	79.9	75.0	74.6	67.8
At age 65				
1900	12.2	11.4	11.5	10.4
1990	19.1	17.2	15.2	13.2
1998	19.2	27.5	16.1	14.4

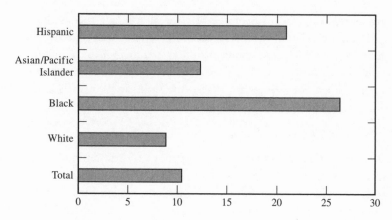

Figure 8.1. Percentage of Older Americans with Incomes Below Poverty: 1998

dard of living far above what income alone would allow. Net worth is defined as assets minus liabilities. Financial assets can include stocks, bonds, mutual funds, and bank accounts, but nearly 50% of the assets of older adults are tied up in home equity, which is difficult to use for daily expenses or emergencies. Median net worth of households with heads aged 65 and over was around $130,000 in 1998, but minority older adults have far fewer financial assets. Over one-third of older Americans receive no income from assets, with women and ethnic minorities particularly likely to have little or no income from assets.

Future projections for the economic status of older adults present a mixed picture. Baby boomers are less likely than current generations of older adults to have savings and are likely to have higher debt and less appreciation of home values. Financial planning is an essential component of preparation for successful aging, but an area that many younger individuals ignore.

Ethnicity and Aging

With increasing number of ethnic minority population and trend of multiculturalism, ethnic minority issues have received greater attention. Today, ethnic minorities comprise 16% of the population over age 65. By 2030, this number is expected to increase to 25%, and by 2050, minorities will constitute 33 percent of the older population. Among the diverse elderly population in 2050, around 30% of the elderly will be African American, 36% will be elderly Hispanics, and Whites will constitute around 40% of the population of the elders. This trend suggests the importance of targeting services to meet the needs of ethnic minority elders.

Ethnic minority elders have been characterized by the term, "double jeopardy," in emphasizing the double disadvantages of growing old and being part of a minority group that may be subject to socioeconomic and racial discrimination. Older adults who are immigrants may also face acculturative stress. However, there is also some evidence that many minority older adults have certain strengths such as relatively strong family ties, coping skills gained via coping with adversity, and informal support networks. Some minority elders also come from cultures that grant particularly high esteem to older adults and high expectations that younger family members will provide care and support. However, the increased acculturation of younger generations to American norms can cause intergenerational conflicts.

Greater attention to racial and ethnic diversity among older adults will be essential in adapting to the "graying of America." Minority elders often differ dramatically from White elders in their attitudes about such areas as health care, nursing homes, and the role of family caregivers.

Fundamental Issues

Before reviewing the physical and psychological changes that can occur with aging, it is important to note several fundamental issues that should guide our thinking about aging. These include the distinction between age and cohort groups, the difference between normal aging and disease, the distinction between usual and successful aging, and increasing heterogeneity among older individuals.

Age Versus Cohort

It is vital that we understand that older adults today differ from younger persons not only in age but also in cohort. A cohort is a group of individuals born during a given historical period (such as 1920–1930) that has experienced many of the same life experiences and historical events. This is an important concept in that the older adults of the future may be quite different from the older adults of today. Many characteristics that are commonly thought of as being related to older age, such as tastes in music, religiosity, and attitudes toward money, are likely to be more closely related to the cohort or generational differences than due to aging per se. For example, in the future the music in nursing homes in the year 2040 will most likely include the Beatles and Rolling Stones rather than Lawrence Welk!

Understanding the experiences of different age cohorts is likely to improve relationships across generations. For example, older adults of today are likely to have been profoundly affected by such historical events as the Great Depression and World War II during their formative years. Baby boomers were raised during an era of unprecedented affluence and opportunity and are more likely to enter old age with better health and economic status. Baby boomers will also have very different social networks due to deferred marriage, reduced childbearing, and greater likelihood of divorce and remarriage. In summary, we should view aging as an experience that can differ dramatically, depending on historical changes and their effects on successive generations.

Normal Aging Versus Disease

Gerontologists distinguish between the effects of aging and the consequences of age-related disease. For example, in considering changes in memory with aging, Alzheimer's disease leads to severe memory deficits far beyond those found in normal aging individuals without this disease. Similarly, while lung capacity is generally somewhat reduced in older adults as a whole, people with a lung disease such as emphysema have much more severe limitations.

This issue is important in that the effects of age-related disease have often been attributed to "senility" or "old age," when, in fact, they may be due to preventable and treatable disorders. It should not be considered "normal" or inevitable that older adults suffer from physical and mental decline. Instead, age-related disease should be aggressively prevented and treated. Attributing decline to "aging" alone can lead to unnecessary pessimism in an era when many age-related diseases can be successfully treated or managed.

Successful Aging Versus Usual Aging

Examination of what happens with aging "on average" can be misleading. There has been increasing interest in the concept of successful aging with growing numbers of older people who have avoided chronic health problems and declining cognitive skills and maintaining active lifestyles late in life. As will be reviewed in detail below, many changes in physical and mental functioning, which are common or usual among older adults, are not due primarily to the process of aging alone but to such processes as lack of physical and mental activity and environments that are insufficiently challenging. Successful aging has been defined as a combination of physical and functional health, high cognitive functioning, and active involvement with society. The important implication is that older people who remain physically, cognitively, and socially active can achieve successful aging. Thus, both at a personal and societal level, we can strive to promote successful aging rather than allowing preventable physical and mental decline to limit our lives as we age.

Heterogeneity of Older Adults

When discussing older adults, there is a tendency to treat them as a homogeneous group. However, today's elderly population is a highly diverse group and becoming more so. In fact, when examining physical and psychological parameters across age groups, a common finding is that older persons show greater variability. Health and well-being in late life can vary from the active and independent senior who has the assets to spend their time traveling and golfing, to the frail and dependent elder living in a nursing home. Thus, we must avoid stereotyping people on the basis of their age and look closely at their individual characteristics.

This variability indicates that planning to meet the needs of this heterogeneous population is a difficult task, in that age-based policies may fail to accommodate for this diversity. For example, efforts to limit problems related to older drivers may be unfair to healthy older persons with excellent health, vision, and driving records. Older adults may be victimized by job discrimination, even when they are fully capable of productive employment. Age alone should not be utilized as a basis for such decisions; instead, we must recognize the uniqueness of the person and take account of their individual capacity.

Physical and Sensory Changes and Age-Related Disease

The perception of physical and sensory changes, once solely attributed to the "ravages of age," has changed dramatically as myths of aging have been systematically replaced by facts based on scientific research and empirical evidence. More precisely, much of what was once considered to be inevitably linked to the aging process has been found to be preventable. Also, advances in the medical arena have not only extended life expectancy but have also produced an elder population that has less functional disability and that is more physically and cognitively fit than in previous times. In the following section, we examine some of the physical and sensory changes that have been linked to aging, major age-related diseases, as well as some of the preventive measures that may be taken to curb these negative changes.

Functional Health

Besides specific changes in organ systems and in rates of disease, a common denominator in viewing health and aging is looking at functional disability. Functional health, concerning the degree of impairments of the individual, is getting more attention since the nature of diseases with age has shifted from acute to chronic conditions. The prevalence of functional disability increases substantially with age measured by activities of daily living (ADLs) such as ability to bathe, dress, and feed oneself, and instrumental activities of daily living (IADLs) such as the ability to independently manage finances and transportation. For example, about 10% of women over age 70 are unable to perform at least one ADL, and about 23% are unable to perform at least one IADL. For women over age 85, over 22% are unable to perform at least one ADL and over 43% are unable to perform at least one IADL. These functional impairments require assistance, which is most commonly provided via informal care (such as by family and friends) or by formal, paid assistance. The compression of morbidity (i.e., a short period of illness directly proceeding death) is an ideal that has become more reachable with continuing advances in medical technology and research into the causes of diseases associated with aging. Efforts to delay the onset of disability have tremendous implications for improving the quality of life of older persons and decreasing health care costs.

Skin and Hair

Among the most prevalent changes linked with growing older are those involving appearance, including changes in skin and hair. However, many of these changes involving the skin (e.g. wrinkling, change of skin texture, loss of elasticity, discoloration, etc.) are affected not only by aging but also by such environmental and behavioral factors as sun exposure and smoking. Some sun/age-related changes (i.e., photoaging) occur primarily in sun-exposed areas, such as the face and hands, and may be minimized by limiting exposure to the sun and using sun block. Also, advances in plastic surgery and dermatology have allowed those persons already suffering from photoaging certain corrective options. Changes in skin texture and the development of lines around the mouth have also been linked with smoking. More directly related to the aging process itself are those changes related to the hair, including hair graying, hair loss, and baldness.

The Musculoskeletal System

Significant and common changes found with aging include loss of bone mass, bone strength, increased levels of pain and restriction of joint movement, and loss of muscle strength. However, research in nutrition and exercise has shown that many of these problems are correctable or preventable. It is now thought that sufficient consumption of calcium during the early years of life (i.e., ages 9–30 approximately) may go a long way to preventing osteoporosis or loss of bone density; and the use of calcium and estrogen in postmenopausal women has been helpful with this high-risk group. In addition, the idea of older adults "pumping iron" has gained considerable favor. Weight-bearing exercise has been shown to produce increases in bone density even in the oldest-old, strengthen muscles, improve balance, and promote walking and climbing stairs without assistance as well as helping to prevent falls. Also, mild exercise is believed to relieve arthritis pain in the joints.

Osteoporosis and osteoarthritis are the two most common skeletal disorders in late life. Osteoporosis is characterized by a gradual, progressive bone change, causing the porous bones to become fragile and brittle. Usually, there are few symptoms of osteoporosis until a fracture occurs. Osteoarthritis, referred to as degenerative joint disease, is the most common form of arthritis and is one of the leading causes of disability among older adults.

The Sensory Systems

Generally speaking, visual acuity decreases with age, often with a significant increase in farsightedness called presbyopia due to the decreased elasticity of the lens and lessened tone in the suspensory ligaments and ciliary muscles. There may also be a decrease in light and dark adaptation with the aging process. Older adults require more light to adequately stimulate visual receptors and are more sensitive to glare. This may be perceived as more of a nuisance than a functional problem, since it makes things such as night driving and dining in a dimly lit restaurant more difficult. Also, not all persons suffer the same loss of vision with aging. Some research has shown a strong correlation between free radicals and conditions such as cataracts (which affects 17% of older adults) and macular degeneration of the retina (affecting 9%), which are often associated with old age. Overexposure to sunlight may also be a culprit when it comes to cataract formation on the older eye. This has led to speculation that some vision problems might be prevented simply by wearing protective eyewear and taking antioxidants such as vitamins C and E, beta-carotene, and selenium; however, further research on these theories is needed before generalizable conclusions can be drawn.

Auditory loss with age, called presbycusis, affects primarily the perception of high frequency tones. While some of these changes are due to aging alone, exposure to noise is an important environmental factor that accelerates hearing loss. There is great concern among gerontologists that future generations of older individuals may have particularly high levels of hearing difficulties due to exposure to loud music.

The Nervous System

Contrary to popular belief, growing old for most people means maintaining full mental function. There is a loss of neurons with age, although the amount and location of the loss varies. Moreover, some neurons may shrink with age rather than being completely lost. There are considerable individual variations in the patterns of brain changes with some increase in amyloid plaques and neurofibrillary tangles even in the normal aging process. Also, the transmission efficacy of the central nervous system decreases with age and sleep patterns change. Preventable lifestyle choices, such as smoking, overeating and/ or poor nutrition, lack of exercise, and lack of mental (cognitive) exertion may all play a part in reduced mental function.

In terms of age-related neurological disease, the most common neurologically related diseases among older adults are strokes and dementia. Stroke is the third leading cause of death and the leading cause of adult disability in the United States. Stroke increases exponentially with age, which might be due to atherosclerosis or a hemorrhage from a ruptured artery in the brain. Dementia also increases with age, being relatively uncommon among 65-year-olds, but affecting up to 4 million Americans with particularly high rates in individuals over 85. Dementia is characterized by the irreversible development of memory impairment, cognitive disturbance, and behavioral problems. Alzheimer's disease is the most common type of dementia, which is characterized by an increase in neurofibrillary tangles and amyloid plaques and a massive loss of neurons. The causes of Alzheimer's disease are not well understood, but it is clear that such factors as genetics, head injury, low educational attainment, and lack of brain reserve are risk factors for Alzheimer's.

The Cardiovascular System

The most apparent aging effects on the cardiovascular system are revealed when the hearts of older adults are needed to beat faster than normal. Older heart muscle requires a longer time to recover after each heartbeat. Moreover, the aging process results in the decreases in cardiac output and limited oxygen to be delivered to tissues and organs. The functions of the conduction system, which is responsible for the coordination of the heartbeat, decline with age and the arteries and veins get more rigid and less elastic with age. Most of these conditions can be lessened through prevention (e.g., cessation of smoking) and/ or treatment. The latter may be as extensive as treatment for hypertension and the use of estrogen-replacement therapy in older women to simple measures such as taking one aspirin each day. Also, high cholesterol, which has often been cited as a major factor in heart disease, is far less a risk factor for older adults than those persons in middle age.

As the major cause of death in older adults, killing one in four, considerable attention is given to the cause and prevention of heart disease. In terms of age-related disease in the cardiovascular system, hypertension increases with age and is the most common medical diagnosis in people over the age of 60. About 71% of non-Hispanic Blacks and 60% of non-Hispanic White Americans age

60 and over have hypertension. Hypertension is a major risk factor for coronary artery disease, which is the leading cause of morbidity and mortality in late life.

The Respiratory System

Lung function is thought to be a biomarker of the aging process, with lung capacity being a predictor of longevity. The aging process results in decreases in the quality of gas exchange in the lungs due to the changes in pulmonary structures in both airways and lung tissue, thereby causing limited elastic ability to resist expansion. Thus, with age, less oxygen is delivered to the body cells; and the reserve capacity in the respiratory system is lessened. Exercise, however, may make a considerable difference and serves to emphasize the variation among individuals. For example, a study of former athletes (mean age 53) who had been sedentary for 10 years found that they still had an average maximum oxygen uptake 20% higher than expected for their age group. A comparable group of athletes who had not stopped training was an additional 25% higher than the sedentary group, far beyond normal expectation for their age. Therefore, it is not surprising that a program of aerobic exercise to increase lung function, as well as cardiovascular performance is often recommended for older adults. It is also thought that increased lung function, due to physical exercise, may be instrumental in preventing cognitive impairment. Indeed, a sedentary lifestyle may be the greatest risk to lung function.

The Reproductive System

With the ending of ovulation and menstruation, the estrogen and progesterone levels in female older adults are decreased. There are increases in the sizes of prostate glands in male older adults. While some changes in sexual functioning are related to aging, a decline in sexual activity is related to many other factors besides age, including general health status, reaction to medications, and availability of suitable partners. Many older adults remain sexually active well into their 80s.

The Immune System

Immune system functioning is reduced with age. The function of T cells' destroying antigens is less effective with age due to the degenerating thymus gland. Nk cells, K cells, and macrophages generally retain their functioning into old age. Again, factors other than age (e.g., stress) may contribute to problems with immune function.

Summary

To say that age is not responsible for physical changes in the human animal would be denying the obvious. However, as research into the aging process becomes more sophisticated, the concept of usual aging as a time of universal physical decline has come under close scrutiny. The result has been to closely examine the interaction between conditions formerly attributed to age and to determine which of these may be attributed to environment and lifestyle, thereby rendering them preventable or modifiable, and to produce healthier older adults. In short, physical aging just isn't what it used to be. All of us can do a great deal to shape our destiny and to age successfully.

Psychological Changes with Aging

Aging can also have profound effects on us psychologically. In viewing the interaction between physical and psychological aging, it is important to remember that it is not only important what kind of disease the patient has, but also what kind of patient has the disease. In the sections below, we will review a number of areas of psychological functioning including personality, intelligence, memory, and mental disorders, all of which are important for successful aging.

Personality

The term personality refers to the organized, distinctive pattern of behavior that characterizes a particular individual. Personality develops out of an interaction between a person's innate dispositions, capacities, and temperament on the one hand and the physical and social environment on the other.

Earlier theories of personality suggested that development takes place only during childhood and adolescence and stabilizes by early adulthood. Erik Erikson is the stage theorist who extended the psychoanalytic theory of ego development into the adult years, describing three stages in later life focused on intimacy, generativity, and ego integrity. Erikson's work raised the possibility that personality can evolve and grow throughout life and sparked interest in life cycle human development.

A contrasting viewpoint is offered by trait theories of personality. Trait theorists suggest that personality is largely stable in adulthood and late life. One important implication of trait theory is that, before we attribute an older person's characteristics to age alone, we should consider whether their behavior is consistent with a life-long pattern. For example, at one time is was thought that older adults generally withdrew from social interaction with aging, and that efforts should be made to engage older people in social interaction regardless of their preferences. We now know that such efforts should consider fundamental personality differences in introversion–extraversion. While extraverts may find high levels of social activity rewarding, a life-long introvert may be comfortable in solitary pursuits.

Life-span theories of development try to reconcile these contrasting views in that they predict both change and stability, depending on which segment of the life course is being examined, the domains that are being studied, and the social and cultural context of the individual. In addition, these theorists note that cohort differences in personality can occur as generations are faced with different historical realities during formative years, and as social contexts change over time in societal attitudes about such milestones during life such as employment, marriage, and retirement.

Personality and individual differences are also increasingly recognized as important in adapting to stress in later life. For example, older persons who are optimistic, and have high levels of mastery and sense of control, generally cope well with stressful life events and chronic strains in late life.

Intelligence

While intelligence has been a central concept in psychology, there have been major problems in studying intelligence in older adults. The most commonly used scales purporting to measure intelligence were developed primarily for purposes of predicting performance in school and work settings, and not in the contexts of major importance to older persons. Intelligence tests have been criticized for being ethnocentric (biased toward the major culture), sexist (biased toward sex), and ageist (inadequate measures of applied knowledge). Differences in intelligence test scores by age can be dramatically affected by cohort differences in educational attainment and extraneous variables such as health. Early research on intelligence tended to be overly pessimistic about age-related changes in intelligence because they compared relatively healthy and well-educated younger persons with less-educated older adults, who were more likely to have age-related disease that can affect cognition.

More recent research has used better research methods in studying intelligence and aging, including longitudinal studies, which allow gerontologists to assess changes within individuals over time, eliminating biases related to cohort groups. These studies find that changes in intelligence with age are much smaller and generally limited to specific domains of cognitive functioning. One important concept in evaluating intelligence is the distinction between fluid and crystallized intelligence. Fluid intelligence refers to the ability to rapidly solve novel problems, and crystallized intelligence refers to factual knowledge acquired through experience and education. Studies report that fluid intelligence, which depends highly on speed of cognitive processing, declines some with age, although these declines are not universal even with advanced age. However, in general, older adults are disadvantaged compared with younger persons in rapidly learning new technological skills such as use of computers, although they can clearly gain such skills with sufficient training and effort.

In contrast, crystallized intelligence declines little with age and, in fact, may show increases if older persons are in stimulating environments that promote new learning. This is important in that older persons may remain highly capable in areas in which experience and expertise are necessary. For example, studies of scholars in such areas as history show that older persons may have considerable advantages in that they have accumulated greater knowledge than younger colleagues.

Many researchers believe that tests measuring decision making in real-life situations are more accurate measures of intelligence in older adults. In terms of daily functioning, the skills measured on standard intelligence tests may be far less useful than such skills as interpersonal judgment, wisdom, and everyday problem solving.

Memory

It is commonly believed that aging is often associated with deterioration in memory efficiency. However, recent knowledge makes it clear that only specific aspects of memory decline with normal aging. For example, immediate memory, such as the ability to remember a phone number for a brief period of time, shows little change with normal aging. Older individuals have greater difficulty than younger individuals in recalling information after a delay, but these differences are eliminated when memory is assessed via a recognition (multiple choice) test. Heterogeneity is important in this domain as well, as some older adults escape memory loss altogether and retain excellent memory functioning well into old age.

Memory functioning can also be improved by a number of factors. Studies report that memory problems can be managed at least to some extent by effective prevention and training. For example, when older adults are given instructions to use certain types of encoding strategies, age differences between young and older adults' memory performance are reduced or eliminated.

Finally, gerontologists increasingly appreciate that older adults can function effectively, even with age-related memory decline. For example, lists can be used to compensate for an inability to remember a lengthy grocery list; medications can be placed in presorted medipacs to enhance compliance; and technology can be utilized to issue reminders for appointments. Because the magnitude of age-related memory decline is not generally sufficient to interfere with most occupational and social roles, it is important that older adults keep such declines in the proper context and avoid catastrophizing over lost keys or forgotten names as indications of the onset of Alzheimer's disease.

Mental Disorders

In general, the present cohort of older adults have lower rates of major depression than middle aged and young adults, but older adults have rather high rates of milder depressive symptomatology, typically related to difficulties adapting to impairments in physical health. Only 1 to 2% of community-dwelling older adults experience major depressive disorders. However, depressive symptoms are very common among older adults. Depressive symptoms are defined as having some, but not all, of the symptoms of major depression such as insomnia, loss of interest or pleasure in usual activities, fatigue, feelings of worthlessness, self-reproach, or excessive inappropriate guilt, although symptoms may be below the severity threshold of major depression defined by the *Diagnostic and Statistical Manual of Mental Disorders, Fourth Edition (DSM-IV)*. Among community-dwelling older adults, the prevalence of depressive symptoms has been found to range from 11 to 44%. Depression is strongly associated with medical diseases, functional disability, and high mortality. The causes of depression are multiple, including biochemical factors, social and environmental factors, and functional disability and physical disease. Depression among the elderly is a potentially modifiable and preventable condition. With appropriate antidepressant medication and psychotherapy, depression of the elderly can be effectively controlled. Contrary to common notions, the group with the highest suicide rates in the United States is White males over age 65, thus, suicide prevention is a particularly important issue for these individuals.

Anxiety is another common mental disorder of older adults. The prevalence rates have ranged from 6 to 33% in older populations. There are some overlapping presentations of anxiety, depression, and physical diseases, which make anxiety difficult to diagnose. Anxiety and depression share several common symptoms. Moreover, the two classes of disorders usually coexist. Anxiety is caused by the complex interactions of biomedical, psychological, and social factors. Anxiety can be effectively controlled by the use of medications and psychosocial interventions.

Another disorder that is frequently ignored is alcohol abuse in the elderly. Older adults are especially sensitive to the effects of alcohol, and problem drinking may be hidden, despite close links to other health and psychological problems. For two-thirds of older problem drinkers this is a chronic problem, but for the other one-third alcohol abuse begins in late life and has a particularly good prognosis for successful treatment.

Aging and Role Functioning: Work, Family, and Retirement

Perhaps one of the most ambiguous aspects of aging and how it affects individuals is in the area of role changes. While society demands certain behavior from persons throughout much of the life course, few expectations are assigned to those persons in the latter part of life. In fact, much has been made of retirement, albeit from formal or informal employment (i.e., motherhood and the "empty nest" syndrome), and the implications of the loss of these roles has been subject to debate.

There is currently considerable interest in older persons' continuing productive involvement in society. Popular belief holds that continuation of work may be beneficial to a person's physical and mental health, and many famous people have produced some of their best work during the latter years of their life. However, current research in the field has presented an unclear picture. Studies of the relationship between health and retirement indicate that, contrary to popular belief, health is not adversely affected by retirement. On the other hand, continued employment into old age is generally associated with longevity, happiness, and higher morale. Also of note is the fact that persons in their 60s (i.e., the older working group and the younger retirement group) self-reported ability to work has improved; diseases causing disability in the aging person have decreased; and attitudes toward working with a disability have become more positive. However, differences in ability to work reported by gender, race/ethnicity, education, and occupation do exist.

Health and disability issues aside, not all older persons who wish to continue to work find it easy to do so. Although law prohibits the termination of employees strictly on the basis of age, age bias in the workplace still exists. In fact, legislation has renewed interest among management in measuring performance (i.e., with failure to "measure up" a grounds for dismissal); and the "pension carrot," where increased pension benefits are provided for those who retire early, remains a favored tool of management to coax older workers from the workplace.

At the core of the work versus retirement debate is the issue of role changes. Old age is mistakenly viewed by many as a time of role loss or role discontinuity rather than role changes. While younger people tend to progress from one role to another (e.g., student to workforce, child to parent), old age brings roles that are terminated by retirement or death. Several positive approaches to aging and employment will be noted.

One response taken by some elders is to create a new subculture based on the idea that older persons are most comfortable living with their peers (i.e., the advent of retirement communities during the latter part of the twentieth century). Others follow up their primary careers with informal work chosen on the bases of preference, flexibility, and personal satisfaction. Still others create a life of leisure activities that mirror the activity level of their postretirement years, while maintaining continuity between pre- and postretirement lifestyle.

A certain segment of the aging population (i.e., women in midlife) are "bucking the trend" by returning to the workplace. While the percentage of men age 54-plus has continued to show a continuous drop in the last half of the century, since 1950, participation of women age 55–64 has increased from 27 to over 40%, and participation of women age 65–69 has remained stable at 15%. While much of this may be attributed to economic need, some of these women are obviously creating a "second career" for themselves. Whatever their choice of activity or role creation, it is obvious that many older persons are actively rejecting the disengagement theory of aging, which claims that the separation of older persons from active roles in society is normal and appropriate for both society and the individual.

However, the question still exists—does retirement make sense? The answer to this question once again reinforces the concept of heterogeneity of older persons. Broad generalizations regarding the elderly and retirement fail to hold true when this group is broken down into subcategories and analyzed as to who does not retire. In older persons, certain factors seem to indicate who will and who will not choose to remain in the workforce. These include race and education (i.e., minority elderly and the less educated are more likely to retire earlier, possibly due to the nature of work available), as well as health and strength of work ethic. The issue of working or not appears to eventually come down to the microlevel.

Other role changes include the issue of family and social support. Where the family and the workforce once provided considerable social support for the individual, retirement and changes in family structure may have altered this support system. It is thought that social bonds and a sense of being loved is important to good health and that persons who are "connected" tend to live longer. Therefore, it is essential that that older adults maintain contact with friends and family or, in the alternative, find replacements wherein they can continue to avail themselves of social support throughout the lifespan. For older adults, the spouse may be the major source of support; the sad eventuality of aging is that death of a spouse brings about the end of this support. However, other roles, such as grandparenthood, may provide not only a sense of familial belonging but also, especially when grandparents are asked to exercise parenting responsibilities for the grandchild, a sense of being needed.

Other important roles for older persons include family caregiving and volunteer activities. These roles provide valuable services that cannot be offered via paid health care and social services and can also serve to enhance the sense of well-being. It is up to the individual to find new activities and relationships to replace the old, and to pursue activities, which continue to expand both mental and physical horizons. Those persons who accomplish this may even enjoy increased activity and creativity in their latter years; those who choose to do less, often age less well than their physically and mentally active counterparts.

Changing demographics have revised the concept of the nuclear family, and migration of retirees has contributed to the geographical distance between aging parents and their children. Therefore, although the family may also play an important supportive role, a circle of friends may be just as important. Successful "agers" usually report an extensive network of persons with whom they feel socially connected and can share activities. Both socioemotional support (i.e., expressions of affection and respect) and instrumental support (e.g., help with activities of daily living) are important to older persons, although the degree of importance may vary with time and circumstances.

It is evident that the interrelation of work, retirement, role changes, and social support for the older adult is quite complex. However, as America ages, more and more older adults are creating new identities for themselves, finding new outlets for their need for activity, creating new social networks, and rejecting the disengagement theory of aging.

Health Care, Social Services, Family Caregiving, Long-Term Care, and End-of-Life Issues

As described above, the majority of older adults are able to function well and even more can be done to promote successful aging. However, because older adults are at higher risk of having multiple medical and psychosocial problems, realistically, we must be prepared to provide special approaches to care to face these challenges. Conventional medical care has a number of limitations in dealing with the problems of older adults. Many physicians have not been sufficiently trained in geriatrics and are unprepared to diagnose and treat such problems as Alzheimer's disease, or to recognize differences in reactions to medications seen in older patients. Older patients with multiple illnesses also risk receiving fragmented care via health care delivered by numerous specialists. In reaction to these issues, a number of innovations have developed that are important for everyone to understand who is dealing with older family members, friends, or their own aging. One valuable reform is the evolution of the specialty of geriatric medicine. Specialists in geriatric medicine (also known as geriatricians) have special training in the problems of older adults and are accustomed to working on interdisciplinary teams with psychologists, social workers, nurses, and other health care professionals. Geriatricians are particularly well qualified to provide either consultation or long-term management of patients with disorders common to aging (such as Alzheimer's disease) or patients with multiple chronic illnesses. In addition, specialists in such areas as clinical geropsychology, geriatric psychiatry, and neurology are of special value in providing specialized care for such problems as geriatric depression and dementia. Medical services are also increasingly available in the home setting, through such programs as visiting nurse organizations.

In addition to medical and psychological services, older adults often need social services that may be essential. These can include such programs as Meals on Wheels (meals delivered to the home), adult day care, chore services, and so on. Because such social services are often difficult for consumers to identify, there is an increasing trend for geriatric case managers, who are trained to identify necessary services to be utilized as vital resources. Often older adults can remain at home, even with disease and disability, if there are sufficient services made available to provide support and care.

The greatest resource available for most older adults in their efforts to live independently is their family members. Family members provide over 80% of the care for impaired older adults. Family caregiving can range from occasional efforts to provide assistance with shopping or household chores to full-time efforts at total care. Family caregiving can be extremely stressful, and caregivers often need social services and emotional support to prevent them from developing depression and health problems as a consequence of caregiving stress.

When family caregiving is not sufficient, there are a number of options for long-term care for older adults. Nursing homes are the institution most commonly thought of for long-term care but are not the only available option. Other options include assisted living facilities (or ALFs), which allow older adults to live in greater independence than nursing homes but with additional assistance available. Another option is the continuing care retirement community (CCRC). In a CCRC, older adults can live either in independent living, assisted living, or nursing home facilities depending on their current level of need.

Increasing attention is being paid to the delivery of quality care at the end of life. One option that is available is hospice care. Hospice is available for individuals with 6 months or less of life expectancy. Hospice care emphasizes not prolonging the length of life but improving the quality of life. Hospice teams commonly include physicians, nurses, and counselors who work to improve such areas as pain management and comfort care. Hospice also emphasizes the psychological aspects of terminal illness, providing support to both the terminally ill patient and their family members. Bereavement services are also offered after the time of the death of the patient.

Although all of us will die eventually, the denial of death causes many Americans to avoid planning for their own impairment and demise. Without advance planning, families and health care providers experience considerable conflict and turmoil in determining appropriate levels of care at the end of life, particularly in cases where the patient is incapacitated and unable to voice their preferences. A number of steps are available to assure that one's wishes are considered in the context of incapacity and terminal illness. Such options as wills, living wills, and durable power of attorney should be initiated after consultation with an attorney and frank consideration of one's values and preferences.

Summary and Conclusions

From the time of birth, all of us are aging. Rather than view old age as a separate time of life, and older people as distinct from younger individuals, we need to consider all of life as existing along a continuum. Aging is a journey that is influenced not only by factors beyond our control but also by our lifestyles and personal choices.

Negative stereotypes about older adults will be increasingly destructive as the older population grows in numbers in the years ahead. We should all endeavor to judge people not by their age but by their unique assets and potential contributions. Older adults have the potential to be fully functional on the job, in social roles, and in our society. Only when we repudiate ageism and honestly accept our own aging will we have overcome the unnecessary barriers that have been placed before aging individuals. A touch of gray can only strengthen the tapestry of America.

References

Administration on Aging (1997). *Profile of older Americans: 1997.* Program Resources Department, American Association of Retired Persons and the Administration on Aging, U. S. Department of Health and Human Services.

Atchley, R. (2000). *Social forces and aging: An introduction to social gerontology.* Belmont, CA: Wadsworth.

Blazer, D. G. (1993). *Depression in late life.* St. Louis: Mosby.

Bortz, W. M., II, & Bortz, S. S. (1996). Prevention, nutrition and exercise in the aged. In L. L. Carstensen, B. A. Edelstein, & L. Dornbrand (Eds.), *The practical handbook of clinical gerontology* (pp. 36–53). Thousand Oaks, CA: Sage Publications.

Butler, R. N., and Sulliman, L. G. (1969). Ageism: Another form of bigotry. *The Gerontologist, 9,* 243–246.

Cavanaugh, J. C., & Whitbourne, S. K. (Eds.), (1999). *Gerontology: An interdisciplinary perspective.* New York: Oxford University Press.

Crimmins, E. M., Reynolds, S. L., & Saito, Y. (1999). Trends in health and ability to work among the older working-age population. *Journals of Gerontology: Social Sciences, 54B*(1), S31–S40.

Ekerdt, D. J. (1994). The busy ethic. In H. R. Moody (Ed.), *Aging: Concepts and controversies* (pp. 328–336). Thousand Oaks, CA: Pine Forge Press.

Haley, W. E., & Bailey, S. (1999). Research on family caregiving in Alzheimer's disease: Implications for practice and policy. In B. Vellas & J. L. Fitten (Eds.), *Research and practice in Alzheimer's disease, Vol. 2.* (pp. 321–332). Paris, France: Serdi.

Hooyman, N., & Kiyak, H. (1996). *Social gerontology: A multidisciplinary perspective.* Boston, MA: Allyn and Bacon.

Lynn, J., & Harrold, J. (1999). *Handbook for mortals: Guidance for people facing serious illness.* New York: Oxford University Press.

Mace, N. L., Rabins, P. V., & McHugh, P. R. (1999). *The 36 hour day: A family guide to caring for persons with Alzheimer disease, related dementing illnesses, and memory loss in later life.* (3rd ed.). Baltimore: Johns Hopkins University Press.

Moody, H. R. (1994). Does old age have meaning? In H. R. Moody (Ed.), *Aging: Concepts and controversies* (pp. 395–403). Thousand Oaks, CA: Pine Forge Press.

Mor-Barak, M. E., Scharlach, A. E., Birba, L., & Sokolov, J. (1995). Employment, social networks and health in the retirement years. In J. Hendricks (Ed.), *Health and health care utilization in later life* (pp. 77–91). Amityville, NY: Baywood.

Morris, V. (1996). *How to care for aging parents.* New York: Workman.

Rowe, J. W., & Kahn, R. L. (1998). *Successful aging.* New York: Pantheon Books.

Saxon, S. V., & Etten, M. J. (1994). *Physical change and aging: A guide for the helping professions.* New York: Tiresias Press.

Schulz, R., O'Brien, A.T., Bookwala, J., & Fleissner, K. (1995). Psychiatric and physical morbidity effects of dementia caregiving: Prevalence, correlates, and causes. *The Gerontologist, 35,* 771–791.

Schulz, R., & Salthouse, T. (1999). *Adult development and aging.* Upper Saddle River, NJ: Prentice-Hall.

Smyer, M., & Qualls, S. (1999). *Aging and mental health.* Malden, MA: Blackwell.

U.S. Census Bureau (1997). *Statistical abstract of the United States: 1997* (117th ed.). Washington, DC: U.S. Government Printing Office.

U.S. Census Bureau (1999). *Statistical abstract of the United States: 1999* (119th ed.). Washington, DC: U.S. Government Printing Office.

U.S. Census Bureau (2000). *Statistical abstract of the United States: 2000.* Available online at http://www.census.gov/statab/www

Williams, M. E. *The American Geriatrics Society's complete guide to aging and health.* New York: Harmony Books.

Zarit, S. H., & Zarit, J. M. (1998). *Mental disorders in older adults: Fundamentals of assessment and treatment.* New York: Guilford Press.

9

DOUGLAS C. HALDEMAN
ROBIN A. BUHRKE

Under a Rainbow Flag

The Diversity of Sexual Orientation

The parade may begin with a corps of bare-breasted lesbians riding motor-cycles. They are followed by drag queens in full regalia waving from elegant floats, power-suited businesswomen and men representing the local gay Chamber of Commerce, family members of lesbian, gay, bisexual, and transgender people, groups performing instrumental and choral music, and representatives of just about every professional, political, religious, athletic, and social endeavor known to humankind. This is just a partial list of what our community looks like, for sexual orientation cuts across all races, genders, ethnicities, generations, ability statuses, and socioeconomic levels. There are lesbian construction workers and lesbian models; gay designers and gay stevedores. For when it comes to sexual orientation, no one is excluded. The rainbow flag is symbolic of the diverse contributions that lesbian, gay, bisexual, and transgender people bring to our culture, and of the diversity within the domain of sexual orientation itself. We are a microcosm of American society.

Our intent is to offer some basic information about how people come to identify as lesbian, gay, or bisexual, and once they do, what issues they are likely to face in their lives. In so doing, we will explore the richness of this diversity, both within the community and in the larger social context. It is important for anyone who has a helping, educational, or management role in our society—as teacher, therapist, health care worker, social service worker, clergy person, or employer—to understand this diversity. Lesbian/gay/bisexual and transgender individuals can be found in nearly every school, office, church/synagogue/mosque, hospital, work environment, and extended family in America. If even the most conservative estimates of the lesbian/gay population are used to estimate the actual numbers in our society (roughly 5%), we still comprise over 15 million people. The phrase "we are everywhere" is used to remind people that it may not be obvious, due to the sometimes invisible nature of sexual orientation, but that gay/lesbian/bisexual and transgender people truly *are* everywhere, and it is a mistake to assume that the whole world is heterosexual.

So What Do We Mean by Sexual Orientation?

First, a few definitions: *sexual orientation* refers to the complex dimensions describing an individual's erotic, romantic, and affiliative attractions and/or attachments. Although overly simplified, typically, persons who experience the greatest attractions in these areas toward members of the same gender are considered homosexual, while those attracted to the other gender are considered heterosexual. Individuals who may be drawn in either direction often identify as bisexual. Sexual orientation is not solely determined on the basis of an individual's behavior but also includes the individual's fantasy, emotional, and social lives. *Sexual identity* refers to the way in which people interpret their own erotic and affiliative experiences. This identification may be congruent with the individual's sexual behavior and history or it may not be. For instance, an individual may identify as gay or lesbian, and yet be heterosexually married, with no history of homoerotic, or same-sex, behavior. Both sexual orientation and sexual identity may be experienced by some as fluid throughout the lifespan. For instance, a woman who has always had romantic relationships with men, and identified as heterosexual, may fall in love with another woman at midlife. She may or may not then identify as lesbian. Similarly, a heterosexually identified man may go through periods of having homosexual interactions with other men. While he may acknowledge that his erotic interests are both homosexual and heterosexual in nature, the concept of a gay identity may be meaningless to him, and he may identify as bisexual or heterosexual. *Gender identity* refers to the individual's intrinsic experience of gender: this may be male or female, and it may not necessarily be congruent with the individual's genetically assigned sex, as is the case for many transgender individuals. Persons who cross gender-norms may describe themselves as *transgender*, which is an umbrella term encompassing a wide range of behaviors, attitudes, and beliefs that break gender norms and stereotypes. Transgender individuals range from "masculine" women and "feminine" men at one end of the continuum through those who cross-dress through individuals who desire or complete a chemical and/or surgical sex change. Gender identity is independent from sexual orientation, that is, transgender individuals may be lesbian, gay, bisexual, or heterosexual. Lesbian, gay, bisexual, and transgender individuals often share a commonality in the way they are treated or stereotyped. For example, gay men are often accused of being "womanish" and lesbians as being "mannish." In the case of many transgender people, there is an abiding sense, usually from early childhood, that one's identity—and all of the social, behavioral, and emotional factors that implies—does not match one's genetic sex.

Everyone assesses themselves on these constructs, either consciously or unconsciously. Furthermore, the process in making this assessment can be experienced as thoroughly intrinsic or determined by social factors. Most heterosexuals may not even be aware of the process because of the prevalence of heterosexual values in our culture. Most lesbians, gay men, bisexuals, and transgender individuals are more aware of this process. Finally, for some, the felt or chosen identifications may change over time. Given the numerous options of these three constructs, it is no wonder that the lesbian/gay/bisexual/transgender community (hereafter referred to as "the Community") reflects such a degree of diversity.

The End of the Mental Illness Model

Historically, homosexuality had been viewed as a form of mental illness, arising from an arrest of normative psychosexual development. It has been speculated that this purported developmental arrest was due to the disruption in the normative patterns of attachment owing to a particular dysfunctional family situation. There had never been, nor is there still, any empirical justification for this position. The first researcher to challenge it was Evelyn Hooker, who found that the personality test scores of matched groups of heterosexual and homosexual males did not differ. This opened the door for an extensive literature that shows that lesbian and gay individuals do not differ from heterosexuals on any number of psychological measures of well-being. Furthermore, the literature attempting to demonstrate that homosexuality is a mental illness was extremely flawed methodologically. When it became clear that the diagnosis of homosexuality was simply an expression of prevailing social prejudice, the organized mental health associations removed it from the list of mental disorders. This ushered in the era of viewing homosexuality as a normal variant of the human experience. Since then, it has become clear that the lesbian/gay/bisexual individuals most likely to enjoy optimal psychological functioning are those who have most effectively come to terms with their sexual orientation.

Coming Out

Once an individual has determined that her/his sexual orientation is other than heterosexual, she or he is faced with a decision: whether or not to disclose this, that is, to *come out*, and if so, to whom? Some view coming out as a necessary step in the development of a healthy gay, lesbian, or bisexual identity. Nevertheless, it can be a mixed emotional experience for many, particularly those who have been raised in an atmosphere of strongly anti-gay attitudes. Anyone who knows a newly out individual, whether counselor, teacher, pastor, employer, friend, or family member, can assist them in identifying and overcoming whatever shame and anxiety she/he may have internalized about a gay, lesbian, or bisexual identity. This assistance may come in the form of a nonjudgmental, open response and suggestions for ways to participate in the Community.

The disclosure of sexual orientation is, for most lesbian, gay, and bisexual individuals, a lifelong process. Due to the invisibility of a same-sex sexual orientation, many family members, friends, neighbors, and coworkers may incorrectly assume that the lesbian/gay/bisexual individual is heterosexual. The individual is then faced with continual choices about disclosure, which may be expressed in different ways depending on the situation. For example, an individual may be "out" to close friends and family, but not to coworkers, as most lesbian and gay workers' jobs are still not protected against discrimination on the basis of sexual orientation. That is, in most jurisdictions, lesbians and gay men can be fired from their jobs simply because they are gay, regardless of their performance. At the same time, coming out provides opportunities for personal growth. Individuals often report feeling more solid with their sense of identity, improved self-esteem, and a sense of pride and relief when they are able to acknowledge their sexual orientation. It has further been suggested that the Community itself serves as a surrogate family, helping to develop a positive lesbian/gay/bisexual identity. In addition, the more people who come out, the more visible lesbian/gay/bisexual people become. An added social benefit is that what has been shown to reduce sexual prejudice and stigma on the part of nongay individuals is personal knowledge of a lesbian, gay, or bisexual individual.

Sexual Prejudice and Culture

Over thirty years have passed since the advent of the "gay liberation" movement, and in that time our society has seen profound changes in its willingness to embrace people of all sexual orientations. The work in this regard, however, is far from done. It has been suggested that the progress we have seen in societal anti-gay attitudes is in reality a diminishment of previously higher levels of hostility. The one thing that everyone, regardless of sexual orientation, has in common is that we have all grown up in a culture that devalues and stigmatizes lesbian/gay/bisexual/transgender people. The term *sexual prejudice* has recently been used in reference to "negative attitudes toward an individual because of her or his sexual orientation." This replaces the more familiar but less accurate term, *homophobia*, in examining the motivation behind the still-widespread mistreatment of individuals based on their actual or perceived sexual orientation. The effects of sexual prejudice may vary greatly from person to person, but nearly every lesbian/gay/bisexual/transgender individual has their own stories of harassment, discrimination, or violence to report. The stress associated with these experiences, along with their tendency to cause high levels of emotional distress in lesbian/gay/bisexual/transgender people, has been extensively documented. National as well as personal events also affect an individual's social stress response. The 1998 murders of Matthew Shepard and Billy Jack Gaither, both because they were gay, had a chilling effect on the entire Community. This effect not only encompasses the grief and outrage in response to these horrific events, but also the fear that accompanies the recognition that *this could have happened to any one of us or our loved ones.*

Person to Person

Family members, friends, and colleagues of lesbian, gay, bisexual, and transgender persons need to know that due to social stressors, lesbian/gay/bisexual individuals are frequent consumers of mental health services. Recently, the organized mental health professions have offered guidance to practitioners and the public alike. Both the American Psychological Association and the American Psychiatric Association have adopted policies that reject portrayals of lesbian and gay people as mentally ill on the basis of their sexual orientation. These organizations also reject treatments based on the premise that homosexuality is a mental illness. In 2000, the American Psychological Association adopted guidelines for practitioners of psychotherapy with lesbian, gay and bisexual clients. They guide competent practice with lesbian, gay, and bisexual clients by establishing a "consciousness," or attitude set, that is useful in helping practitoners respond to the needs of their lesbian, gay, and bisexual clients. The knowledge base they provide, about a variety of important issues, creates a minicourse in lesbian, gay, and bisexual cultural literacy.

Homosexuality and bisexuality are not mental illnesses. Therefore, when a person voices discomfort about being lesbian, gay, or bisexual, the reasons for this discomfort need to be discovered. For example, the individual's history of anti-gay victimization, the support, or lack thereof, from family and friends should all be investigated. People who have come from strongly homophobic backgrounds would understandably be conflicted about being gay, lesbian, or bisexual. Often, people in this position feel a need to choose between their family and/or culture and their gay, lesbian, or bisexual identity. One needs to examine one's own biases about sexual orientation and be aware of the fact that an inaccurate or prejudicial view of being lesbian, gay, or bisexual may affect the individual's self-concept.

The examination of personal attitudes and knowledge is relevant to a variety of situations. In medical and legal settings, for example, it is useful for workers to understand that the families of lesbian/gay/bisexual and transgender individuals may include persons who are not legally or biologically related. Thus, it is helpful for the physician to be respectful of the importance of lesbian, gay, and bisexual relationships. In this regard, the physician might inquire as to the relationship of a gay/lesbian patient's family member, so that those individuals can be consulted and apprised of treatment options. Lawyers who are familiar with the specific legal protections needed in most jurisdictions to safeguard the primacy of the gay or lesbian relationship are an invaluable asset.

Educators who are sensitive to the plight of many lesbian, gay, bisexual, transgender, or questioning youth serve an invaluable function in the lives of young people. Such young people experience special risks and difficulties and are at increased risk for a number of personal and academic problems. The incidence of anti-gay harassment continues at epidemic levels in our schools, most of which goes unreported. A compassionate teacher or school counselor recognizes that it is not just the individual faced with such marginalization who needs help, but the school culture as a whole that must be addressed.

One of the more difficult arenas in which helping professionals interact with lesbian, gay, and bisexual people is the religious setting. The Christian churches, in particular, have been responsible for exacerbating much of the social prejudice that has been the basis for attempts to deny civil rights to lesbian and gay individuals. Gay and lesbian members of any number of religious denominations have frequently been hounded to enter ineffective ex-gay ministries or excluded from religious communities altogether. Yet, for many lesbian and gay people, a sense of spiritual identity is as intrinsic as the sense of sexual orientation. For them, it is important to seek out religious or spiritual environments that are affirming of all sexual orientations and of all loving relationships. There is an increasing trend, even among some conservative Christian denominations, toward publicly identifying some congregations as open to members who identify as gay, lesbian, or bisexual. We now turn our attention to some of the more specific aspects of diversity within the Community.

Diversity Within the Community

The use of the term "community" to refer to lesbians, gay men, bisexuals, and transgender individuals is something of a misnomer. That is, community implies commonality, similarity, or sameness among its members and difference from nonmembers (i.e., heterosexuals). In reality, members of the lesbian, gay, bisexual, transgender community are no more similar than those of the so-called Black community, the Hispanic community, or even the heterosexual community. That is, gay men, lesbians, bisexuals, and transgender individuals are a very diverse group with, in many ways, very little in common. Furthermore, there are more similarities overall with the heterosexual community than there are differences. While it may sound clichéd, the concerns of most lesbians, gay men, bisexuals, and transgender individuals are no different than those of most heterosexuals, that is, concerns about bills, taxes, school systems, mortgages, jobs, loved ones, and so on. There are, however, some differences experienced by gay men, lesbians, bisexuals, and transgender individuals.

Gender Issues

Gay men are often incorrectly stereotyped as effeminate, "femme," and interested in traditionally feminine endeavors, while lesbians are often stereotyped as masculine, "butch," and interested in traditionally masculine activities. While some gay men are more feminine and some lesbians are more masculine, in reality, gay men and lesbians span the continuum of sex-role behaviors and identities in the same way that heterosexuals do. That is, gay and heterosexual men are as likely to be football players, businessmen, nurses, or hairdressers.

Relatedly, gay men and lesbians are often incorrectly stereotyped as "men who want to be women" and "women who want to be men." This may, in part, come from the heterosexist assumption that all people really want to be with persons of the other gender. Therefore, if a man wants to be with another man or a woman wants to be with another woman, they must really not want to be the man or woman that they are. Most people develop their gender identity very early on, and in general, long before their sexual identity. In most cases, gender is one of the first, if not "the" first, characteristics noted of a newborn. Generally speaking, the first questions after the birth of a new baby are not "what color is her hair?" or "is he healthy?" but rather, "is it a boy or a girl?" And there is a powerful socialization that ensues. Just as male and female socialization impacts heterosexual relationships (hence, the plethora of references on Martian Men and Venusian Women), gender socialization impacts same-sex relationships. Men who are traditionally raised to compete with one another and to repress their emotions, a la "boys don't cry," may have difficulty experiencing and expressing intimacy. Women, on the other hand, who are traditionally raised to cooperate with one another and to express and communicate emotions may find themselves relationally enmeshed. Regardless, differences between and conflicts within same-sex and other-sex relationships may be due, in large part, to the gender socialization of the participants.

Contrary to popular stereotypes, most (but not all) same-sex relationships do not conform to traditional male-female or "butch-femme" roles. That is, most partners share roles and tasks based on personal preferences, individual tastes, and negotiated or tacit agreement rather than assigned role. In that way, same-sex relationships may offer more sex-role flexibility in that roles, tasks, and chores can be assigned by individual talent and relational negotiation rather than by socialization alone.

Multiple Minority Statuses

Race and Ethnicity

As previously noted, sexual orientation cuts across all races, ethnic groups, and cultures. Some racial, ethnic, and cultural groups are more embracing or tolerating of sexual orientation differences than others. In addition, in American culture, some racial, ethnic, and cultural groups are more "favored" than others. Many gay, lesbian, bisexual, and transgender people face complex and difficult choices about coming out within their cultures and/or when their racial, ethnic, or cultural heritage is in conflict with their sexual orientation. For example, some African Americans believe homosexuality is a "White person's problem," and therefore, there are no gay or lesbian African Americans. This invisibility can make it difficult for gay and lesbian African Americans to come out. In addition, just as sexual orientation cuts across all races, racism cuts across all sexual orientations. African American, Native American, Latino/a, and Asian American lesbians, gay men, bisexuals, and transgender individuals also face racism within the community as well as in the society at large. Lesbian, gay, bisexual, and transgender people of color face multiple stigmas, including the prospect of being alienated from their race and ethnic cultural groups for being gay and alienated from the gay community for their race. Furthermore, they face oppression from the mainstream, heterosexual, White community for their race, sexual orientation, and for women, their gender.

Ability Status

In addition to race, ethnicity, and culture, lesbians, gay men, bisexuals, and transgender individuals vary across the spectrum of ability/disability. That is, as with heterosexuals, lesbians, gay men, bisexuals, and transgender individuals are faced with the effects of aging, chronic illness, debilitating accidents, and disability. Stereotypically, persons with disabilities are inaccurately not considered to be sexual beings and therefore cannot be lesbian, gay, bisexual, or transgender. Thus, their sexual orientation may be invisible to both the heterosexual and the lesbian, gay, and bisexual communities. In addition, people with disabilities face access difficulties and oppression from the able-bodied community.

Bisexuality: Caught Between a Rock and a Hard Place Versus the Best of Both Worlds

Bisexuals, individuals who are attracted to either same- or other-sex partners, may find themselves ostracized from the heterosexual community for their same-sex attractions and relationships and alienated from the lesbian and gay community for their other-sex relationships. The term *heterosexual privilege* is used to describe the social benefits derived from being in, or giving the appearance of being in, a heterosexual relationship. These benefits accrue from participating in a relationship that is socially sanctioned and validated. While some people self-identify as bisexual while in transition from a heterosexual to a lesbian or gay sexual orientation, most bisexuals, contrary to stereotype, are not "in transition" or "indecisive." Bisexuals are often stereotyped as being promiscuous, in part because of the connotation that they are attracted to both genders and thus have partners of both genders. In reality, bisexuals are as promiscuous as any other sexual orientation group—heterosexuals, lesbians, or gay men. Most bisexuals more accurately describe themselves as able to be attracted to "either" gendered partners rather than "both."

Generational Differences

Sexual orientation crosses age boundaries as well. With the availability of role models and resources, many lesbians, gay men, bisexuals, and transgender individuals are able to come out to themselves and others at an earlier age. While coming out at a younger age affords youth the opportunity to claim their identities, it also opens them to certain vulnerabilities. It is not unusual for some newly out teenagers to be kicked out of the family home, to have college tuition rescinded, and to be in physical danger from unaccepting family members and others. Given that coming to terms with a homosexual sexual orientation can be traumatic, it is important that young people questioning their sexual orientation have safe and affirming places to explore their identities.

At the other end of the age spectrum, lesbian, gay, bisexual, and transgender senior citizens may face a number of difficulties. As with people with disabilities, senior citizens are often stereotyped as asexual. If they are considered sexual beings, they are often described as "dirty old men." Like their heterosexual counterparts, many lesbians, gay men, bisexuals, and transgender individuals continue to have happy, healthy sex lives throughout their lifetimes. Because of the focus on physical beauty and youth in the American culture, some older lesbian, gay, bisexual, and transgender individuals may struggle with finding affirming support networks and resources. Furthermore, older lesbian/gay/ bisexual/transgender individuals may have come out as lesbian, gay or bisexual at a time when social attitudes were vastly different than they are at present. This may affect a wide range of issues, from the internal (self-concept) to the external (legal and medical issues).

Considerations Relating to Families

The concept of family is as important to the lesbian, gay, bisexual, and transgender community as it is for the heterosexual community. Because families of origin may not accept or be aware of the sexual and gender orientation of their lesbian, gay, bisexual, and transgender relatives, many lesbian, gay, bisexual, and transgender individuals create their own families, defined by affinity rather than by biology. For many, the lesbian, gay, bisexual, and transgender community functions as an extended family, particularly for those who are estranged from their families of origin.

It is inaccurate to assume that individuals in same-sex partnerships do not want children. Many same-sex couples have children, either from previous heterosexual relationships, by adoption, or by some form of insemination. Some people worry that children raised in same-sex households will be harmed by not having in-house parents of both genders. Some go on to further worry that these children will be more likely to grow up gay, lesbian, bisexual, or transgender (as if, even if it were true, it would be something to worry about). However, we know from the research that such families are as happy and as healthy as heterosexual families, and that children raised in same-sex households are no more likely to be gay, lesbian, or bisexual than are children raised in other-sex households. It is important never to make assumptions about the family status of lesbian/gay/bisexual/transgender individuals, but to inquire who the individual considers their family to be. Viewed in the appropriate context, all other decisions—from child-rearing practices to decisions about education to where the family spends the holidays—become much clearer.

Summary

It's apparent that what we refer to as the gay/lesbian/bisexual transgender community includes individuals with diverse characteristics indeed. People of every color, gender, generation, social class, cultural background, and ability status are part of our Community. This is what makes the rainbow flag such an appropriate symbol: bright bands of different colors represent our differences.

The flag itself represents our unity. It's also apparent that the past thirty years of gay liberation have brought tremendous social change. At one time, most Americans didn't know, or didn't know that they knew, a lesbian, gay, or bi-sexual person. Now, most Americans indicate that they know at least one person living under the rainbow flag. As a result, Americans are becoming less preju-diced against gay/lesbian/bisexual people and more inclined to support pro-tection against discrimination in housing and employment on the basis of sexual orientation.

It all sounds as though things are moving in the right direction. Two cau-tionary notes, however: first, we aren't yet even close to where we need to be in terms of social integration. Despite volumes of scientific evidence to the contrary, and the positions taken by every major mental health organization, there are still those who inaccurately characterize homosexuality and bisexu-ality as forms of mental illness. From this antiquated perspective it is extra-polated that therefore, lesbian, gay, and bisexual individuals are incapable of leading fulfilling, productive lives. Though there is no evidence to support this position, there is still an active effort in a conservative margin of society to devalue sexual orientation as a "choice" and therefore undeserving of civil rights protection. Such positions must be assertively countered, for they are the well-spring of ongoing abuse and violence against lesbian, gay, bisexual, and trans-gender individuals. Millions of people in the United States have suffered such abuses, ranging from harassment to violence, all due to their sexual orienta-tion. The Community needs help from its heterosexual allies to educate the entire culture that sexual prejudice is wrong, whatever its basis, and that be-havior based on homophobia will not be tolerated.

Confronting and examining one's own homophobia is a necessary first step. Heterosexuality is still considered the norm in our culture, thus, heterosexuals hold special privilege. Therefore, the Community needs active support from our allies if we are going to work together to create a more reasonable, toler-ant world. For as long as our youth are driven out of their homes and schools and on to the streets, for being—or being presumed to be—lesbian, gay, bi-sexual, or transgender, we haven't done our job in making the world safe enough. As long as workers have to cringe in embarrassment as they endure a colleague's recitation of yet another gay joke, we haven't done our job in making the world respectful enough. And as long as stable lesbian and gay relation-ships are denied the opportunity for the same social and legal benefits as het-erosexual relationships, we haven't done our job in making the world as fair, and as loving, as it ought to be.

Lesbian, gay, bisexual, and transgender people have their own healing work to do in this time of social change. We are used to calling for the end of ho-mophobia because of the injurious and discriminatory behavior to which it leads and the poisonous effect it has on heterosexuals' same-gender relationships. But lesbian/gay/bisexual and transgender people have their own hetero-phobia to deal with—the understandable but nonetheless destructive tendency to fear and avoid heterosexuals. Creating bridges with the dominant hetero-sexual society cannot be a one-way street. We should encourage a reaching out, whenever possible, to our heterosexual allies. This reverses a familiar les-bian/gay/bisexual/transgender theme: personal knowledge reduces prejudice. It works both ways.

The second cautionary point about the future has to do with the lesbian/gay/bisexual/transgender community's preservation of its distinctiveness. Les-bian cartoonist Alison Bechdel recently commented, "I'm having assimilation anxiety. What kind of subculture will we be writing about when there's no more subculture?" The ultimate goal, of course, is not for the Community to disappear or to simply be "accepted" or "tolerated" by the dominant society. Rather, the goal is to join the mainstream intact, in celebration of the many distinctive features represented by the bright bands in the rainbow flag. For those of us carrying the rainbow flag, the intention is not to drop it and blend into society but to leave our place on the sidelines, marching in the parade of our human family, proudly carrying our colors aloft.

10

STEVEN M. TOVIAN

BOWYER G. FREEMAN

ABDUL R. MUHAMMAD

One God, One Faith, One Humanity

Perhaps what is most remarkable about God is that each person is able to relate to God in a slightly different way from his or her neighbor, in a manner that speaks most directly to his or her needs, aspirations, and ability. If God is truly beyond limit, then it is the ultimate Godlike ability to respond to each individual as singular and special (Artson, personal communication, 2000).

In this chapter, we will provide a review of issues relevant to working with persons of a different religious background. We will also highlight the issues one should be aware of for many of the more common religions. We will focus mainly on three sections in this chapter. We will discuss interaction between people of different religions, provide some definitions to foster a basic understanding of the religions within our society, and expand on religious stereotypes that face persons of the non-Christian faith. The Islamic faith will be discussed in this last section and in so doing highlight how religious stereotypes can interfere with human interaction.

Religion is now an integral part of the human diversity spectrum and needs to be afforded the same consideration in the workplace and in other human interactions as all other forms of diversity. The diverse and fundamental character of religious experience is an essential part of the tapestry of American society. Contemporary religious pluralism adds to the strength and character of our culture.

On your next commute to work, count the number of churches you pass. You might be very surprised if you underestimate the significance of religious congregations or religious systems to individual and community life. There is clear evidence of the importance of religion in American life. A survey reported that 92% of all Americans say that they have never doubted the existence of God, and 85% consider religion important in their lives (Gallup and Castelli, 1989). Moreover, 82% of all Americans reported having received religious instruction as children. In addition, religious systems contribute three times more to philanthropy than any other social institution. A 1990 poll found that 66% of respondents agreed that prayer is an important part of their daily life, and 88% reported that they have prayed to God (Princeton Religious Research Center, 1990). More recently, a 1992 national survey found that 86% of Americans believed in God 70% believe that there is a God who answers prayers, 64% consider themselves to be religious, 49% attended a religious service in the past week, and 47% consider faith to be relevant to the way they live their lives (Barna, 1992).

Importance of Religious Systems

These statistics highlight the prominence of religion, but they do not convey the functions religion serves in our society. Religious systems share many functions with other systems. Like educational systems, religious congregations attempt to socialize and instill a set of values in their members. Like family systems, religious systems try to provide their members with a sense of belonging and support. Like human-service systems, religious congregations offer their members concrete resources and assistance when needed. And like judicial systems, religious settings provide their members with a set of rules to live by (Pargament, 1997).

The power of religion is unique in its capability to respond to so many needs in so many different ways. Religion can provide meaning to one's life, give a sense of direction, or act as a coping aid when faced with challenging life situations. For instance, in a two-year longitudinal study of a community sample, researchers found that attendance at religious services buffered the effects of increased numbers of undesirable life events on subsequent psychological distress (Williams, Larson, Buckler, Heckmann, & Pyle, 1991). In addition, a study has found that religion has a positive effect on meaning and purpose and that respondents with higher levels of religious commitment felt greater well-being and reported being more satisfied with their lives (Chamberlain & Zika, 1992). Furthermore, prayer was ranked seventh in effectiveness among a field of 25 possible coping behaviors mediating life events and depression (Parker & Brown, 1982). Finally, researchers have demonstrated the positive relationship between religious commitment and physical health (Ferraro & Koch, 1994).

Religious systems also function in other distinctive ways. They are uniquely accessible to people. Traditionally, clergy have been among the first "gate-keepers" sought out by people when they are facing serious problems. Places of worship are often integrally involved in most of life's key transitions through-out the life span; births, "coming of age" celebrations (e.g., Bar/Bat Mitzvot, confirmations), marriages, divorces, and deaths. As mentioned previously, re-ligious systems are particularly accessible to people during times of stress and crisis. When faced with problems in life, many people feel less stigma in turn-ing to religion for help, as opposed to mental health professionals. In addition, active outreach by both clergy and congregation members to others in times of stress is part of the long tradition of religious helping (Pargament, 1997).

Medicine and religion have worked hand in hand in the process of healing for thousands of years. In ancient societies (as in some societies today), illness was perceived as primarily a spiritual problem. Religious and medical author-ity were vested in the same person who might himself become an object of worship (e.g., Imhotep, Ascelapius, Jesus, etc.).

From the early Christian era through the Reformation, the relationship between medicine and religion remained close. The first hospitals were founded in monasteries, and the missionary movement linked physical healing with spiritual conversion. By the seventeenth century, rifts between medicine and religion emerged, because of the challenges to church authority and the rise of empirical science. Science claimed the body (and later, the mind) as its pur-view, while religion held onto the soul. Critics of religion arose over the years, for example: (1) "the opium of the people" (Marx); (2) "a universal obses-sional neurosis" (Freud); and (3)"equivalent to irrational thinking and emo-tional disturbance" (Ellis).

By the late twentieth century, a growing disillusionment with the limita-tions of science had once again opened up the possibility of a rapprochement between medicine and religion, the twin traditions of healing. It is important to help us better understand the role that religion/spirituality plays in health as well as in mental health and to build on the growing research findings linking religion and medicine.

Our society has freely interchanged the theological concepts of religion and spirituality. One of the challenges we face when considering religious and spiri-tual issues is the fact that our pluralistic society has merged, synthesized, and made synonymous various terms. Because of society's attempts to be inclusive, we have diluted the historical understanding of these terms. Today's language blends such terms as religious/religion and spiritual/spirituality. So what does it mean to be a religious person? What is spirituality? According to Ulmer (1993):

> To be religious is to be devoted to a religion. Religion for many people con-notes an established system and institution. A person is called religious if he

or she is committed to a set of theological principles or a certain philosophy. The religion's structure may be highly sophisticated or organizationally simplistic. It may be a given set of rules for life passed down through the ages as highly intricate and often complicated written literature, fully understood by only a few, but passed on to the masses of its constituency. Or, it may be an equally valid series of narratives woven into the very fabric of a given society by generations of storytellers. (p. 19)

We hear the word "religion" and tend to think of nicely wrapped bundles of beliefs or truths. There is a bundle of beliefs named Christianity and a bundle wrapped as Buddhism and so on. There is a historical development of this word "religion," however, with which we should be at least somewhat familiar. The word *religio* is a Latin word meaning "to bind together," but it is a word notoriously difficult to define. There is a bewildering array of definitions, none of which seem to satisfy a consensus. Humankind everywhere and in every time has been what we would call "religious," and yet, there have been in the past relatively few languages in which the word "religion" could be translated outside of Western civilization. "The phenomena that we call religions undoubtedly exist, yet perhaps the notion that they constitute in themselves some distinctive entity is an unwarranted analysis" (Smith, 1994, p. 17). Indeed, Smith argued for dropping the term altogether.

The word "religion" was used infrequently prior to the period of the Enlightenment and when it was used, it seems to have referred to some obligation or act demanded by or prohibited by the deity. By the fourth century, there seems to be a correlation between the frequency of use and the historical situation of pluralism. Which is to say, humankind began to become aware of the rival ways of looking at and ordering the world. The word emerged in the modern period, beginning with the Renaissance, expanding with the Reformation and fully developed in the Enlightenment and on into the nineteenth century. It is this modern period that has shaped our current understanding of the word.

Religious systems also provide their members with unique sources of support. Theologies attempt to offer answers to a number of key questions: the purpose of life, why there is suffering, the nature of good and evil, the meaning of death. These beliefs may provide meaning, hope, and esteem to people confronted with serious challenges in life. As a medical patient once noted to one author of this chapter, after several surgeries for cancer, "each time I knew everything would be alright because I asked God to carry me through. He embraced me and I felt His support." Other religious beliefs may exacerbate rather than help solve significant problems in life. For example, the belief that an illness represents a punishment from God for the person's sins can add to the stressful weight of that event.

One author recently had an interesting experience while leading a prayer the other day. A friend and fellow chaplain's father was critically ill and in the

ICU. He reported the progress of his friend's dad and volunteered to lead the group of chaplains (64 chaplains) in a prayer for the dad's recovery. Although no one walked out of the prayer, a few chaplains were uncomfortable with a Muslim, non-Christian leading the group of predominately Christian chaplains in prayer. Their discomfort later prompted an intense discussion and debate. The real concern was not so much the response to who was leading this prayer, but that too often this type of subtle prejudice or lack of acceptance exists. It is difficult for ministers at times to be cognizant of their faults and realize they are as human as those to whom they minister—meaning prejudices exist. In the previous example, it appeared initially that religious prejudice was perhaps the motivation for discomfort. However, after some thought and discussion with a few African-American chaplains, racial prejudice may have also played a role in this scenario. Even among the Christian denominations, bias and prejudice exists simply due to racial prejudice and/or stereotypes. Black chaplains of the Christian faith often don't appreciate being labeled as "the Gospel Chaplain" or the one who must lead the Gospel service regardless of faith group or denomination.

A part of the calling to ministry is to assist others in coming to grips with their stereotypes. This has opened another door in the history of American life and free exercise within our pluralistic society—that is, the door that allows all Americans to worship as they choose, and when necessary, worship as a single group. This door will enable Buddhists, Hindus, and others to come forth and fulfill their role in service to their faith, communities, and the nation, as one humanity.

When we use the word "religion," we tend to use it in four ways as expressing:

1. *A personal piety.* We use this sense when we say things like "He is more religious than he was ten years ago." Or when we remark that in every religion there are those whose religion is harsh and narrow and those whose religion is warm and open.
2. *A system of beliefs*, practices, values, or ethical considerations.
3. *There is an ideal system and there are the other empirical phenomena*, which is historically how the religion has in fact been practiced. Smith notes, "Normally people talk about other people's religions as they are, and about their own as it ought to be."
4. *Religion in general.* There is a use that sees religion as a generic summation to differentiate from other aspects of life like art or economics. (Smith, 1997, p. 48)

Crucial for us from the outset then is to be aware that there is no clear-cut definition of the word "religion" geographically and culturally.

Remember the original root of the word "religion" is *religio*—to bind together. This has dynamic significance in crisis, and bereavement counseling. When illness, shattering crisis, or loss fragments one's life, vital religion helps one to reorient, thus restoring some sense of coherence and meaning. The crisis of facing illness or death brings many people face to face with their existential beliefs and values. Religion can aid in the process of reordering, reorienting, and restoring important meaning to the events in our lives.

Nevertheless, religion represents a resource to many of those with the fewest resources. Congregations provide a community to identify with and belong to, an opportunity for meaningful involvement, and a source of optimism for many marginal, minority, or disenfranchised groups (Pargament, 1997).

In short, religious systems represent a significant personal and social resource in our culture. The findings discussed above indicate the centrality of religion for many individuals. If most people incorporate religion in their lives, either through prayer, attending religious services, or other spiritual means, it should be expected that religious values and beliefs will certainly emerge in work and other interpersonal settings.

Complexity of Religious Systems

Our earlier commute and ride past the many religious congregations cannot reveal the rich, complicated life going on inside. Religious congregations, and the respective theologies from which they emerge, are embedded in the lives of the surrounding community and the lives of their own members. These individual congregations are both active and reactive, shaping life in the surrounding community and life among its members. However, they also respond to the changing demand and challenges from the larger, diverse community, its own congregational members, and often the larger parent denomination institution (i.e., the Vatican in Catholicism). In this sense, religious systems can be thought of as dynamically changing systems influenced by change from within and from outside and from the near community and from afar in the world community as well.

Spirituality

Spirituality is something that everybody seems to want these days. It is so sought after that it has become a contemporary buzzword. But no one seems to know exactly what it is. Nonetheless, it is vigorously pursued. While many in society are careful to avoid "religion," the interest in things spiritual is seemingly at an all-time high. So what does *spirituality* mean?

At its most basic meaning, to seek spirituality is to hunger and thirst for things beyond the mundane—to, as Webster put it, seek things "of, relating to, consisting of, or affecting the spirit." No one would argue that to have spirituality is to be mindful of the things of the spirit. But this is where the definition gets muddy. What spirit should we be mindful of? How does being mindful of spirit fit into religious beliefs, life philosophy, or just everyday living? It's easy to see how the meaning of *spirituality* quickly becomes elusive, and there are many reasons why. One simple reason is that the word means many different things to many different people. Bradley Holt (1998) writes:

> Spirituality—this ambiguous six-syllable term is new to many and objectionable to some. Although it is a clumsy word, it is used too much because it seems to do a task that no other word does. Religion for many people connotes an established system and institution, whereas, *spirituality* implies personal involvement. *Spirituality* is a trans-religious word; it is not tied to any one single faith tradition. (p. 16)

Spirituality, broadly defined as that which gives transcendent meaning to a life, is central to the human experience and is often the dominant issue for patients in an acute care setting or at the end of life. As people deal with crisis situations which challenge their definition of personhood, spiritual questions oftentimes arise.

Illness is a major life event; such events frequently cause people to question themselves, their purpose, and their meaning in life. It disrupts their career, their family life, and their ability to enjoy themselves (three areas that Sigmund Freud said were essential to a healthy mind). The significant prospect of dying—a natural outcome of many illnesses—simply amplifies these concerns. From a spiritual standpoint, healing does not turn solely on the question of recovery. It involves the restoration of wholeness which may manifest itself by a transcendent set of meaningful experiences that help people become more peaceful with their situation(s).

With respect to theology and worldview, some religious systems focus on "other-world" concerns, such as preparation for the world to come. Others stress the significance of working in this world to improve individual and social life. Some theologies offer religious writings as a strict guide for living. Others stress personal freedom and responsibility in choosing paths of life. While some theologies focus on the soothing, comforting qualities of faith, others challenge the individual to seek radical personal and social change. Various sections of this chapter describe similarities and differences between various religions or religious systems.

The Difference Between Religion and Spirituality in the Ethnic Minority Community

> What a strange fellowship this is, the God-seekers in every land, lifting their voices in the most disparate ways imaginable to the God of all life. How does

it sound from above? Like bedlam, or do the strains blend in strange, ethereal harmony? Does one faith carry the lead, or do the parts share in counterpart and antiphony where not in full throated chorus? We cannot know. All we can do is try to listen carefully and with full attention to each voice in turn as it addresses the divine. (Smith, 1997, p. 2)

A dear professor said that he learned another language not in order to speak to someone but to listen to someone. With this emphasis on listening, we come close to what the phenomenological method of studying religion is about. Phenomenology is a school of philosophy whose principal purpose is to study the phenomena, or appearances, of human experience, while attempting to suspend all judgment of their objective reality or subjective association.

It is not simply religious identification alone, however, that must be accounted for when attempting to understand religious systems and diversity. The unique history, culture, and sociological experience of potential subgroups in a religious system need to be understood. For example, religious or orthodox Jews can differ from one another along many dimensions, one of which is cultural as well as religious commitment. The pluralism in orthodox Jewry results in descriptions of "Modern" Orthodox and "Committed" Orthodox, while others even designate "right," "left," and "center" groups on the basis of religious commitment and cultural basis. Another example involves cultural-regional differences of Latin immigrants, where a devoted Catholic from Nicaragua may have different practices from a devoted Catholic emigrating from Haiti (Levitz, 1989).

Diverse missions or purposes of congregations follow from religious theologies. In terms of their effect on outside communities, many congregations support the social structure of the surrounding community and seek civic harmony. Other congregations encourage radical, systematic social change in their search for social justice. Still other congregations espouse an evangelistic mission and seek social change through personal religious change and conversion. Finally, other religious systems establish more isolated or separate communities as a means of avoiding the evils of society or assimilation of its members. Of course, some congregations may direct themselves to more than one or various combinations of these missions.

Equally diverse are the person–oriented missions of religious systems. Central to the purpose of many congregations is the development of the members' personal relationship with God. Other congregations place more emphasis on living by religious rules and traditions. Many congregations encourage personal growth among their members. Still other congregations try to provide their members with a supportive milieu that helps them cope with the world. In short, each religious system, congregation, and individual member has a unique identity made up of a special history, social context, membership, language, view of the world, purpose, and set of organizational structures and processes (Pargament, 1997).

As caregivers to such a diverse, multicultural tapestry of people, it is extremely important that we utilize a phenomenological approach when we encounter the religious beliefs and practices of those we serve. Phenomenology of religion, unlike philosophy of religion, is not looking for a common ground beneath the cultural forms. Although it is interested in the essence of things, it does not try to find a common natural religion beneath the forms of religion. The purpose of this approach is to raise the level of the conscious, reflective awareness, of that which is taking place as religious activity/conversation. Its main concern is to describe religious behavior rather than to explain it. The goal then is not a theoretical validation of religion but an existential participation. The truth of the matter is left open. Highlighted in this method of approach are people, including their beliefs, literature, traditions, practices, cultural preferences, and their geographical setting. Table 10.1 serves as a reference for different religious groups and their salient features.

Biases and Stereotypes

When one enters into a meaningful relationship with religious people or with people whose religions differ from our own, one must examine biases and stereotypes that may exist about the nature of religiosity or specific religions. Beliefs, attitudes, or other cognitive schemata operate overtly or covertly to influence our behavior and decision-making processes. If we can identify them through our thoughts, language, and behavior, we can control and modify our decisions for the common and individual good. People tend to behave as we expect them to, and it takes substantial effort to change this assumption. The willingness to examine our personal beliefs about religiosity and religious individuals is a necessary initial step opening communication and developing close, positive relationships. Exploring our biases and stereotypes and exposing them to review and revision is an important first step.

Muslims, who interact with those of many denominations and faith groups (both Christian and non-Christian), have experienced rewards and displeasures of ministry. This is perceived as intolerance and insensitivity, perhaps stimulated by fear, misunderstanding, and oftentimes misinformation of the Islamic faith. An example of this is the continued misunderstanding that Arabs or people from the Middle East are the majority group within the Islamic world. The Arab world is comprised of less than 30% of the total Islamic population or roughly 200 million people. The people of Indonesia are the largest single Muslim group in the world, numbering slightly over 300 million people. Another common sterotype is equating Islam with terrorism or random violence.

TABLE 10.1. Religious Groups and Their Salient Features

Name of Religious Body	Name of Founder	Date Founded	Name of Primary Deity	Inspirational Writings	Doctrines
Aboriginal religions	Unknown	Unknown	a Creator god	Learn sacred history during initiations and meetings	Creator god withdraws into a distant realm of heaven where humans cannot reach
Buddhism	Prince Gautama	6th Century B.C.	Buddah "The Enlightened One	The Sutra; Vinaya; and Abhidharma	Man must rely entirely on himself for salvation. State of "Nirvana"
Celtic religion	Celts of Iberia, Ireland, and Britain	5th Century B.C.	Mercury or "Lugh" Teutates, Esus, and Taranis	Forbidden to write their secret knowledge	The Celts performed human sacrifice to three divinities
Christianity	Jesus	1st Century C.E.	Trinitarian Godhead	Bible	All humankind are sinners; God's son Jesus sent to reconcile humankind back to God
Christian Science	Mary Baker Eddy	1879	God	Science & Health w/key to the Scriptures; Bible	Immanent spiritual realities & the Divine mind expunge illness caused by limitations of the human mind
Church of Latter Day Saints (Mormon)	Joseph Smith	1830	God	Bible; Book of Mormon; The Doctrine & Covenants; The Pearl of Great Price	Though Jesus is believed to be the Messiah, humankind's works are also key to redemption
Confucianism	K'ung Fu-tzu	6th Century B.C.	Confucius	Ching or "The Classics"	Discovery of the Middle Way (Tao) in human society and in individual actions. The Way that would guarantee balance between the will of earth and the will of heaven
Hellenistic religion	Aristotle	300 B.C.	Unknown	Stoic Philosophy; Greek science	No postmortem hell for punishment of wicked. Connection between astral movements and the system of human life
Hinduism	Brahma	1400 B.C.	Brahma "Universal Spirit"	Bhagavad Gita	Believe that physical is just an illusion. There is no reason or purpose to what goes on around us

Hittite religion	Hattic, Hurrian, Semitic, Indo-Euro, Hittite people	1500 B.C.	Teshup (weather god); Telepinu (his son); Sun goddess of Arinna	"Kingship in Heaven"; "Song of Ullikummi"	Divination played prominent role. Ranged from interpretation of royal dreams to extispicy
Islam	Muhammad	622 B.C.E.	Allah	Qur'an and the Hadith	The uniqueness and might of God and the nature and destiny of humans in relation to God
Jainism	MAHAVIRA (Great hero) aka Vardhtmana	6th Century B.C.E.	The Mahapurusa	The Svetambaras and the prakaranas	Man can obtain omniscience or Perfect Gnosis; and One who obtains this is free from all constraints
Jehovah's Witness	Charles Taze Russell	1872 A.D.	Jehovah	New World Translation of the Christian Greek Scripture	Expecting an imminent end to Satan's rule; a great judgment & reign of Christ over a perfect earth
Judaism	Descendants of Amorites	2000 B.C.E.	God, YHWH, Elohim	Torah nebi'im we ketuvim aka The Tanakh; Mishnah; Talmud	Monotheistic; view themselves as the chosen people of God
Minoan religion	King Minos	2000 B.C.E.	A great goddess of nature	Unknown; artistic motifs	She is a mistress of animals, but also of mountains & sea, agriculture & war, reigning over the living and the dead
Oceanic religions (Pacific Islands)	Micronesians; Melanesians; Polynesians	1600 C.E.	Tangaroa; Tane; god Oro	Unknown	Most of the gods are ancestors living in another world and pay frequent visits to the human sphere. The heavenly creator god is inaccessible
Religions of the Bantu	Bantus of Central Africa	Unknown	The creator god	"Royal Oracles"	At the center of Bantu religions are spirit cults and propriatory magical rituals
Shinto	Ono Yasumaro	712 C.E.	The Kami (omnipresent manifestations of the sacred)	The Kojiki; the Nihongi	Strong purification emphasis; worship of ancestors
Spiritualist	Fox Sisters of Hydesville, NY	1848 C.E.	Unknown	National Declaration of Principles	Spiritualism does not rest on the Bible but the Bible rests on spiritualism

(continued)

TABLE 10.1. (continued)

Name of Religious Body	Name of Founder	Date Founded	Name of Primary Deity	Inspirational Writings	Doctrines
Taoism	Lao-Tzu	6th Century B.C.E.	Emperor Huang Ti	Tao TE Ching; the Chuang-tzu	Developed doctrine of defied human beings, eternal representatives of the way, and warrants of truth
Unity	Myrtle Fillmore	1886 C.E.	God	Daily Word; Weekly Unity	A school rather than a church, Unity seeks to help anyone "to find health, peace, joy, and plenty. While Bible may stimulate revelatory insights, it is not God's word
Zoroastrianism	Zarathushtra	1200–500 B.C.E.	Geush Urvan; Ahura Mazda	The Avesta; the Pahlavi Writings	Beneficent spirits (virtues) surrounded Ahura Mazda and individuals who chose the Truthful Order "asha"

The fact is, like other groups, some Muslims have been responsible for acts of violence. However, the majority in the Islamic world have been peace-loving people, despite years of oppression and exploitation from others outside the Islamic world. Literally, Islam means "submission or the surrendering to the authority and Will of Allah (God), and when one does so, he/she enters into a state of peace" (Emerick, 1997, pp. 135–238).

There are many difficulties in being a "trail blazer"; counseling non-Muslims involves sacrifices such as not being able to wear a beard and shaking hands with females. Many Muslim males would never make such sacrifices. However, to sacrifice the smaller things in the faith affords the opportunity to bring about the greater good. A verse in the Holy Qur'an (The Final Revelation according to Islam) increases understanding in this area. It reads, "So, verily with every difficulty, there is relief: Verily with every difficulty there is relief. So when you are free from your immediate tasks, continue to work hard, and to your Lord turn all of your attention" (Ali, 1999, 94:5–6). Another verse reads, "To each is a goal which Allah (God) turns him; then strive together (as in a race) towards all that is good. Wherever you are Allah (God) will bring you together. For Allah (God) has power over all things" (Ali, 1999, 2:148).

These two verses have symbolized the very foundation of the ministry and counseling: to maintain a healthy balance, serving God as a Muslim and yet serving the country as an American. It continues to amaze some people how such is possible. People often ask, "how to do you pray for people outside of the Islamic faith?" Simply, in a language that we can mutually understand, English! When people are in crisis or in need, it normally doesn't matter in what form the help, care, or human compassion comes. Most people, especially those in real need, generally accept and appreciate the motto, a "chaplain is a chaplain, is a chaplain." At the same time, there are occasions when requests are made for a chaplain of one's own faith group. This area is generally understood by all good and sincere chaplains. In fact, it is an expectation, that is providing support for others outside of our faith is integrally a part of the military chaplain's function and responsibility. As a Muslim chaplain, this aspect of the job is enjoyable, that is, selflessly serving others outside of Islam in whatever manner one is called. At times requests are made, for example, when a patient wants to take the sacrament or simply pray in the manner dictated by their faith group or denomination, that is, praying in Jesus' name. Most people may not know every aspect of the fundamentals of Islam, but most know it is forbidden for Muslims to drink alcohol, eat pork or pork by-products, and pray in Jesus' name.

The belief that God is One must therefore be translated into action, that is, being able to minister to all of God's humanity without hesitation or reservation. According to the Qur'an, God says, He will be the one to determine those areas where we differ and be the final judge of it all on the last day. Although there are fundamental theological differences among the various religions of the world, the world religions have more in common than not. Therefore, as a general rule, one simply does not argue about whose faith is right and whose faith is wrong as a part of daily ministry. One must have great respect for Christians, as well as Jews, Buddhists, Hindus, and all of God's people. One does not choose whom to provide ministry, yet one respects and honors those times when people simply want a chaplain of their particular faith group. On this subject the Qur'an says: "O mankind! We created you from a single (pair) of male and female, and made you into nations and tribes, that you may know each other (not that you may hate or despise each other). Verily the most honored of you in the sight of Allah (God) is he who is the most righteous of you. And Allah (God) has full knowledge and is well-acquainted with all things" (Ali, 1999, 49:13).

People often tend to oversimplify religions and religious systems. One way this is expressed is through the view of religion as either "all good" or "all bad." This oversimplification is a failure to distinguish between types of religious beliefs and practices. For example, while many people speak of God as a controlling force in their lives, they may mean different things by this statement. For some people, the report of control by God refers to a process of partnership and support. For others, this sense of control refers to a process in which the individual waits passively for God to solve his or her problems. A reasonable approach to this bias and most others is to know as much as possible about the religion *and* the individual who practices this religion (Pargament, 1996).

Another bias involves the belief that religiosity is equivalent to "rigidity" in belief and action. As discussed earlier, pluralism within religious subgroups supports the notion of liberal and conservative movements within a religious system.

Our language, with its power to reinforce bias and shape thought, can still preserve stereotypes. The role of appropriate communication is to examine that language and select alternatives that recognize broadening religious diversity. For example, it is important to be aware of those words, images, and situations that suggest that all or most members of a religious group are the same. Certain practices and even physical dress may be similar among members of a religious group, but stereotypes lead to assumptions that are insupportable and offensive. They cloud the fact that numerous attributes may be found in all religious systems and groups.

Concerns of the Religious

In an attempt to achieve greater empathy, as well as build and sustain relationships with the religious individual, several issues need to be considered. While religious individuals may strive for the same goals as others from diverse groups—namely, self-actualization and self-expression, security, equal opportunity in a nonhostile environment, to name just a few—their religiosity can pose unique problems.

Religious individuals may view helping professionals in the workplace, for example, not as potential sources of help but as potentially threatening outsiders. They may choose instead to turn to their traditional structures, for example, family, congregational clergy, or other culturally syntonic sources. The stigma of a religious individual receiving assistance or guidance from outside helping sources may be seen as negative or "unfaithful" by others in the congregation.

Another class of factors relevant to the religious individual relates to his/her ontological and existential concern for their religious system. Many religious individuals fear assimilation with the majority culture. This concern with the survival of their religious system and identity can lead to further isolation, mistrust, and misunderstanding with others.

The criteria for sufficient pleasure and effective living in society are often psychosocial in nature. In other words, we tend to determine how well off we are by comparing ourselves to external criteria—often others that surround us. For many religious individuals, personal goals and expectations are often measured with two yardsticks, as the religious often live in two societies. Living in two cultures, one is often exposed to conflicting, unnegotiable expectations from both. Those professionals who work with the religious individual and who are sensitive to their potential sources of psychological distress can move more readily along the path to change described.

Recommendations

As we enter a new century where culture and diversity prevail, the area of religion as a form of diversity must not be overlooked. It can be concluded that religion is an important aspect of many individuals' lives. For many individuals, then, religious or spiritual issues may potentially play an important role in work and other interpersonal endeavors. As a result, those in personnel management, counseling, human resources, and related fields need to be sensitive to religion as an area of diversity and have greater awareness of religious issues in interpersonal relations. Specific recommendations made to ensure this is done in an ethically appropriate and sensitive manner include:

1. Ask individuals about any religious concerns or expectations during early encounters. If an interest in religion exists, increase your sensitivity toward the needs of that individual and how it affects his or her behavior and interaction with others.

2. Become more aware of your own religious or spiritual beliefs and values, how they have evolved, and how they impact your interactions with others.
3. Maintain an awareness of the use of spirituality and religious belief by others for strength, support, and the finding of meaning and values in life.
4. In the workplace, obtain training in diversity issues to include religion and spirituality.
5. Seek professional continuing education and keep current on recent developments, trends, and issues on religious diversity.
6. Seek supervision and consultation when needed in the workplace on religious diversity issues. Establish relationships with individuals in the religious community and use them for consultation, collaboration, and referral when needed.

Those individuals in the helping professions realize life is not a straight road. Often it is more like a maze, and it often seems to be a contradictory process in which good and evil, the comic and tragic, cowardice and heroism are intermingled. The ancient Greeks said, "Know thyself." They understood self-knowledge as one of the paths to wisdom. Knowing others in an undistorted way is another path. Both of these—knowing both yourself and others in caring, genuine, reflective, unvarnished ways—will assist in developing the wisdom that enables one to move beyond the mere technology of helping and toward a more authentic, genuine helping alliance. Experience can be either a teacher or a despot. The ability to befriend the dark side of oneself, coworkers, clients, or neighbors, without becoming its victim, is not the fruit of raw experience. Experience with religious diversity needs to be wrestled with, reflected on, and learned from. Then it becomes a teacher and friend. Wrestling with yourself, your biases, and those biases of your colleagues on issues of religious diversity will provide you with both painful and rewarding experiences and will go far in helping the skilled helper in you become the wise helper.

Conclusion

All people are unique. And that unique difference of each person makes sense not only psychologically but from the perspective of theology as well. Religious writings remind us that we are made in the image of God. If God is infinite, then every creature made in God's image will reflect a different finite aspect of that infinite source of life. That each new person presents a new aspect of God's image is a consequence of God's creative energy.

Everyone is different, and those differences are to be cherished, nurtured, and cultivated. Rather than seeing this individuality as a threat to society, perhaps we, in our places of work and in our communities, can celebrate diversity as yet another mark of the abundant fullness of Divine presence in our midst, infusing us and all with passion, energy, justice, kindness, wonder, and life.

References

Ali, A. Y. (1999). *An English interpretation of The Holy Qur'an, 10th edition.* Beltsville, MD: Amana Publications, pp. 1974–1975, 60, 1593.

Barna, G. (1992). *What Americans believe: An annual survey of values and religious views in the United States.* Ventura, CA: Regal Books.

Chamberlain, K., & Zika, S. (1992). Religiosity, meaning of life, and psychological well-being. In J. F. Shumaker (Ed.), *Religion and mental health* (pp. 138–148). New York: Oxford University Press.

Emerick, Y. (1997). *What Islam is all about.* New York: International Books and Tapes Supply.

Ferraro, K. F., & Koch, J. R. (1994). Religion and health among black and white adults: Examining social support and consolation. *Journal for the Scientific Study of Religion, 33,* 362–375.

Gallup, G., and Castelli, J. (1989). *The people's religion.* New York: Macmillan.

Holt, B. P. (1998). *A brief history of Christian spirituality.* Ventura, CA: Regal Books.

Levitz, I. N. (1989). Orthodoxy and mental health: Suggested parameters for empirical studies. *Journal of Psychology and Judaism, 4,* 87–100.

Pargament, K. I. (1996). Religious methods of coping: Resources for the conservation and transformation of significance. In E. P. Shafranske (Ed.), *Religion and the clinical practice of psychology* (pp. 215–240). Washington, D.C.: American Psychological Association.

Pargament, K. I. (1997). *The psychology of religion and coping.* New York: Guilford Press.

Parker, G. B., & Brown, L. B. (1982). Coping behaviors that mediate between life events and depression. *Archives of General Psychiatry, 39,* 1386–1391.

Princeton Religious Research Center (1990).

Smith, H. (1997). *The world's religions: Our great wisdom traditions.* San Francisco: Harper San Francisco.

Smith, W. C. (1994). *The meaning and end of religion.* Minneapolis: Fortress Press.

Ulmer, K. C. (1993). *Spiritually fit to run the race.* Nashville, TN: T. Nelson.

Williams, D. R., Larson, D. B., Buckler, R. E., Heckmann, R. C., & Pyle, C. M. (1991). Religion and psychological distress in a community sample. *Social Science and Medicine, 32,* 1257–1262.

11

IRENE W. LEIGH

PATRICK J. BRICE

The Visible and the Invisible

Nondisabled Americans do not understand disabled ones.

—J. Shapiro

Within the spectrum of diversity, we tend to immediately see different hues of ethnicity and race and culture as part of the tapestry of America. Then we may think of gender, of sexual orientation, of age, of religion, all as interactive components of ethnicity, race, and culture. Disability is rarely in the forefront of our minds, even though disability permeates every classification that society has defined for humanity with the exception of the "nondisabled." Only when we experience the immediacy of a disability upon seeing a wheelchair user cross the street in front of us, a blind person walking toward us with a white cane, or a Janet Reno projecting herself on a television screen with symptoms of Parkinson's disease, do we then experience a fleeting awareness that people with disabilities have lives to live and do exist within our society.

Sometimes, we may take a moment to focus on the disability and think of what life must be like for these persons with disabilities. Likely, we think about their difference, their loss, their helplessness, or heroism. We picture, for example, Christopher Reeve, embedded in the public eye as Superman, now physically immobilized and taking on himself the role of spokesperson for those with spinal cord injuries, searching for possible miracles, and soliciting donations for spinal cord research. How many of us really understand who these people with disabilities are, what they actually experience, and what their lives may be like? How many understand that a good number of individuals with mobility disabilities feel the value of their lives are denigrated when people see them as "victims" (Lynch & Thomas, 1999). How many of us know someone with a disability that says, "I'm doing just fine, thanks!" and really means it? Considering that approximately 50 million Americans, or 14% of the general U.S. population, are persons with disabilities (Mackelprang & Salsgiver, 1999; Olkin, 1999), this ignorance needs to be rectified. As a matter of fact, Olkin (1999) states, "Persons with disabilities constitute the largest minority group in the United States" (p. 16)!

The fact that the 1990 Americans with Disabilities Act (ADA) has been enacted into law should suffice to inform us of the extent to which discrimination against people with disabilities has permeated our society, thus necessitating attention through civil action. Television programs reveal how landlords avoid renting apartments to this group of people. Doctors' offices are often not set up to facilitate the transfer of wheelchair users to the typical high-standing examination table. Deaf individuals who rely on sign language to communicate encounter obstacles when competing with hearing peers for psychology internship slots. The list goes on and on.

Why is that so? People with disabilities are human beings who live with a disability, like we all live with something we perhaps could do without. They want to work, to play, to love, to live their lives to the fullest. But it does not happen as a matter of course, as it should. Carolyn Vash (1998) tells the story of a young man from New Zealand, severely disabled by cerebral palsy, who does a weekly radio show on disability. When he and his traveling companion visited the United States and were taken to Disneyland, he returned to his hosts and exclaimed that now he knew what people meant by happiness! Why did he have to wait that long to find out?

All too often, perceptions of disability are framed within the constructs of powerlessness, incompetence, bodily violations, deviations from society's idealized norm, and forced dependency on others. Many of us may harbor myths about disability that stigmatize individuals with disabilities and subtly give rise to discriminatory attitudes. A man with atrophied muscles or spastic movements that result in drastically limited mobility may, in the mind of a naïve observer, trigger the thought that he is not too bright, when, in fact, there is potentially a brilliant brain behind the spastic front. That person could be a lawyer, even a Stephen Hawkins. Unfortunately, these negative myths have perpetuated the centuries old oppression and rejection of people with disabilities (Davis, 1995; 1997; Mackelprang & Salsgiver, 1999).

Or we may admire people with disabilities because they have had to overcome significant hurdles in order to succeed. This attitude can be laced with pity. Difference in the guise of disability is not idealized. This also can lead us to deny and possibly even denigrate the disability by stating to a particular person that we would have never known that person was disabled or that we "forgot" about the disability. This could be interpreted to mean we are focusing on the person and not the disability. But, in reality, "forgetting" the disability could be a significant inconvenience when a hard-of-hearing person is inadvertently excluded during an animated group discussion.

If we make an appointment with someone sight unseen and then discover upon initial contact a person with a disability, how the specific disability influences our perception of that individual depends very much on the disability myths or perceptions we harbor. Olkin (1999) says that the attitudes of others, or specifically the able-bodied, are important in terms of affecting the lives of persons with disabilities. In other words, it's the able-bodied who make life a headache for people with disabilities. They invent a "normal" category that excludes people with disabilities, who are then delegated to the "abnormal" category (Davis, 1995; 1997) and thereby rejected or victimized. The able-bodied are the ones who are not comfortable with disability. They create accessibility problems and make people with disabilities the problem instead of part of the spectrum of diversity. They use negative language like cripple, handicapped, or impaired, all of which imply that the person being referred to is defined by the deficit, when, in fact, the person is a person who happens to have a condition (disability) with variable consequences in daily living, depending on the nature of the disability.

Disability: An Integral Component of the Diversity Spectrum

Disability as a form of diversity is a concept whose time has come. Publications on disability have exploded in recent years. Specific topics cover civil rights, accessibility, identity, sexuality, employment, health care, ad infinitum, related to the lives of people with disabilities. Able-bodied people take these topics for granted, and people with disabilities are claiming ownership as well. Many are now saying that with improved accessibility, their disability becomes one part of life that they have to handle rather than an unremitting burden that takes over their lives. Only with frequent exposure to people with disabilities living full, enriched lives can we understand how that is possible.

Many people with disabilities think they would do just fine if they were seen as part of the normal expected diversity in the general population. Society would then be more accommodating, particularly in terms of environmental accessibility. For example, deaf individuals say they can function as well as anyone else if their environment provides sufficient visual input, such as closed captions in television programs. What curb cuts on sidewalk corners mean is that wheelchair users can now navigate urban outdoor environments without major headaches. What human beings fail to recognize is that these improvements benefit more than just people with disabilities. In the process of learning to read English, immigrants can take advantage of closed captioned television programs. Curb cuts in sidewalks are a godsend for baby carriages, bicycles, and suitcases with wheels. Hence, what is good for individuals with disabilities is good for all! So design the environment with everyone in mind, using the "universal design" approach (Shapiro, 1993)

What Is Disability?

Disability as a difference from ability is not easy to conceptualize. Do we focus on physical anomalies? Skill areas? If one is not able to play football, is that person disabled? Some of us have seen amputees skiing down mountains. Are they disabled? How so? Nelson Rockefeller had dyslexia. Do we consider him disabled in life? Wheelchair users frequently ride the subway. They get around as we do. So, in essence, who is disabled and how do we conceptualize disability?

This category is an extraordinarily unstable one (Davis, 1995; Linton, 1998). There are the more obvious physical and sensory disabilities. Then there are the less visible disabilities, including psychiatric, learning, and developmental disabilities. People are born with disabilities or they become disabled as a consequence of diseases such as polio or multiple sclerosis that limit functional abilities. In addition, what is often overlooked is that many individuals are going to experience disability at some point in their lifetime, either through the aging process, accidents, or disease. Disability can be either temporary or permanent, depending on its nature. Lastly, not everyone whom "society" perceives as disabled may necessarily identify as disabled. Those deaf individuals who communicate using American Sign Language generally see themselves as part of a linguistic minority, not as a group with a disability, society's perception of them notwithstanding (Lane, Hoffmeister, & Bahan, 1996; Leigh, 1999). Many individuals with diagnosed learning disability find it difficult to juxtapose their hidden disability with the general notion of disability as something different and obvious.

Because of the complexities inherent in defining the exact point whereby individuals move into the disability category, disability laws have focused on a functional definition of disability. The most recent law is the 1990 Americans with Disabilities Act (ADA). In that law, the diagnosis is not the focal point. Rather, the focus is on the functional impairment inasmuch as it affects daily living. Specifically, the ADA defines disability as a physical or mental impairment that substantially limits one or more of the major life activities of such an individual, a record of such an impairment, and being regarded as having such an impairment. For those who are interested, the ADA is posted on the Internet at http://www.usdoj.gov/. Also, explanations of what the ADA means for people with disabilities can be found in, for example, Bruyere and O'Keefe (1994), Mackelprang and Salsgiver (1999), and Olkin (1999).

Disability Groupings

People with disabilities generally perceive themselves as having a common experience in life and are often more interested in accessibility than in labeling of disability-related conditions. However, society's typical tendency is to categorize these individuals into disability groupings in order to explain various disabilities per se. As we have clearly indicated, what constitutes a disability is subject to question. Consequently, disability labels continue to be debated. Committees that focus on disability have difficulty agreeing on, for example, who falls into the visible disability category or even who is disabled. While it is easy to assume that people with physical disabilities qualify, what about deaf individuals whose inability to hear often goes undetected? What about the individual going through an active psychotic episode and clearly acting out of the ordinary if psychiatric disabilities are considered invisible?

Additionally, the variability is mind-boggling. For instance, those who may fall into the mobility disability group may range from those with minimal limitations to those who are completely immobile. Individuals in this group have drastically different needs, and it behooves us to respect how they wish to identify themselves. Also, we need to consider various factors that influence disability categories, such as what bodily systems are affected (e.g., visual, cardiovascular, etc.), what bodily functions (e.g., the ability to see, to walk, to control leg movements, etc.) are not present, at what stage of development the disability occurs (the life experience of one born with a disability is not the same as that of one experiencing onset later in life), and so on. For these reasons, it is impossible to be comprehensive within the brief scope of this chapter. All these concerns notwithstanding, the average reader will benefit from some understanding of disability categorizations with the caveat that stereotyping of individuals within each category is to be avoided at all costs. Having said that, we move on to a consideration of general groupings.

Persons with sensory disabilities include those who have visual disabilities and blindness as well as those who are deaf, hard of hearing, and deaf-blind. Visual disabilities can range from those who have vision in the better eye at 20/80 or less when corrected to those who are legally blind, which is defined as corrected vision of 20/200 or less in the better eye. Total blindness is rare; many can perceive at the very least the existence of light. Often the individual with visual disability is considered unable to do activities that require sight (a critical consideration for legal blindness). What society often forgets is that there are techniques to overcome the requirement of sight in a large variety of activities. For example, individuals who are blind can whip up a meal in their kitchen based on strategies developed to accommodate their needs. Some accommodate well and function independently. Others don't. Society often sees visual disability as a stigma, but those who grew up with it can accommodate to it as part of life rather than as a tragedy that deprives them of happiness.

From a medical perspective, labeling a person as deaf or hard of hearing is based on definitions of hearing acuity. These range from mild to severe to profound levels. Hard-of-hearing individuals hear within the mild to severe range, while deaf individuals place in the severe to profound levels of hearing loss. Total deafness is rare; most deaf individuals have some residual hearing that can be amplified by hearing aids. Whether they benefit from hearing aids beyond environmental sound awareness depends on whether they have some hearing in the speech range and obtain training in the recognition of speech sounds. An increasing number of deaf persons now have cochlear implants, which require surgery. It is important to understand that even with hearing aids or cochlear implants, normal hearing is not restored. Users are still deaf or hard of hearing, though to different degrees. Age of onset varies; the earlier the hearing loss, the more difficult it is to acquire a spoken language, and the need to rely on visual avenues for language learning becomes more critical. Communicating with these individuals requires some understanding of what they need. This might be speaking slowly, raising one's voice (this is *not* always appreciated), making sure eye contact is maintained, using some form of sign language system such as signed English, which follows English word order, or American Sign Language, which is a visual language with its own grammatical structure, or writing back and forth, depending on individual usage.

Deaf-blind individuals are those who have varying degrees of vision and hearing loss in combination. If they cannot discriminate the spoken word or see sign language communication, they can rely on various methods of tactile communication through feeling the hand shapes of the communicator who is signing to them. They navigate their environment as persons with visual disabilities do.

There are many variations of mobility disability based on etiology and on what part of the body is affected, too numerous to count or specify here. For example, those born with arrested development in the spinal cord and vertebrae resulting in spina bifida will have various types of mobility impairment; multiple sclerosis may gradually affect the entire body; amputations affect either arms or legs, in whole or part, and strokes affect one side of the body. Each situation will require attention to different ways of achieving mobility. Some require prostheses for arms or legs. Some walk differently but without assistance; others require canes, crutches or walkers, even scooters, and the rest depend on wheelchairs. While many wheelchair users use wheelchairs simply to get around, others become wheelchair athletes, competing in races and other events. Whatever the case may be, these constitute what society generally terms the "physically disabled." There is no standard approach in terms of how they can best navigate their environment and what accommodations they require, since much depends on the nature of the mobility disability, etiology, and age of onset.

Cognitive disabilities cover a broad range of disabilities, ranging from those resulting from traumatic brain injury to learning disabilities, intellectual disabilities, and attention deficit disorder with or without hyperactivity. A number of developmental disabilities such as autism (which can involve cognitive and socioemotional deficits), Down's syndrome, and other mental retardation categories, do fall under the rubric of intellectual disabilities. While cognitive disabilities can occur at birth or at any time during the life span due to accidents, disease, or aging, developmental disabilities are usually evident during the early years of life and interfere with critical developmental aspects that have long-term consequences for individual learning and daily functioning. Individuals with developmental disabilities often require long-term support. Self-determination issues have been problematic over a wide range of disabilities, but for individuals with cognitive and developmental disabilities, this is a pervasive problem. Typically, attention is paid to their limitations, not their potential. This makes it more difficult for them to learn how to make decisions about their daily lives or achieve autonomy to the greatest extent possible.

Last but not least, we consider psychiatric disabilities, which involve disturbed perceptions of the self and the environment. Symptoms vary at any point in time, may occur unexpectedly, and can include hallucinations and delusions, upheavals in typical thinking processes, immobility or frenzied movements, and other behavior and personality changes that make it very difficult or impossible to maintain normal activities and social interactions. Successful treatment cannot be achieved without careful consideration of treatment approaches, including psychotherapy, since symptoms and responses to medication, including side effects, are very much individualized. Individuals with schizophrenia, bipolar disorders, and major depression have historically been stigmatized and incarcerated. Today people with schizophrenia are increasingly visible on the streets due to deinstitutionalization policies. Celebrities with major depression and bipolar conditions have begun coming out to the public, thereby putting society on notice that psychiatric disabilities can happen to anyone and should be dealt with. However, if a candidate for political office acknowledges any sort of psychiatric history such as depression, his or her qualifications for office are automatically questioned, even if symptoms have long since been absent. The stigma of psychiatric disabilities is very difficult to escape.

Diversity Training

Diversity training is hot now. Private companies, public institutions, health care settings, educational settings—you name it—all have gotten into the act.

Sensitizing people to the implications of ethnicity, race, culture, and religion is paramount. Issues related to sexual orientation and aging are increasingly being addressed. All of these have profound consequences for human interaction, as this book so clearly demonstrates.

Disability, however, appears to be the lost child in diversity training. Both Lennard Davis (1995; 1997) and Simi Linton (1998) accuse the academic establishment of literally denying the existence of people with disabilities through relegating this group to afterthought status. In this way people with disabilities are marginalized, and study of this group is marginalized as well. In her review of this topic, Olkin (1999) cites studies showing the extremely limited attention paid by professional training programs to disability as a component of diversity. However, the tide appears to be changing. Linton notes that resistance to disability studies is beginning to crumble with the recognition that the understanding of disability underlies human relations. In other words, we all have disabilities of one form or another, whether these are medically related, personality related, based on unaccommodating environments, or a mismatch between environment and individual; these factors impact on how we interact with each other. Disability is now evolving into a more positive term, thanks to the actions of disability activists.

Perceptions of disability have profound implications for training and service provision. For example, an analogue study conducted by Kemp and Mallinckrodt (1996) demonstrated bias on the part of psychotherapists who emphasized different treatment themes, depending on whether or not the client had a disability after viewing videotapes of disabled and nondisabled clients with the same presenting problems. However, those psychotherapists who had even a small amount of training in disability-related issues revealed significantly less bias in case conceptualizations and treatment themes. Clearly, some understanding of disability paradigms will help all of us as we encounter people with disabilities and start interacting with them in mutually beneficial ways.

Views of Disability

There are three basic lenses through which to view disability. The one with the longest history is the moral model, which defines disability as the embodiment of evil or as a punishment visited on those who have transgressed or sinned. This perspective continues to be expressed by, for example, parents who find out they have a child with a disability and ask, "Why me? What have I done wrong to make God do this to me?" On the other side of the coin, the moral model also encompasses the perspective that disability is a divine gift for those who are given the challenge of overcoming adversity in very special ways. The moral model is largely dependent on religious and cultural paradigms that serve to explain conditions for which there is no obvious answer.

The medical model of disability incorporates the perception of disability as a medical problem. In essence, disability is a pathological condition in need of "fixing" because it differs from the "norm," whatever that means. Key words include treatment, healing, cure, amelioration, and rehabilitation in dealing with a sick or chronic condition. This model, also termed the functional limitations paradigm, has reinforced the concept that the person with a disability is a victim or a burden that needs to be "taken care of" and is therefore subject to charity. This paternalistic perspective has made it very difficult for people with disabilities to take charge of their own lives. In exploring political implications of disability definitions, Hahn (1999) tells us that activists have increasingly challenged the notion that disability is a problem within the individual.

The challenge of these activists is based on the premise that the sociopolitical environment unnecessarily gives rise to a pathological perspective of disability that encourages dependency on society. To them, this smacks of oppression. On this basis, they have increasingly adopted the social/minority model of disability. Specifically, this model views individuals with disabilities as part of a minority group that has to deal with discrimination and oppression. The blame is not on the person's disability but on his or her surroundings. The focus is not on the pathology but on one's strengths in dealing with society's imposition of environmental and interpersonal obstacles and with life in general.

This model has given rise to a collective consciousness of disability (Barnartt, 1996). Within this frame, similarities in the disability experience are emphasized. Self-determination instead of dependency on others is a key concept. The victim status is rejected. People with disabilities are now fighting for what they perceive as their rights, primarily recognition and accessibility. Examples include blockades across streets to demand greater access to public transportation and the 1988 barricading of Gallaudet University (the world's only liberal arts university for deaf students) during the Deaf President Now movement, when the Gallaudet University Board of Trustees selected a hearing candidate for the presidency over deaf candidates.

The existence of a disability culture is increasingly advocated. It is defined by those who are part of the disabled community and who see themselves as bicultural, as Rhoda Olkin (1999) does. She had polio early in life and sees herself as able to navigate the world of the able-bodied and the world of the disability community. Barnartt (1996) questions the construct of a disability culture because it does not really fit the anthropological meaning of the word "culture." She makes a case for defining the disability way of life within the collective consciousness frame. At this point, disability culture is still a concept in evolution, and as Disability Studies programs begin to emerge within academic settings, we can expect to see further discussion of the existence of disability culture, as it becomes more widely used to frame the disability experience. However, we cannot leave this discussion without again mentioning Deaf persons, who consider themselves a linguistic minority, not a "disability" minority, since they share a common language (American Sign Language) and a Deaf-World way of life (Lane, Hoffmeister, & Bahan, 1996) that sets them apart from the majority hearing society. The use of Deaf (upper case) to represent membership in a culture, specifically Deaf culture, is contrasted with the use of "deaf" (lower case) to represent the audiological condition of not hearing or a sensory disability. Not every deaf or hard-of-hearing individual considers themselves members of Deaf culture, and it is necessary again to avoid stereotyping.

Implications for Human Interactions

So, what do we do when we encounter individuals whom we recognize as having a disability? This is clearly more salient in terms of overt, visible disabilities. It is also salient when we become aware of a disability that is "hidden." How do we deal with the disability in the course of the interaction? How do we avoid being patronizing? If we do not understand the disability experience, whether it be lifelong or due to trauma, we run the risk of unintentionally giving offense. If we keep in mind that the way we react to persons with disabilities is dependent on which model of disability we carry within us, the first thing to do is evaluate within ourselves what our attitude to disability is. Only with self-awareness can we enter the world of the person with disability in a way that imparts respect and validation.

The starting point for developing any sort of working relationship or any significant interaction with another individual is communication. Communication occurs on many levels or layers, with much of what we "say" to each other being nonverbal in nature. As our society increases dramatically in diversity, more attention is paid to interaction dynamics between different cultural groups. Understanding how cultures view each other, the stereotypes that underlie interactions, and the various attitudes that come into play is a starting point for analyzing relationships between able-bodied persons and those with disabilities.

A critical point to understand when considering relationships between able-bodied people and people with disabilities is the nature of the cultural difference. In most families, the culture and cultural traditions of the parents are passed on to the children. There may often be conflicts, particularly in countries like the United States where immigrant parents strive to preserve their native culture in their children, while the children work to acculturate.

However, it is still a given that the possibility of the children remaining in the same culture as the parent exists. If these children have disabilites, by nature of having a disability, they thereby enter into a community or culture, specifically disability culture, to which their parents most likely do not belong. Those parents also may carry cultural attitudes toward disability that constrain potential for a "full life" as society typically means. The attitudes, beliefs, and values of the disability community, and those things that tie people together, may not be the same attitudes as those of the family of origin. This same dynamic occurs in hearing families that have deaf children. There is the distinct possibility that the children will enter a culture where the parents may have limited or no access. In fact, some hearing parents will express fears of losing their children to Deaf culture. This sets in motion system responses to keep the family intact and functioning, though sometimes at the expense of the child.

With disability culture, membership is "open." That is, anyone may be joining at any time, depending on those random events that life brings. Olkin (1999) points out that when able-bodied individuals interact with disabled individuals, a whole host of responses come into play. There is often a need to understand how the individual came to have a disability. People do not want to believe that life can deal arbitrary blows that can lead to a disability. Instead, we strive to give some meaning or explanation to how it happened. This is obvious in the news media, when coverage of major catastrophes such as the Columbine shootings focuses at length on what instigated the event. People feel better when there is some reason for why things happened, particularly when that implies that we can control and perhaps ensure that it does not happen to us.

A second reaction is often guilt, particularly in family members. Siblings may feel guilty that they are able-bodied and their siblings are not, or that they survived accidents without injury while others were badly hurt. People may even feel guilty for feeling angry or jealous toward other friends or family. The point is that guilt can be experienced in a number of ways and expressed in a variety of behaviors.

These reactions can influence how able-bodied people react and interact with people with disabilities. If we are striving to find explanations, we are likely to ask the person with a disability what "happened" to them or to react with sympathy or regret for things that are no longer relevant to the disabled person. For example, a graduate student once talked of how she lost both her parents by the time she was 12 years old. She said the hardest part was everyone saying how tragic that was and how hard it must have been. Her recollection was that her extended family and siblings were all incredibly supportive and that life went on. She did not have the sense of intense tragedy that seemed to be the universal reaction to her story.

As we consider interactions between people, and in particular, between people who have disabilities and other people, the concept of countertransference is useful. Those who have been involved in counseling or psychotherapy are surely familiar with this experience, where our own internal and personal reactions to our clients become very much present. It can influence how much we like our clients, how we respond to them (both positively and negatively), and how we make decisions about treatment. It becomes very important to evaluate our own countertransference toward people with disabilities as we enter working or personal relationships with them. A starting point for this assessment, suggested by Olkin (1999), is the internal model of disability that we possess.

As described earlier, the three lenses through which to view disability have been described as the moral, medical, and social minority models. Our own internal working model or representation of disability will influence how we relate to people with disabilities. To the extent that we believe that things happen for a reason, that people are given hardships either because of their past actions or as tests, we will hold people with disabilities responsible for their circumstances. This may not even be at a highly conscious level, but even below the surface it will influence our interactions. If we subscribe to the medical model, we will tend to see people with disabilities as having shortcomings or problems or challenges that they need to work to overcome. This almost precludes the notion of acceptance of the person as he/she is and focuses on efforts to change them.

The medical model is quite pervasive, not only in able-bodied people but also in people with disabilities. It can be represented by the work of Jerry Lewis on behalf of the Muscular Dystrophy Association. The Labor Day Telethon that he has conducted for years raises money that goes into research for treatment and a cure. However, in recent years, people with muscular dystrophy have protested the patronizing attitude involved in the fund raising (they are all "Jerry's kids"), and the lack of attention to the everyday care necessary in the lives of many of these people. While the money raised may well be going to a worthy cause, it means that even adults with muscular dystrophy are seen as "kids."

While there is currently no research on how many people subscribe to which models, the likelihood that very many able-bodied people internalize a social minority model of disability is not strong. Yet, this model, which emphasizes strengths, functionality, and options, makes much more sense for almost all human interactions. An emphasis on, or search for what is wrong, often leads to the conclusion that there is nothing that can be done on a psychosocial level. For example, a depressed woman, in talking about her situation, can find no external reason for feeling depressed. She states that she does well in school, is popular and has friends, has a fine boyfriend, and is physically healthy with a warm supportive family. Since there is no reason to feel depressed, it must be genetic or biological. That leaves no room for intervening or working on a psychosocial level. However, if the question is changed just slightly, from what reason is there to be sad, to what reason is there to be happy, the work changes. Instead of searching for the elusive and unhelpful "cause" of the depression, searching for ways to add joy or happiness to life is very possible and gives direction to work.

Do we ask people with disabilities about their strengths, what they are able to do, how they can add meaning to their lives, and what they can contribute? Do the people with disabilities with whom we work ask themselves these questions? In discussing the various models of disability, Olkin (1999) points out that not all disabled people will subscribe to a minority model. Thus, in addition to asking ourselves how we approach disabilities and what our reactions are to people with disabilities, we must be open to people having various and diverse views of themselves.

Besides our internal working models of disability, our attitudes toward people with disabilities and the beliefs that serve as the foundations of the attitudes will influence our interactions with these individuals. We know that there is a ranking of acceptance regarding disabilities, with some being more acceptable than others. It is not clear on what basis able-bodied people make that judgment (or other disabled people as well). Physical disabilities seem more acceptable than sensory impairments, which are more acceptable than psychiatric or cognitive impairments (Olkin & Howson, 1994). However, this does not always hold in a consistent manner. Much depends on the experiences and characteristics of all the people involved. The personality characteristics of the person with a disability will interact with things like amount of education or cultural background. A physically attractive and socially charming individual with a disability will leave a different impression on others than someone who is less physically attractive or socially gruff. In addition, we all bring different tolerances for different things based on our own experiences. Examining those tolerances, as we might for any sort of human interaction, is vital.

A few beliefs are common in the belief systems of able-bodied people and should be considered. Linton (1998), for example, describes the stereotype that people with disabilities should strive to overcome their disability. The highest compliment in this sense is that others stop thinking of the person as "being disabled." There are pitfalls in this belief, in that it leads to diminished social responsibility and less emphasis on civil rights. Another belief that Olkin (1999) discusses is that people with disabilities should be cheerful. Many people consider a positive outlook and a pleasant demeanor a must. Anger, frustration, or hostility is seen as signs that these individuals have not accepted their disability, that they are in denial, or that they need to adjust/adapt in some way. These emotions are either not allowed or are considered a stage in the mourning process. This leads to another belief that Olkin discusses, which is that all people with disabilities must go through a mourning process. Some do not necessarily mourn a "normal" state that they have never experienced.

When we decide to truly enter into a relationship with people with disabilities, whether for professional reasons, political, or other, one must take the time to look at the issues described here. They play a strong role, albeit one that is often not visible or obvious. Beliefs, attitudes, internal working models, or other cognitive schemas unconsciously direct and influence our behavior and decisions as well as our interactions. We can see them, if we take the time, in our language, in our actions, and in our decisions.

Communicating with Persons with Disabilities

Entering the community of people with disabilities can be a richly rewarding, yet challenging endeavor. As with all human relationships, attending to the various layers of communication is critical, starting with the most obvious layer, that of having our words understood in and of themselves. This is clearly an issue when working with people who have a different native language than our own. However, it is often an issue when working with people with disabilities. Many people with a variety of disabilities exhibit communication problems, ranging from deaf and hard-of-hearing people, to people with severe cerebral palsy, to those who experienced head injuries, to the severely learning disabled.

Technology is greatly enhancing the communication abilities of those with certain kinds of disabilities. Computer systems that can speak for individuals who are unable to control their oral-motor movements are becoming more commonplace, more sophisticated, and easier to use. People are now able to express much more than they were previously. In addition, the need for communication access is more widely acknowledged, with sign language interpreters seen much more regularly in a wide variety of settings, such as medical and legal. This is not to say that the situation is perfect or that all people have access. Quite frequently, people assume that a deaf or hard-of-hearing person can understand them clearly because they nod their heads in assent or because the deaf person's speech is understandable. This is often erroneous. Yet these beliefs persist.

Various aspects of communication that we often do not think about need to be examined more carefully when we communicate with people with disabilities. Facial expressions, for example, can have multiple meanings. With deaf and hard-of-hearing people who relate stories or describe events using sign language, facial expressions carry many nuances of meaning. Hearing people, unfamiliar with this, can easily misinterpret the amount of emotion or affect involved in conversations. Similarly, due to a whole host of physical conditions, people may make different sorts of facial expressions, interrupt what they are saying in midsentence, or do any number of other actions almost unconsciously. While sometimes there may be some underlying psychological issue at work, very often people are responding to things such as chronic pain, the need to move around in wheelchairs to prevent pressure sores, the need to adjust themselves in response to changes in lighting, or any number of things. This brings a new layer to communicating, both in therapeutic as well as other situations.

Another layer of communication, probably strongly related to the one just discussed, is the willingness of people to engage in communication. Communicating with someone through an assistive device or through an interpreter is more time consuming than straight, face-to-face verbal conversation in the same language. While technology is helpful, one still must be willing to use it, to learn the systems, to adapt one's own communication style to the person using the device. Turn taking in conversation is one characteristic that changes. While in verbal discourse, people will often interrupt or intrude into another speaker's turn, particularly within group situations. When using assistive devices or interpreters, that cannot happen. When it does, it becomes very difficult if not impossible to follow who is saying what. And usually the people being left out are the individuals with disabilities, who either cannot follow what others are saying, or who are not able to participate at the rate that other people are participating either because of interpreter lag or an inability to jump in quickly during discourse. Patience and a willingness to put in time to communicate and ultimately have a relationship with someone are very significant here.

A word about the relation between communication and beliefs (or judgments) is relevant here. Human beings are constantly taking in and processing a great deal of information about the people around us and trying to organize and make sense of that information. Personal beliefs serve to simplify the organizational process, providing shortcuts to conclusions about people and what roles they play or can play, and how we should deal with them. One major belief relates to how we speak or communicate with each other. People who are articulate are often considered to be bright and intelligent, meaning that their thoughts and opinions should be listened to. As the old investment commercial said, "When E. F. Hutton speaks, people listen." If E. F. Hutton were to garble his words, repeat himself, stutter, or take an exceptionally long amount of time to make statements, very few people would be listening.

We often make judgments about people based on how they speak. This can lead to our inaccurately judging someone with slow, labored speech to be less intelligent. Even when using assistive devices, the imperfections in the devices can lead people interacting with disabled individuals to judge them as less intelligent, less interesting, and as having less to offer. And since what we believe about the world is more important than any "objective" truth, people tend to find what they expect to find. We usually find that people behave as we expect they will, and it takes something a bit out of the ordinary to challenge our assumptions. Once again, a willingness to examine our personal beliefs about disabilities and people with disabilities is a necessary first step in opening communication and developing relationships. Exploring our own stereotypes, such as that all deaf people read lips or people with cerebral palsy are mentally retarded, and opening them up to scrutiny is a first step. Honestly looking at what we expect from these people in terms of participation in society, what we believe their role to be, and how we feel about ourselves in relation to people with disabilities serves as the groundwork or foundation for building working relationships.

Service Provision

When thinking about people with disabilities, we are often thinking about service provision. This might include vocational rehabilitation services, physical and occupational therapy, social services such as help with housing, personal care attendants, obtaining and managing social security or disability income, or personal counseling as well as psychotherapy. The latter services are often related or thought to relate to adjustment to the disability.

A deaf client intentionally selected a therapist who specialized in the specific problem for which the client was seeking help. During the first session, after preliminary discussion between the therapist and the client, the therapist inquired of the client whether she felt the deafness was a factor. The client made it clear the deafness was not an issue, and the therapy proceeded to focus solely on issues related to the presenting problem. For the client, this approach was very validating; it meant the focus of treatment was not on the client's "difference," that is, deafness or pathology, but rather on the client's issues in navigating life stages. This is how the disability should be treated in society, according to Blotzer and Ruth (1995).

The first step in discussing service provision with disabled individuals is the issue of accessibility. The word "accessibility" has a broad range of meanings in terms of working with disabled individuals. It can mean ensuring that buildings have easy access for wheelchairs, have elevators, restrooms with doors that are wide enough to accommodate a wheelchair, and other physical or structural features to guarantee that people who use wheelchairs can get to where they need with no obstacles. It can mean provision of printed materials in Braille or in large print formats so that people with limited vision or people who are blind can have access. It can also mean having the means and willingness to provide sign language interpreters for deaf clients and having a TTY (a telephone communication device for deaf people) on the premises.

Accessibility, however, is more than just physical or structural features that allow a person with a disability to make contact with a service provider. Accessibility is an attitude. A common complaint voiced by deaf consumers is that TTY numbers are printed in the literature and a TTY may, in fact, be available. However, when someone calls on the TTY, no one is trained in its use and it usually goes unanswered or an answering announcement is simply put on the machine. That reflects an attitude issue, not a problem with access. In other words, the importance of TTY access is denigrated and its mere presence is assumed to take care of "accessibility."

It is too easy, sometimes, to provide physical or structural access and then claim that accommodations have been made. However, this can serve to cover up underlying feelings of resentment regarding the extra work or time that needs to be committed or the additional activities to be undertaken. One starting place is to realize that having mixed feelings toward those with disabilities is not unusual. Whether these feelings come from resentment, fear, or some other discomfort, the feelings themselves are not harmful. What is harmful is *not* acknowledging those feelings and accepting the need to work with them.

Accessibility also means that the person with a disability is not seen in a pathologizing way, but as a person with strengths and weaknesses, virtues and foibles. When a person with a disability is immediately put into that category of someone who needs to overcome something, adjust to something, mourn something, there is diminished accessibility. Olkin (1999) further points out that accessibility implies that counselors or therapists understand the disability well enough to make recommendations that are not counterproductive to the individual's overall well-being.

When we work to recognize and see people with disabilities as people first, one issue that arises is what the effects of having the disability might be? For example, when assigning a psychiatric diagnosis using the *Diagnostic and Statistical Manual* (*DSM-IV*), diagnoses are made on several axes or levels, with each one representing a different aspect of the person's life. One of the axes or levels of diagnosis (Axis III) asks about physical disabilities. Comments here are supposed to indicate how the person's physical condition *relates to the psychiatric disorder*. This would imply that seeing someone with muscular dystrophy for an anxiety disorder would not automatically lead to an Axis III diagnosis incorporating muscular dystrophy. If, however, the person stated that part of what made them anxious was how people would react to their physical condition, then an Axis III diagnosis makes sense. The basic question is how much of what the person shows the world (whether in a clinical sense or not) is truly a manifestation of the disability that the person has.

One of the authors once worked with a young man who had received a head injury in a motorcycle accident that left him with serious brain damage. He was ambulatory, had reasonable language skills (though spoke in a monotone at all times), and managed his life with minimal assistance. One major complaint from people at the workshop where he worked had to do with his attempting to touch women around him. Some people attributed this lack of inhibition to the brain damage he had received. However, when looking into his life and his history, what emerged was that he had a long history of sexual acting out, drug use, and other related criminal activity. His postaccident personality was really not very different from his preaccident, nondisabled life. Attributing his behavior to the injury and subsequent impairment missed the point.

A related issue has to do with enabling people with disabilities, and whether ultimately protecting them from natural and logical consequences does them a disservice. One young man with mild mental retardation continually missed work at his job in a mailroom of a large company. His parents, social worker, and rehabilitation counselor kept intervening on his behalf to prevent his being fired. Meanwhile, counseling focused on helping him understand the seriousness of his behavior and looking at what "might" happen to him if he lost his job. All of this went to naught, as he ignored everyone's admonitions to go to work and was finally fired. After he had spent several months unemployed (and with great difficulty finding new employment), he could no longer afford to do the things he enjoyed, such as going out on Monday nights to watch Monday Night Football or buying sports paraphernalia. It was at this point that he truly began to understand what having a consistent job meant. When he obtained employment (in a different company's mailroom), he was much more aware of the importance of employment, as it now had personal meaning for him. It was not just something his parents or counselors preached.

A common issue that is discussed among families and professionals providing services to people with disabilities, especially developmental disabilities that can affect cognitive abilities, is how to "protect" them. While we know that people with disabilities are more vulnerable and more likely to experience abuse, being "overprotective" also does a disservice. Finding the balance between support (and perhaps protection) while allowing individuals to learn from life's lessons is not easy. However, what must be recognized is that there is an implicit message that is communicated to people when they are protected too much, and that is that they are not capable. If they get that message often enough, they will come to believe it. If, on the other hand, we express our belief in them and our willingness to support them, their full potential is more likely to be realized.

A question that sometimes comes up is how service provisions or human service work should be modified for people with disabilities. For example, can one do psychodynamic or human-centered psychotherapy with people with mental retardation or are behavioral approaches the only ones that make any sense? Similarly, does our work change if the person with whom we are working has recently acquired a disability, as compared with working with a person who has had a disability for a long time? This relates again to the question of what role the disability may play in the person's life, as well as to our own beliefs about what is important or helpful to people. Blotzer and Ruth (1995) write in a highly compelling manner about work with people with developmental disabilities from a human-centered approach. While behavioral principles are not ignored, the importance of a supportive, empathic relationship with a helping professional is seen as equally important.

It is not possible to make blanket statements about the kinds of problems clients will bring to counseling or therapy or to any kind of interactive setting. It is more likely the case, however, that if working with someone with a long-standing disability, other life issues may be more central than the disability. This will not always be the case, and sometimes people with more recent disabling injuries will have issues other than adjustment to the disability. It is wise to proceed with an open mind and not assume that we know what will be important for any particular client to discuss or work through.

Whether working with someone who has recently acquired a disability, or someone who has had one for a long time, counselors, therapists, and others becoming involved with the disability community will quickly become impressed with the large number of systems that are present and working in some more or less coordinated way. In addition to any number of medical professionals, there are often rehabilitation professionals, physical and occupational therapists, providers of assistive devices (ranging from mechanics who alter cars and vans, to prosthetists who make the braces and artificial limbs, to those who manufacture and sell hearing aids and TTYs), as well as personal care assistants. Time moves at a different pace and in a different way in the disability community. This is one of the first things that many able-bodied people will notice. Simple decisions, such as where to meet or where to eat, can take quite a while to resolve and even longer to actually make happen.

So where do all these issues leave us? Probably the most important point to conclude with is an emphasis on disability as a social construction (Linton, 1998). It is what we think about disability, what society mandates in terms of views toward disability and people with disability that must be engaged, understood, and challenged. Disability exists, and it has to be acknowledged as a multi-layered experience that is part of the composite of life, not as the whole person. Too many of us tend to focus too much on the disability, or to "ignore" it, neither of which bodes well for interactions between the able-bodied and the person with a disability. Working with people with disabilities requires flexibility and a willingness to examine our beliefs about disability. And to be ready to put ourselves to the test, we must show our willingness to enter into an equal partnership, and not just say that is what we should do.

References

Americans with Disabilities Act of 1990, Public Law 101–336, 42 U.S.C.12111, 12112.

Barnartt, S. (1996). Disability culture or disability consciousness? *Journal of Disability Policy Studies, 7,* 1–19.

Blotzer, M., & Ruth, R. (Ed.). (1995). *Sometimes you just want to feel like a human being: Case studies of empowering psychotherapy with people with disabilities.* Baltimore, MD: Paul Brookes.

Bruyere, S., & O'Keefe, J. (Eds.). (1994). *Implications of the Americans with Disabilities Act for psychology.* New York/Washington, DC: Springer/American Psychological Association.

Davis, L. (1995). *Enforcing normalcy: Disability, deafness, and the body.* London, UK: Verso.

Davis, L. (Ed.). (1997). *The disability studies reader.* New York: Routledge.

Hahn, H. (1999). The political implications of disability definitions and data. In R. P. Marinelli & A. E. Dell Orto (Eds.), *The psychological and social impact of disability, 4th edition* (pp. 3–11). New York: Springer.

Kemp, N., & Mallinckrodt, B. (1996). Impact of professional training on case conceptualization of clients with a disability. *Professional Psychology: Research and Practice, 27,* 378–385.

Lane, H., Hoffmeister, R., & Bahan, B. (1996). *A journey into the Deaf-World.* San Diego, CA: DawnSign Press.

Leigh, I. W. (1999). *Psychotherapy with deaf clients from diverse groups.* Washington, DC: Gallaudet University Press.

Linton, S. (1998). *Claiming disability: Knowledge and identity.* New York: New York University Press.

Lynch, R. T. & Thomas, K. R. (1999). People with disabilities as victims: Changing an ill-advised paradigm. In R. P. Marinelli & A. E. Dell Orto (Eds.), *The psychological and social impact of disability, 4th edition* (pp. 212–219). New York: Springer.

Mackelprang, R., & Salsgiver, R. (1999). *Disability: A diversity model approach in human science practice.* Pacific Grove, CA: Brooks/Cole.

Olkin, R. (1999). *What psychotherapists should know about disability.* New York: Guilford.

Olkin, R., & Howson, L. (1994). Attitudes toward and images of physical disability. *Journal of Social Behavior and Personality, 9,* 81–96.

Shapiro, J. (1993). *No pity.* New York: Times Books.

Vash, C. (1998, October). *Disability attitudes for all latitudes.* Paper presented at the meeting of the 5th International Congress of the World Leisure and Recreation Society, São Paulo, Brazil.

12

SAMUEL M. TURNER
DEBORAH C. BEIDEL

The Enriching Experience

When people think about research, different images may come to mind. Some think about laboratories and scientists who wear white coats, such as Madame Curie or Louis Pasteur. Others may picture census takers or surveyors at the local shopping mall, armed with a clipboard and asking questions of those who agree to participate. Still others may imagine Indiana Jones at an archeological dig in the desert. Actually, all these images depict individuals who are in the process of gathering information, and although their actions may seem very different, all are engaged in the process of science at some level. Despite the differences in the images described here, those who conduct research share a common endeavor—the pursuit of knowledge.

In school, children are taught that science is objective. However, scientific discoveries are the work of scientists and thus, science has a human face. As others have noted, this means that the scientific process is affected by all the usual human virtues and frailties that characterize the human condition (National Academy of Sciences, 1989). Thus, despite the often quoted dictum that science is a purely objective process, nothing could be further from the truth, as scientific pursuits are embedded within a cultural context and are influenced by all the associated cultural values, beliefs, and biases. This includes not only the manner in which studies are planned and conducted, but also how the resulting data are interpreted. The scientific method, taught in virtually every science class, may appear to be a rigorous, cut-and-dried process with little opportunity for deviation. Reality is very different, however. In the case of psychology, conducting research involves many different decision points, rang-ing from study design, to participant selection, to instrumentation, and to the interpretation and presentation of results. Each of these involves a human deci-sion, which is, in turn, influenced by prior knowledge as well as the scientist's values, personal style, and particular worldview. In this chapter, we will address the process of research and how the current status of psychological science has been influenced by researchers' decisions regarding issues of diversity.

The Current Status of Our Knowledge Base

An interesting fact is that the vast majority of all the world's mental health research is conducted in the United States, and many of these studies are con-ducted with college students who are Caucasian (Sue, 1999). What this means is that most of our knowledge about human behavior is based on a small subset of the U.S. population, which, in turn, represents less than 5% of the world population. Thus, much of what we generalize to be true about human be-havior (not just the behavior of those in the United States but the behavior of everyone) is based on a very nondiverse and unrepresentative group, the U.S. college student. This is very problematic because we really do not know how this "knowledge" applies to individuals from other countries or even for those living in the United States, who did not attend college or who might not be Caucasian and of European descent. We will address this issue in more detail later in this chapter.

Recently, at least within the United States, the unrepresentativeness of samples used to generate our understanding of human behavior has been recog-nized. The National Institutes of Health, for example, now includes a require-ment that participants in research projects funded by the federal government must include women and racial/ethnic minorities. Nevertheless, the fact re-mains that the majority of research publications report the use of primarily Caucasian samples or do not bother to report the ethnic makeup of the sample. In many cases, when the samples do include representatives of non-Caucasian groups, the data are not analyzed with this in mind.

A second issue relating to the current status of research and diversity is the distinction between investigators who conduct research "on" rather than "with" cross-cultural groups. For example, Rogler (1999) described how during the 1950s, researchers from the United States mainland went to Puerto Rico to conduct research. Although recognizing the need to translate their surveys and interviews into the Spanish language, the scientists came to Puerto Rico, quickly collected their data, and then returned stateside. As Rogler (1999) noted, whether or not the researchers were aware of it, their behaviors created the impression that except for translating the assessments instruments into Spanish, there was no need for them to understand any aspect of Puerto Rican culture, its relevance for the data they collected, or the phenomena they sought to study. This insensitivity, or perhaps a lack of respect for the culture of the research participants, almost certainly guarantees difficulty in correctly interpreting the resultant data. It also presents an image of the researcher as someone who does not value or respect the culture of others, but rather treats them as mere scientific curiosities to be measured or studied.

Some researchers have noted the need for cultural sensitivity in all aspects of research, including conceptualization, design, sample selection, treatment development, and treatment outcome evaluation. Rogler (1989) even goes as far as to suggest that "pre-testing" the research objectives should include direct immersion in the particular culture of the research participants. Although it is unclear that this latter suggestion will ever be implemented, in the remainder of this chapter we will discuss the issue of diversity and cultural sensitivity in the conduct of research endeavors.

Issues of Subject Recruitment

Even researchers who make a concerted effort to conduct sensitive, cross-cultural research face many challenges. Many minority groups have good reason to be suspicious of research and researchers. We cannot forget that for the purpose of "research," treatment for syphilis was withheld from African American males in the infamous Tuskegee study without their knowledge or consent. Thus, many minority groups distrust the motives of researchers, and this distrust is not without reason.

Even if they do not have preconceived suspicions about research participation, some members of minority groups may be unfamiliar with the research process. They also may experience conflicting cultural values and therefore, respond with data that may be of only limited value. For example, Okazaki and Sue (1995) discussed the difficulties trying to determine whether a measure of depression used with Caucasian-Americans would be appropriate to assess for depression among Chinese-Americans, and the effort was fraught with a number of problems. First, the research was conducted by telephone survey. This form of data collection was unfamiliar to older Chinese women (i.e., being questioned over the telephone by a stranger about personal experiences and mood) and probably made at least some of the women uncomfortable and no doubt influenced their response in some cases. Yet, they would not have refused to answer because, within the Chinese culture, that behavior would have been viewed as impolite. There is no way to determine how their uncomfortableness might have influenced the information provided. It is possible that they quickly denied the presence of symptomatology in order to end the interview. Similarly, among middle-aged Chinese men, endorsing positive mood would be viewed as immodest and frivolous, again leading to questions about the validity of the data collected (Okazaki & Sue, 1995).

These examples provide just a minimal illustration of how inattention to the values of a different culture might be perceived as a lack of respect for research participants. Furthermore, when collecting data across cultures, inattention to specific cultural parameters can negatively impact scientific knowledge. That is, not only might the researcher be perceived as insensitive but this also could affect the data obtained, and importantly, the manner in which data are interpreted. It is likely that the Chinese participants in the study described earlier did not feel comfortable answering the questions and yet felt equally uncomfortable about refusing to answer the questions. Therefore, it is impossible to know how accurate the data might be. These examples illustrate the scientist's need for cultural sensitivity when recruiting research participants and when collecting research data. Because of differing values and behaviors toward authority, individuals from different cultural groups may feel unable to refuse research participation or may feel uncomfortable when providing data, using methodologies commonly accepted by Caucasian Americans.

Issues Related to Data Collection

As previously noted, even researchers who, in terms of their other actions, might be considered "culturally insensitive," appear to understand that the assessment instrument must be translated into the research participant's native language. This might well be due to the fact that it would be difficult to publish articles in our best journals without at least having had assessment instruments translated into the proper language. This is usually accomplished by having someone translate the measure from the original language into the second language and then checking the translation by translating it back to the original language (back translation). Rogler (1999) noted that current procedural norms insist that standardized instruments must be kept exactly as in the original language version. He goes on to note that in actuality, this insistence on verbatim English language translation represents a form of cultural insensitivity. Many English language idioms don't translate effectively into other languages (e.g., "shake off the blues" has no literal translation into Spanish). The insistence that translations must conform to the original language often results in language that, although technically correct, does not convey the necessary cultural meaning, again a situation that has the potential to result in inaccurate data from which important conclusions are then drawn.

Actually, the issue of translation is only one consideration when contemplating issues of measurement in cross-cultural research. A second and much more complex concern is whether the concepts themselves "transfer" across culture. For example, does the construct of "depression" or "assertiveness" mean the same thing to people of various cultures or ethnic groups? Although anxiety exists in every ethnic group and virtually every country, the disorder appears to be expressed differently by people of various ethnic groups and cultures. Among Caucasians, panic disorder is characterized by a myriad of physical symptoms, including heart palpitations, dizziness, and shortness of breath, among others. Among those of Hispanic descent, there seems to be a related syndrome called ataque de nervios. Although some of the symptoms are similar to those of panic disorder codified by the *Diagnostic and Statistical Manual of Mental Disorders-Fourth Edition* (*DSM-IV*, American Psychiatric Association, 1994), ataque de nervios also includes the symptom of losing control and falling to the floor. This behavior pattern appears to be related to interpersonal, social, or familial distress. Unfamiliarity with this culturally specific presentation of anxiety or stress among Hispanic patients might result in inadequate diagnosis, misdiagnosis, and/or inappropriate interventions.

Another example of different cultural presentations across various ethnic groups is the disorder know as social phobia. In the American and European diagnostic schema, social phobia is characterized by a fear of doing or saying something which others might perceive in a negative light, thus causing embarrassment *to oneself*. Although social phobia appears to be a worldwide syndrome with similar features across various cultural and ethnic groups, the results of recent diagnostic interviews conducted in Asia produced much lower prevalence rates than in American and European countries (Chapman, Manuzza, & Fyer, 1995). Based on the diagnostic criteria used at that time, rates in the United States were 2.4%, 1.7% in Edmonton, Canada, and 3.0% in New Zealand, whereas rates in South Korea were 0.5% and in Taiwan, 0.6%. There may be several explanations for the substantially lower prevalence rate of social phobia among Asians. First, we cannot be sure that the questions were asked in such a manner as to convey the standard meaning of this disorder (i.e., perhaps there was a translation problem). A second reason for the difference could be that the diagnostic interview used for the study (constructed in the United States) did not assess for symptoms of taijin kyofu-sho. This syndrome, first reported in Japan and common in Korea and perhaps other East Asian countries, is a fear of causing offense or embarrassment *to others* by blushing, emitting body odors, or displaying unsightly body parts (Chapman et al., 1995). These fears appear to be unique to East Asians and may reflect a cultural emphasis on politeness rather than the importance of making a positive impression (see Beidel & Turner, 1998, for a discussion of this issue). To summarize, this interesting and apparently different manifestation of a disorder, common in the United States and Europe, highlight the importance of culture in the manifestation of a major psychiatric syndrome. Thus, even though the individual who is embarrassed by the person's behavior differs across cultures (i.e., embarrassment of self in Western cultures versus embarrassment of others in Eastern cultures), these two conditions share symptomatology and could represent the same underlying disorder. However, without attention to differing worldviews, it is easy to see how an assessment for social phobia using the "Western" definition could result in underreporting in Eastern cultures.

How does this lack of attention to whether concepts transfer across cultures affect research? Actually, it may have several different effects. First, as we noted, prevalence rates for various disorders may be underestimated (or overestimated) in different ethnic and cultural groups because of the lack of attention to variations in symptoms that may exist across cultures. In turn, research and research funding decisions could be based on these inaccurate data. Second, research that is insensitive to cultural diversity may lead to inaccurate conclusions that certain groups do not "get depressed," as one example. Thus, intervention efforts might not be developed for, or delivered to, these individuals. This problem often is referred to as "ecological validity"; that is, the degree to which the intervention has the properties it is assumed to have (Bronfenbrenner, 1977, p. 516).

Issues Related to the Quality of the Research Design

Many of the issues cited above might be addressed through more careful education and training in cultural diversity and research design. However, what is not so easy to change is what might be perhaps the overarching obstacle. That is, it will be necessary to change attitudes and values regarding what constitutes "good research." In 1972, Thomas and Sillen coined the term "scientific racism," which they defined as the ways theories and empirical research perpetuated a biased view of African Americans as well as other ethnic groups. More recently, Sue (1999) noted that science and the scientific method are not the culprits for the perpetuation of scientific racism. Rather, he noted that it is the selective reinforcement of certain scientific principles that emphasize one set of scientific values over another that can lead to research conclusions that are biased. Below, we examine some of the various issues that must be addressed to prevent this bias when designing scientific research.

The controlled study epitomizes the scientific method and requires that an experiment be carefully controlled in order to determine the relationship between "X" and "Y." That is, if one wants to know whether aspirin cures a headache, one would not want headache sufferers also to take acetaminophen or put a cool cloth on their head at the same time that they took the aspirin. If they did all of these at once, it would be impossible to determine whether it was the aspirin, acetaminophen, or the cool cloth that cured the headache. The control of conditions (referred to as independent variables) when conducting research so that their effect on other variables (i.e., dependent variables) is referred to as *internal validity*. However, sometimes the need to gain experimental control (and thus internal validity) means that the scientist must sacrifice other, equally important, considerations (known as external validity). For example, if the research requires the participants to read and complete long questionnaires that are only available in English, then the study will be limited to only participants who can read and understand English. Similarly, studies of children sometimes requires participation of both parents, thus limiting data collection (and conclusions) regarding two-parent families. Limiting who can participate in research (as well as other decisions) limits the *external validity* of the study. That is, it limits to whom the results of the study can be generalized or applied.

Ideally, researchers should attempt to have both high internal and external validity, but this rarely occurs. Rather, as we noted in the introduction, scientists often are forced to make decisions. According to Sue (1999), scientific racism exists because the prevailing scientific values reinforce and reward the focusing on internal validity and do not require the same standards for external validity. In simplest terms, studies that adhere to all the necessary internal controls, even to the point that the study lacks generalizability (the research only applies to two-parent families living in the United States who speak and write English), still receive federal grant funding and get their results published in the "top" scientific journals. Thus, there appears to be no penalty to a scientist's decision to ignore external validity (and thus, cultural diversity) because they continue to get grants funded and continue to publish their findings in top scientific journals. Thus, one method that might be used to encourage more attention to the issue of external validity would be to require attention to this issue in the scientific journals. However, this would seem an unlikely eventuality given the current zeitgeist.

Unfortunately, scientists who decide that generalizability and other aspects of external validity are important, and thus sacrifice some internal validity, find that their studies do not get funded, their results rarely get published, and further research is discouraged (Sue, 1999). In reality, both types of validity are equally important. However, as long as the prevailing scientific norm that internal controls are prized above all is upheld, the result will be a knowledge base based on primarily Caucasian, American college students with little relevance to anyone else. Until there is a change in scientific attitudes and values that demand external validity, while maintaining internal validity, we will remain in the situation that led Robert Guthrie to write his now famous work *Even the Rat Was White* (1998).

Data Interpretation

Finally, we turn our attention to issues of interpretation of research data. First, there are instances in science where research was conducted intentionally to try and prove that one gender or race was "inferior" to another. A study by Bache (1894, cited in Pope & Vasquez, 1998) described a study of differences in reaction time using a "finely calibrated, state-of-the-art magneto electric apparatus" (p. 314). Bache was convinced that men would have faster reaction times than women and that the "Caucasian Race" would have faster reaction times than both the "Indian Race" and the "African Race." He equated (prior to conducting the study) faster reaction times with intellectual superiority. In the first experiment, he found that men had faster reaction times than women, leading him to conclude that men were intellectually superior. However, in the second experiment, Caucasians had slower reaction times than "Indians" or "Africans," but still Bache concluded that Caucasians were intellectually superior! He reasoned that white "intellectuality [had] been gained at the expense of his autonomic capacity" (Pope & Vasquez, 1998, p. 315). Thus, Bache stated that, when examining differences across races, intellect caused a slowing down of reflexes, as indicated by the slower reaction time among Caucasians. He attributed this slowing down of reaction time to the "law of compensation" (i.e., smarter people moved slower). Although this is a very blatant example of forcing research findings to fit or uphold a particular stereotype, Pope and Vasquez (1998) noted that such biases can continue to be found in more recent scientific literature.

In the above example, the author was trying to prove a stereotype by conducting a specific research project, which illustrates rather clearly the influence of his own beliefs and values in interpreting the research data. Even when the results were contradictory to his bias, he reinterpreted his results to support his original position rather than vice-versa. In many instances, there may be legitimate reasons that one would want to examine cultural effects on a specific behavior of interest, even if one did not have a particular stereotype that one wanted to uphold. For example, a researcher may want to examine how various racial/ethnic groups deal with a relative who has an advanced case of Alzheimer's disease. At what point, if ever, would families decide to institutionalize a relative? When it is suspected in advance that there may be important differences between groups with respect to a specific topic, the research effort should be designed to be assured that one can detect these differences. However, considering cultural diversity issues when developing the various phases of a research design seldom occurs (Bernal, Bonilla, & Bellido, 1995). Usually, researchers only pay attention to potential group differences after the research has been conducted. That is, when examining the outcome of their endeavors, researchers may look for different outcomes based on existing group differences (gender, race/ethnicity minority status, and socioeconomic status). Although such efforts should be applauded as an initial first step, cultural biases still often affect how these group differences are interpreted. For example, it is not unusual for detected differences between minority and nonminority groups to be interpreted unfavorably in terms of the ethnic minority group (Okazaki & Sue, 1995). Thus, group differences are not interpreted as "different" but that one group is inferior to the other. Similar to the attitude and values issue raised above, acceptance of various worldviews would mean that minority group behaviors are not interpreted negatively, just because they are different from the nonminority group.

Finally, Sue (1999) raises the issue that even when researchers examine or analyze group differences based on ethnic status, that is where the examination ends. That is, researchers often treat ethnicity as if it were the reason for the difference (e.g., the difference is because one group is African American and the other group is Caucasian). However, such a statement has little explanatory value. Sue (1999) refers to ethnicity as a distal value, which, in and of itself, does not explain much about the behavior. What researchers must do is consider what aspects of ethnicity (e.g., respect for authority, being an individual versus being part of a group) might account for the group differences. Only when we can identify and understand these more proximal variables, will we begin to affirm ethnicity's role in understanding and predicting human behavior. The same is true for gender and socioeconomic status.

Summary and Future Directions

What will it take to change the current state of affairs? These issues have been around for a number of years now, so just continuing to point them out does not seem to be the complete answer. One suggestion is that we need to teach cultural sensitivity in our research training programs. Although this would appear on the surface to be a reasonable training goal, the actual implementation of such a suggestion presents what to this point has been an insurmountable task. For example, in one county in Maryland alone, the local school system has to deal with students who speak 140 different native languages. Given the multitude of cultures that exist throughout the world, not to mention issues of gender, socioeconomic status, sexual orientation, and disabilities, one can see that it would be impossible to train students to be culturally competent in all of these different areas. What would seem possible, however, is to train researchers in an attitude of cultural sensitivity. That is, to train researchers to always be aware of the need to question their own worldview and how that (a) might be different from that of participants or (b) might influence either the design or interpretation of their research. Additionally, although Rogler's

(1989) suggestion that prior to initiating any type of cross-cultural research, researchers should immerse themselves in the "other culture" also may not always be possible, providing students with one cross-cultural training experience certainly is a possibility. Such an experience might be similar to the "semester abroad" experiences offered as part of many undergraduate programs. Providing an opportunity for a student from a majority culture to live as a minority in a different culture might teach the need for cultural sensitivity in a fashion that no course ever could. Of course, this is but one of a myriad of ways that one could devise to teach respect for various cultures. The point is that, rather than trying to train students in all aspects of culture, teaching an attitude that respects various cultures and worldviews is at least a viable training option.

In summary, issues of cultural diversity affect every aspect of the research endeavor from the initial conceptualization of the problem, to recruitment of research participants, to the design of the study and the selection of the methods of assessment, to how the data are collected and then interpreted. Cultural insensitivity, an inability to understand or accept a different worldview, scientific racism (where internal validity is overvalued and a study's limited external validity is ignored), all result in scientific data that can be biased and, in many cases, inapplicable to many individuals. Furthermore, differences that automatically confer inferior status among the minority group members may be seen as a different kind of racism. In reality, there are probably many instances where there are no differences among various racial or ethnic groups when it comes to many aspects of human behavior. However, our current scientific literature does not allow us to address these issues. Until science begins to value alternative worldviews and conduct research designed to examine these influences, our understanding of ourselves always will be limited.

References

Beidel, D. C., and Turner, S. M. (1998). *Shy children, phobic adults: Nature and treatment of social phobias*. Washington, DC: American Psychological Association.

Bernal, G., Bonilla, J., & Bellido, C. (1995). Ecological validity and cultural sensitivity for outcome research: Issues of the cultural adaptation and development of psychosocial treatments with Hispanics. *Journal of Abnormal Child Psychology, 23*, 67–82.

Bronfenbrenner, U. (1977). Toward an experimental ecology of human development. *American Psychologist, 32*, 513–531.

Chapman, T. F., Manuzza, S., and Fyer, A. J. (1995). Epidemiology and family studies of social phobia. In R. G. Heimberg, D. A. Hope, and F. R. Schenier (Eds.), *Social phobia: Diagnosis, assessments, and treatment* (pp. 221–240). New York: Guilford.

Guthrie, R. V. (1998). *Even the rat was white: A historical view of psychology.* (2nd ed.). Boston: Allyn and Bacon.

National Academy of Sciences (1989). *On being a scientist*. Washington, DC: National Academy Press.

Okazaki, S., & Sue, S. (1995). Methodological issues in assessment research with ethnic minorities. *Psychological Assessment, 7,* 367–375.

Pope, K. S., & Vasquez, M. J. T. (1998). *Ethics in psychotherapy and counseling*. San Francisco: Jossey-Bass.

Rogler, L. H. (1989). The meaning of culturally sensitive research in mental health. *American Journal of Psychiatry, 146,* 296–303.

Rogler, L. H. (1999). Methodological sources of cultural insensitivity in mental health research. *American Psychologist, 54,* 424–433.

Sue, S. (1999). Science, ethnicity and bias. *American Psychologist, 54,* 1070–1077.

Index

Aboriginal religions, 166
academic achievement, 42, 66, 68–69
accessibility, 190–91
acculturation, 184
activities of daily living (ADL), 130
ADA. *See* Americans with Disabilities Act
ADL. *See* activities of daily living
adolescents
    African American, 39–45
    American Indian, 87
African Americans, 33–61
    academic achievement, 42–43, 125
    adolescent, 39–45
    bias and prejudice against, 52, 56–58
    biracial, 111–21
    contemporary, 51
    crisis and traditional helping resources, 38
    culturally sensitive modes of helping, 54–55
    Diaspora, 34, 46–47
    and diversity, 45
    experimentation with, 36

extended networks of support, 60–61
family ties, 35, 43, 60
helpers as guides and educators, 53
help-seeking situations, 52–54
impact of racial oppression on help-seeking patterns, 35–37
informal sources of support, 38–39
major subcultural groups, 47
and media, 41, 42–43
nonverbal behavior, 59–60
passing for white, 15, 116
patterns of social disadvantage, 14
sexual orientation, 15–16
skin color, 46–47, 55
statistics on, 34, 113
support from church and family, 37–38, 43
vernacular, 58–59
ageism, 123
aging, 123–42
    and cardiovascular system, 132–33
    and cohort, 127–28
    demographic issues, 124–27
    economic issues, 125–26

aging (*continued*)
  and education, 125
  and ethnicity, 126–27
  and functional health, 129–30
  growth of older population, 124
  health care, 140–41
  heterogeneity of older adults, 129
  lesbian, gay, and bisexual older adults,
    153–54
  life expectancy, 124–25
  and musculoskeletal system, 130–31
  and nervous system, 131–32
  normal versus disease, 128
  physical and sensory changes with,
    129–34
  psychological changes with, 134–37
  and respiratory system, 133
  and role functioning, 138–40
  and sensory systems, 131
  successful versus usual, 128
Alaskan Natives, 82, 85
alcohol abuse, 137
Allah, 169
Alzheimer's disease, 123, 128, 132
America. *See* United States
American Indian Historical Society, 81
American Indians. *See* Native Americans
American Psychiatric Association, 149
American Psychological Association,
    149
Americans with Disabilities Act (ADA),
    176, 178
anger, 12
antioxidants, 131
anxiety, 137
Apology Bill. *See* Public Law 103–150
Asante, Molefi Kete, 111
Asian Americans, 63–74, 120
  cultural characteristics, 65–68
  cultural variables and diagnosis of
    psychiatric disorders, 71
  discrimination against, 70–71
  disparity in health care, 72–73
  feelings of social isolation, 72
  lack of power base, 73–74

  as model minority, 69–70
  professional issues, 72
  role overload, 71–72
  socioeconomic status, 68–69
  statistics on, 63–64, 69
  underemployment, 71
assertive behavior therapy, 57
Assertive Black, Puzzled White (Cheek), 57
assisted living facilities, 141
assistive devices, 189
autism, 181

Bantu religions, 167
Batista, Fulgencio, 29
Bechdel, Alison, 156
behaviors, 6
beliefs, 189
Bering Strait, 25
Berry, John W., 101
bias, 56–58, 161, 165, 169–70
biculturalism, 23, 47, 101
biracial people, 111–21
bisexuality. *See* lesbian/gay/bisexual
    people
Black English, 58–59
Black Hispanics, 50–51
Black Power/Pride, 51
Blacks. *See* African Americans; Black
    Hispanics; Caribbean Blacks
Black, White and Jewish (Walker), 119
blindness, 179
bone, 130–31
Boudinant, Elia, 79
Boyd-Franklin, Nancy, 10
brain, 132
Brown v. Board of Education, 42
Buddhism, 166
Bulletproof Diva (Jones), 114
Butler, Robert, 123

calcium, 130
cardiovascular system, 132
caregiving, 141
Caribbean Blacks, 47–50, 51
Castro, Fidel, 29

cataracts, 131
Catholicism, 164
Celtic religion, 166
Central Americans, 29–30
Cheek, Donald, 57
Cherokee Indians, 79
Chicanos. *See* Mexican Americans
children
  American Indian, 79–81, 87
  biracial, 111–21
  disabled, 185
  Hawaiian, 106
  natural ignorance about realistic
    dangers, 8
  See also adolescents
Chinese Americans, 64, 197–98
Chinese Exclusion Act, 64
Chisholm, Shirley, 47
cholesterol, 132
Christianity, 98, 105, 161, 166
Church of Latter Day Saints, 166
Civil Rights Act (1964), 35
Clark, William, 58
class, 6–7, 40–41
Clinton, William, 36, 95
cognitive disabilities, 181, 187
cohort, 127–28
colleges and universities, 41, 42
Columbus, Christopher, 82
communication, 184, 188–90
computer systems, 188
continuing care retirement
    communities, 141
cool posing, 59–60
cooperation, 67–68
Creek Indians, 79
criminal justice system, 42
cross-cultural competency, 23–24
Crowther, J. H., 38
crystallized intelligence, 135, 136
Cuba and Cubans, 29, 48, 50
cultural differences, 10–11, 55–56
cultural framework, 54–56
cultural responsiveness, 56
curiosity, 8, 107

data collection, 198–200
data interpretation, 202–3
Davis, Lennard, 182
deafness, 180, 184, 185, 188, 190–91
death, 141, 163
dementia, 132
depression, 137, 186–87
developmental disabilities, 181, 192,
    193
*Diagnostic and Statistical Manual of Mental
    Disorders,* 191, 199
differences, 3–19
disability, 175–94
  and communication, 184, 188–90
  culture, 183
  definition of, 178–79
  groupings, 179–81
  and human interaction, 184–88
  as integral component of diversity
    spectrum, 177–78
  medical model, 183, 186
  moral model, 182–83, 186
  service provisions for, 190–94
  as social construction, 193
  social minority model, 183, 186, 187
  views of, 182–84
disadvantaged. *See* socially disadvantaged
discord/discomfort, 11–12
discrimination, 35–37, 70–71
disease, 78, 97, 128
diversity
  and Black Americans, 45
  definition of, 3
  disability as integral component of,
    177–78
  of older adults, 129
  of religion, 157–58, 164–65
  within lesbian, gay, bisexual
    community, 150–51
diversity training, 181–82
Dominican Republic, 48, 50
Down's syndrome, 181

earned power, 10
Ebonics, 58–59

economic issues
  and aging, 125–26
  of aging African Americans, 125
  of American Indians, 87–88
  of Asian Americans, 68–69
  of Black adolescents, 40–41
ego ideal, 11, 12, 13
Elbert, Samuel H., 94
elderly. *See* aging
elders, 65, 107
embarrassment, 199–200
empathy, 170
employment. *See* work
entertainment industry, 42
Erikson, Erik, 134
Eskimos, 82
ethnicity, 14–15, 55, 126–27, 152
Even the Rat Was White (Guthrie), 201
exercise, 130–31, 133
external validity, 201

familiarity, 107
families
  African American, 35, 37–38, 43, 60
  of aging population, 139–40, 141
  American Indian, 80, 89
  Asian American, 65–66
  of disabled, 185
  Hawaiian, 103–4, 105
  of lesbian, gay, and bisexual people,
    154
fear, 5–6
feelings, 5
Fetal Alcohol Syndrome, 87
Filipino Americans, 64–69
Five Civilized Tribes, 79
flexibility, 58
fluid intelligence, 135–36
Frye, Marilyn, 10
functional health, 129–30

Gallaudet University, 183
gender identity, 146–47, 151
generosity, 68
geriatric medicine, 140–41

Gibbs, Jewelle Taylor, 111
glass ceiling/floor, 30, 72
God, 157–58, 164, 169, 170
Gonzales, Elian, 50
grandparenting, 139
group orientation, 88–89
guides, 53
guilt, 12–13, 67, 185
Guthrie, Robert, 201

hair, 130
harmony, 12, 66, 88, 103
Hastie, William, 47
Hawaii and Hawaiians, 82, 93–108
  abolishment of *kapu* system, 98
  annexation and statehood, 99
  assimilation, 101–2
  cultural identity, 100–103
  cultural values, beliefs, and traditions,
    103–5
  effects of colonization, 99–100
  historical overview, 94–100
  impact of sociopolitical changes, 96–
    99
  influence of Christianity, 98
  land tenure system, 98
  languages, 102, 106
  marginalization, 102
  overthrow of monarchy, 98–99
  socialization, 106
  social organization, 105
  time orientation, 106
healing, 159
health care
  of aging population, 140–41
  of American Indians, 86–87
  of Asian Americans, 72–73
health insurance, 87
hearing, 131, 180, 188
heart disease, 132
Hellenistic religion, 166
heterosexual privilege, 13, 16, 153
Hinduism, 166
Hispanics, 21–31, 50–51, 125
Hittite religion, 167

Holt, Bradley, 163
Holzman, Clare, 12
homophobia, 149, 155
homosexuality. *See* lesbian/gay/bisexual
    people
hospice care, 141
hospitality, 68
housing, 41
human service professionals, 17–18
hypertension, 132–33

IADL. *See* instrumental activities of daily
    living
identities, 13, 14, 44, 55
illness, 163
immigration
    and Black adolescents, 39–40
    and disability culture, 184–85
    recent changes in Black, 46–47
Immigration Act of 1965, 65
immune system, 133
Indian Citizenship Act (1924), 85
Indians. *See* Native Americans
Indonesia, 165
institutional privilege, 13
instrumental activities of daily living
    (IADL), 130
intelligence, 37, 135–36
internalized racism, 10, 16
internal validity, 201
interracial marriages, 112–13
Islam, 165, 167, 169

Jackson, Andrew, 79
Jainism, 167
Japanese Americans, 16–17
Jehovah's Witnesses, 167
Jim Crow practices, 35
Johnson, Allan, 9
Jones, Lisa, 114–15
Jordan, Judith, 10
Judaism, 164, 167

Kamaku, Samuel, 97, 98
Kamehameha I (King), 97

kapu system, 98
Kim, Uichol, 101
knowledge, 195, 196–97

labels, 13
language(s)
    of African Americans, 46, 58–59
    Hawaiian, 106
    Native American, 83
    of superiority, 113–14
    translation, 198–99
Latin America, 21
Latinos, 21–31, 50
learning disabilities, 178
lesbian/gay/bisexual people, 145–56
    and ability status, 152–53
    bisexuals' dilemma, 153
    and choice, 14–16
    coming out, 148
    definition of sexual orientation, 146
    diversity within community, 150–51
    end of mental illness model, 147,
        149
    families of, 154
    gender issues, 151–52
    generational differences, 153–54
    in heterosexual society, 13
    mistreatment of, 16
    multiple minority statuses, 152–54
    and opportunity, 7
    personal attitudes on, 149–50
    race and ethnicity, 152
    senior citizens, 153–54
    sexual prejudice and culture, 148–49
Lewis, Jerry, 186
LGB. *See* lesbian/gay/bisexual people
life expectancy, 124–25
life-span theories, 135
Lili'uokalani (Queen), 99
Linton, Simi, 182
listening, 164
Lorde, Audre, 19
Loving v. Virginia, 113
Lowry, Richard, 52
lung function, 133

macular degeneration, 131
Manifest Destiny, 26
Marielle boatlift, 29
maturity, 107
McIntosh, Peggy, 9
media, 41, 42
Medicare, 123
medicine, 159
memory, 128, 132, 136–37
mental disorders, 137
mental retardation, 181, 192, 193
meritocracy, 10
methods of distraction, 22
Mexican Americans, 27–28, 30–31
Minoan religion, 167
minorities, 113–14
Minton, Nalani, 99
mobility disabilities, 180
Mormons, 166
Mountain Ute Indians, 84
"Mulatto Millennium, The" (Senna), 115
multiculturalism, 23, 24, 101
Mura, David, 118
muscular dystrophy, 186
musculoskeletal system, 130–31
Muslims, 165, 169

Na Kānaka Maoli, 93–108
Native Americans, 21, 25, 26, 77–90
   boarding schools, 79–80
   contemporary, 82–83
   early oppression, 77–79
   economic conditions, 87–88
   education, 86
   health conditions, 86–87
   languages, 83
   population, 85–86
   reservations, 79
   stereotypical images, 81–82
   tribal enrollment, 83–85
   values, 88–89
nature, 88
Neal-Barnett, Angela, 38, 39
nervous system, 131

net worth, 125–26
neurons, 131
nonassertiveness, 66
nursing homes, 141

Oceanic religions, 167
Oglala Lakota Indians, 84
older adults. See aging
Olkin, Rhoda, 183, 185–88
"one drop" rule, 112
opportunities, 7, 30
osteoarthritis, 131
osteoporosis, 130, 131
oxygen, 133

personality, 134–35
phenomenology, 164
Philippines, 64, 65
physical disabilities, 180, 187, 191
Pocahontas, 112
political correctness, 22
politics, 30–31
"Postcards From 'Home'" (Tsang), 120
poverty. See economic issues
Powell, Colin, 47
prebycusis, 131
prejudice, 52, 56–58, 148–49, 161
presbyopia, 131
present-time orientation, 88
pride, 67
privileged. See socially privileged
psychiatric disabilities, 181, 187, 191
psychology, 196
Public Law 103–150 (Apology Bill), 93, 95, 96, 99
Pueblo Indians, 89
Puerto Rico and Puerto Ricans, 28–29, 48, 50, 82, 196–97
Pukui, Mary Kawena, 94

Qur'an, 169, 170

race, 14–15, 152
racial profiling, 36

racism, 10, 13, 16, 48–49, 52, 70–71
reciprocal moral obligation, 68
Reeve, Christopher, 175
"Reflections on My Daughter" (Mura), 118
religion, 157–73
    in African American life, 37–38, 43
    in Asian American life, 67
    biases and stereotypes, 165, 169–70
    complexity of systems, 162–63
    concerns of, 170–71
    definitions of, 159–61
    difference from spirituality in ethnic minority community, 163–65
    in Hawaiian life, 98, 103, 105
    importance of systems, 158–62
    relationship with medicine, 159
    salient features of specific groups, 166–68
Reno, Janet, 175
reproductive system, 133
research, 195–204
    current status of knowledge base, 196–97
    data collection, 198–200
    data interpretation, 202–3
    quality of design, 200–201
    subject recruitment, 197–98
residential patterns, 41
resistance, 12
respiratory system, 133
retirement, 138–39
Rolfe, John, 112
Ross, John, 79
Rothenberg, Paula, 12

schizophrenia, 181
science, 195
scientific method, 195, 200
scientific racism, 200, 201
segregation, 35, 51
self-blame, 10
self-identity, 22
senior citizens. See aging
Senna, Danzy, 115

sensory disabilities, 179–80, 187
sexual identity, 146
sexual orientation. See lesbian/gay/ bisexual people
sexual prejudice, 148–49
shame, 67
Shinto, 167
Sillen, Thomas, 200
Silva, Noenoe K., 99
Sister Outsider (Lorde), 19
skin, 130
skin color, 25, 46–47, 55
slavery, 33, 34, 35, 47–48, 51, 64
Smith, John, 78
socially disadvantaged, 9–17
socially privileged, 9–17
social phobia, 199–200
Social Security, 123, 125
social services, 141
socioeconomic status. See economic issues
South Americans, 29–30
Spanish language, 21, 24, 29–30
Spiritualist religion, 167
spirituality, 159–60, 162–65
    See also religion
stereotypes
    of African Americans, 42–43, 56, 57
    of American Indians, 81–82
    of disabled, 187, 190
    of older adults, 129
    religious, 165, 169–70
stroke, 132
suffering, 10
suicide, 87, 137
syphilis, 36

Tahlequah (Okla.), 79
Taoism, 168
technology, 188
teenagers. See adolescents
Texas, 26
Trail of Tears, 79
trait theories, 134

transgender individuals, 146, 150
translation, 198–99
tribes, 83
trust, 53–54, 107
Tsang, Lori, 120
TTY (telephone communication
    device), 191
Tuskegee Institute, 36

United States
  acquiring American identity, 30
  Black adolescents in, 39–45
  Central and South Americans in, 29–
    30
  Cubans in, 29
  Latinos/Hispanics in, 25–27
  Mexican Americans in, 27–28
  Puerto Ricans in, 28–29
  value of diversity in, 12
  See also African Americans; Asian
    Americans; Hawaii and Hawaiians;
    Native Americans
Unity religion, 168
universities. See colleges and universities
unknown, 8

Vash, Carolyn, 176
Virginia, 112
vision, 131, 179

Walker, Rebecca, 119
West Indies, 29, 47, 49
White Americans, 9, 124
White race, 10, 112, 196
white skin privilege, 9, 13
Wildman, Stephanie, 9
Williams, Eric, 47
Wilson, James, 78, 80
women
  Asian American, 71–72
  Black, 38–39, 52
  life expectancy, 124
Woods, Tiger, 119–20
work
  Blacks in workforce, 40
  diversity in workforce, 23
  and older adults, 138–39
  overqualified Asian Americans, 71
  unemployment, 88

Zoroastrianism, 168